A world of my own

The single-handed, non-stop circumnavigation of the world in

SUHAILI

by

ROBIN KNOX-JOHNSTON

CASSELL · LONDON

CASSELL & COMPANY LTD
35 RED LION SQUARE, LONDON, WCI
Melbourne, Sydney, Toronto
Johannesburg, Auckland

© Robin Knox-Johnston 1969
First published October 1969
First edition, second impression, October 1969

S.B.N. 304 93473 9

Printed in Great Britain by
Cox & Wyman Ltd, London, Reading and Fakenham
969

A world of my own

for
SARA

Contents

MAPS

APPENDIXES

Illustrations

---

* Photograph by Robin Knox-Johnston
† Syndication International – a Sunday Mirror
photograph by William Rowntree

K

Acknowledgements

IN preparing *Suhaili* for our voyage, during the voyage, and since my return, I have received help and kindness from many people. In acknowledging some by name, I am well aware that there are many others unnamed to whom I should also address my thanks. I can only hope that this book will in some way help to repay the debt *Suhaili* and I owe them.

For the voyage itself, the chief credit must go to David Waterhouse and George Greenfield; David for his encouragement when the venture was little more than a dream, and George for enabling me to turn the dream into reality.

A young person rarely has the means to pay for a voyage of this kind and nowadays must find sponsors. I should like to thank David Ascoli of Cassell and Mike Christiansen of the *Sunday Mirror* in London, and Charles Barnard of *True Magazine* and Larry Hughes of William Morrow in New York, for having the faith in *Suhaili* and me to persuade their respective companies to back us. The support I have received and the friendships I have made among the staffs of all four companies have been some of the incidental but happiest 'perks' of the voyage.

The Directors and the afloat and ashore staffs of the British India Steam Navigation Company gave me every encouragement throughout; without their co-operation I could never have made the voyage.

For help in preparing *Suhaili* for the voyage I am indebted to David Waterhouse, Clive Henderson, Mike Souter, Richard Carpenter, Ken Parker, Bruce Maxwell, Bill Rowntree, my brother Mike, Hazel Cresswell, Stella and Jim Friend, Will Deas, many of the crew of H.M.S. *Duncan*, Mr McKay of Mills & Knight, Jim Jones and the Deptford Sea Cadets, members of the Beckenham Theatre Centre, Pat Flux, and members of the staffs of Surrey Commercial Docks, Newhaven Marina, and the Falmouth Harbour Board. William Maconachie and George Gardiner of Marconi Marine, Cliff Pearson of the *Sunday Mirror* and Matthew Johnston of the G.P.O. Radio Station at Baldock, organized my radio and my schedules with stations all round the world with tremendous efficiency.

In Falmouth before I departed the '*Suhaili* Supporters Club' – Ken Parker of Cassell, Bruce Maxwell and Bill Rowntree of the *Sunday Mirror* – and Vic Roberts of the *Sunday Mirror* so organized my life that I had little to worry about other than preparing *Suhaili*. The Rev. David Roberts and Ron Stringer of Marconi Marine gave me much appreciated help and encouragement in their specialized fields and I owe a special debt of thanks to Di and Bob Drennan of the Marine Hotel, their staff and many of their customers.

While I was away, Ian Murray, Norman Alexander and George Greenfield handled my affairs with far greater efficiency than I can when I am at home.

During the voyage the staffs of the G.P.O. Radio Station at Baldock, Cape Town Radio, Arawua Radio in New Zealand and Land's End Radio gave great assistance. The *Sunday Mirror*, through Bruce Maxwell in London, New Zealand and finally the Azores, and through Natie Ferreira in Cape Town, went to extraordinary lengths to keep me in touch with news from home and to keep my family informed of my progress.

On my return to Falmouth, and subsequently, Cliff Pearson and the *Sunday Mirror* team, Robert Riddell of the *Sunday Times*, Di and Bob Drennan and the staff of the Marine Hotel, John Lodge, Captain Edwards the Harbour Master, Commodore Fox of the Royal Cornwall Yacht Club, the Falmouth Boat Construction Company, the Supporters Club, and last but far from least my sister Diana and my brothers Dick, Chris and Mike, all weighed in to help with the rush of those first days at home. My thanks are also due to Guy Crossley-Meates and the crew of *Fathomer* (chartered by the *Sunday Mirror*) for performing their escort duties so ably on the run-in, and to Captain Evans and the crew of *Queen of the Isles* (under charter to the *Daily Express*). And whilst remembering the days I spent

ACKNOWLEDGEMENTS

in Falmouth, any words I could find to express my gratitude to the Mayor and Mayoress, Alderman and Mrs Norman Fittus, and through them to the hard-working council officials and to the people of the town for their welcome on April 22nd, 1969, and their continuing kindness to myself, my family and friends in the days that have followed would be wholly inadequate.

Whilst writing the book, I have received advice and assistance from Ken Parker; Gil Pearson did all the typing, managing to take the daily batches of manuscript, decipher them, and return an immaculate typescript to me the next day.

Finally, I should like to acknowledge the support and understanding of my Mother and Father before, during, and since the voyage. In many ways theirs was the most difficult task of all.

Robin Knox-Johnston

Downe, Kent
July 1969

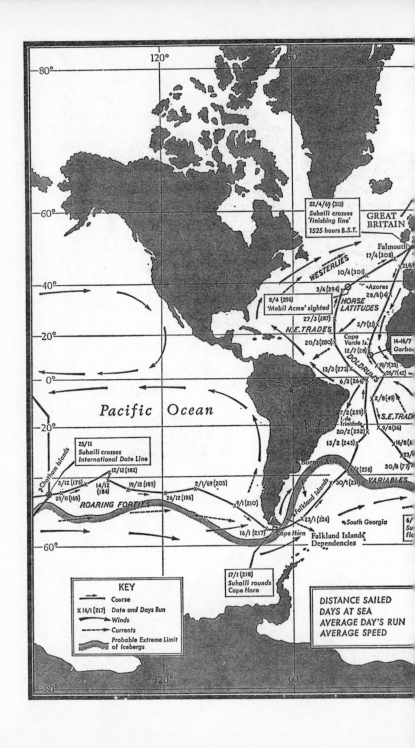

22/4/69 (313)
Suhaili crosses
'finishing line'
1525 hours B.S.T.

GREAT
BRITAIN

Falmouth
17/4 (308)

21/6

WESTERLIES

10/4 (301)

3/4 (294)   •Azores
28/6 (14)

HORSE
LATITUDES

5/4 (296)
'Mobil Acme' sighted
27/3 (287)

5/7 (21)

N.E.TRADES

20/3 (280)

Cape
Verde Is.
12/7 (28)

14-16/7
Garbo

13/3 (273)

DOLDRUMS

19/7 (35)

26/7 (42)

6/3 (266)

2/8 (49)

27/2 (259)
I. de
Trinidade
20/2 (252)

S.E.TRAD

9/8 (56)

Rio de
Janeiro

13/2 (245)

16/8 (6

23/

Buenos Aires

6/2 (238)

30/8 (77)

30/1 (231)

VARIABLES

Pacific   Ocean

25/11
Suhaili crosses
International Date Line

Chatham Islands

12/12 (182)

5/12 (175)   14/12   19/12 (189)
(184)

2/1/69 (203)

Falkland Islands

6/

Su
fla

29/11 (168)

ROARING FORTIES

26/12 (196)

9/1 (210)

23/1 (224)

South Georgia

16/1 (217)   Cape Horn

Falkland Islands
Dependencies

17/1 (218)
Suhaili rounds
Cape Horn

KEY
→   Course
X 16/1 (217)   Date and Days Run
↝   Winds
--→   Currents
〰〰   Probable Extreme Limit
of Icebergs

DISTANCE SAILED
DAYS AT SEA
AVERAGE DAY'S RUN
AVERAGE SPEED

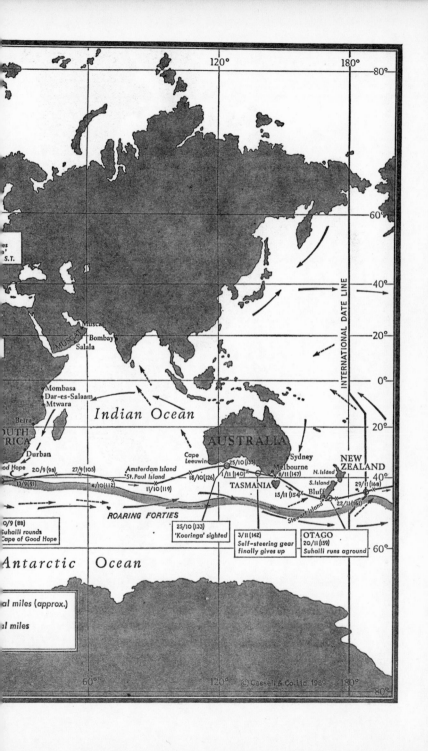

120°   180°   80°

                                                                      60°

                                                          INTERNATIONAL DATE LINE
                                                                      40°

Muscat   20°
Bombay
Salala
                                                                       0°
Mombasa
Dar-es-Salaam
Mtwara   *Indian Ocean*   20°

Beira
SOUTH
AFRICA   AUSTRALIA
Durban   Sydney   NEW
Good Hope   20/9 (98)   27/9 (105)   Cape   ZEALAND
            (13/9(91))   Leeuwin 25/10 (135) N. Island   40°
                        Amsterdam Island   1/11 (140) Melbourne
                        St. Paul Island 18/10(126)   8/11(147) S. Island
                                        11/10 (119)   TASMANIA 15/11 (154) Bluff 29/11 (168)
                        4/10(112)   22/11 (161)
20/9 (88)   *ROARING FORTIES*   Stewart Island
Suhaili rounds
Cape of Good Hope   25/10 (133)   3/11 (142)   OTAGO
                          'Kooringa' sighted Self-steering gear   20/11 (159)
Antarctic Ocean   finally gives up   Suhaili runs aground   60°

al miles (approx.)
al miles

60°   120°   © Cassell & Co.Ltd. 1969   180°   80°

Suhaili

'I SEE that Tabarly is building a trimaran,' my Father said one morning. 'Would that be suitable for the Transatlantic race?'

I was on leave in March 1967, enjoying a quiet month at my parents' home at Downe in Kent, before joining the *Kenya* as First Officer. A couple of weeks before, my brother Chris, Heinz Fingerhut and I had brought *Suhaili* into London at the end of a 15,000-mile voyage from India. *Suhaili* was now laid up in a mud creek at Benfleet in the Thames whilst I decided what to do with her.

'I wouldn't have thought so,' I said. 'Are there any other details?'

'No, but I wonder if he is going to try and beat Chichester's time, or perhaps even go round non-stop. That's about all there's left to do now, isn't it?' He got up and left for the office, leaving me stirring a cup of coffee and thinking.

'That's about all there's left to do now' kept turning in my mind. Going non-stop round the world *was* all that was left to be done in the sailing marathons. Chichester had stopped in Australia, and Alec Rose was planning to do the same. Who would try going round non-stop singlehanded? It would only be a matter of time before someone went, and Tabarly, a strong and experienced yachtsman, might well be planning to go. What was more, he was quite capable of doing it. He had proved his extraordinary ability in the 1964 singlehanded Transatlantic race. I remembered all the fuss in the French newspapers when he had won. 'Frenchman supreme on the Anglo-Saxon Ocean' *Paris-Match* had screamed, the inference being that the Island Race had been proved inferior seamen to the French. This had made my blood boil at the time and I could picture the headlines if Tabarly became the first person to sail right round the world non-stop. We'd never hear the last of it.

Of course, there was no proof that Tabarly had this voyage in mind at all, but he just might, and in any case someone was going to attempt it sooner or later. By rights a Briton should do it first, and in the circumstances he had better get moving.

But who would go? All the names in singlehanded sailing were either at sea or preparing for other voyages. Could I go? Obviously not in *Suhaili*; she was too small and even though I knew her now and she was a part of me, I could never hope to race Tabarly in her. I would need a new boat for the job and boats are expensive. The only way I could possibly afford another boat was by selling *Suhaili* or finding a sponsor.

I began to think over the problems involved in a voyage of this sort, which would mean between seven and ten months on my own, sailing for half of that time in the Roaring Forties of the Southern Ocean, too far from any shipping routes to expect help if I ran into serious trouble.

I wondered if I could manage that long without human company, or if I would go round the bend. I had no yardstick to measure this, since the longest I had ever been on my own was twenty-four hours, but suddenly this did not seem to be very important, and that's when I realized I was hooked.

I am of mixed Ulster and English stock. My Father's forbears, the Knoxes and Johnstons, were Presbyterian farmers who fled from the Lowlands of Scotland to Ireland in the early seventeenth century. Family legend has it that Robert Knox (1640–1720), whose portrait hangs in the Queen's Building at the National Maritime Museum at Greenwich, and which I am supposed to resemble, is one of 'our' Knoxes. While in the East India Company's service, as was his father, he spent nearly twenty years as a prisoner in Ceylon, resourcefully supporting himself by knitting caps and peddling goods round the island; made a famous escape, and after his retirement as a Commander in 'John Company's' fleet, he wrote the still valued first English language history of Ceylon. There is also a dark family story of a Knox who was the last pirate to be hung on the west coast of Scotland, but apart from these three, the Knoxes and Johnstons seem to have had little or no connection with the sea.

Mother's family, the Crees, although Scots in name, were a family of lawyers from Stockton-on-Tees, who somehow came south to Beckenham, in Kent, and in Captain T. Cree, R.N., my godfather, there is a strong naval link, though whether this had any great influence upon my decision to go to sea I don't know.

It is true that Father worked in a shipping company's office before the war, but of the five children – my younger brothers, Dick, Chris and Mike, my sister Diana and myself – I am the only one who has showed any inclination towards a career at sea.

I was born in Putney on St Patrick's Day, March 17th, 1939, which was a source of intense and immediate satisfaction to my paternal Grandfather, after whom I was christened William Robert, with the inevitable Patrick added; to avoid confusion I have always been called Robin.

I can, of course, remember little of the war. We were bombed out of a flat in New Brighton, near Liverpool, and I can recall being lifted out of my bed and wrapped in an eiderdown when the engine of a doodlebug cut out over my Aunt's flat in Putney. I can also remember Father coming home on leave after being wounded in Antwerp, but little else.

After losing the New Brighton flat, we moved to Heswall on the Dee Estuary, and it was here that boats and the sea first caught my interest. When I was four I made a raft from orange-box slats which I carried a mile to the beach. The launching went off without incident but when I stood on my craft it sank at once. I had lost my first command.

My next boat was a 10-foot canoe which I built in my grandparents' attic when I was fourteen and attending Berkhamsted School as a day boy. During builder's trials on the Grand Union Canal, she sank as well – a fact that I now think it is safe to reveal to the sponsors of my round the world trip – but by the time we took her to Selsey in Sussex for the summer holidays, she was seaworthy, and a photograph of the boat and her proud owner appeared in the *Junior Express*.

At seventeen I had made up my mind to join the Royal Navy and I sat the Civil Service Commission's examination. I came through with high marks in geography and history, my choice subjects, but failed in physics, a compulsory subject for the Navy entrants. Looking back on it now, when the subject is an integral and fascinating part of my everyday life in both the Merchant and Royal Navies, I believe the reason for my failure was that I had difficulty in applying the theories and experiments of the General Certificate syllabus to any practical problems that came my way. It was a distinctive trait in my character that when faced with a problem or job in which I was not at once deeply interested, I would do all I could to avoid tackling it, even to taking on a more difficult, even dangerous task which did hold my interest. Although my subsequent training taught me to discipline myself to overcome this, it was still one of my difficulties in preparing *Suhaili* to go round the world, and was at times the despair of my friends. Reading again my diary of *Suhaili*'s voyage while writing this book, I can see evidence of the same tactics, and of the same conscious effort to overcome them. More to my satisfaction, however, I see also that

the only way to overcome my present feeling of depression is to fully occupy myself, so I cleaned and served the remaining bottle screw threads and then gave all the servings a coat of Stockholm Tar. Next I polished the vents and gave them a coating of boiled oil. Whilst I had it out I dabbed the oil on wire and rust patches. . . . *

Failing the Civil Service Commission's exam meant that I could either wait for the next – and there was no guarantee that I would pass then – or go to sea immediately as an apprentice in the Merchant Navy. To my great good fortune I chose the latter and on February 4th, 1957, I joined the British India Steam Navigation Company's cadetship *Chindwara* in the Royal Albert Dock in London as an Officer Cadet.

The *Chindwara* was one of two B.I. 7,500-ton cargo ships which were crewed almost entirely by the Company's cadets. There were some forty of us aboard working under a full complement of officers plus a cadet instruction officer and a

* July 9th, 1968 (Day 25)

bosun, 'Bertie' Miller, who was even then a legend in the Company. While the cadet instruction officer, David Colley, led us through the maze of theoretical and technical knowledge required by Merchant Navy officers, Bertie was responsible for making seamen of us. Bertie, with his enthusiasm and encouragement, taught us our knots and splices, canvas work, rigging, how to work a paintbrush properly, and the thousand-and-one finer practical points that make the difference between the seaman and a hand. It was Bertie who gave us a respect for the materials and the tools we used and took tremendous trouble to see that we set about a job the right way and finished it off properly. Shoddy work had no place in his scheme of things; it never escaped his notice and we soon learned that it did not pay.

I spent three enjoyable years on the *Chindwara* running between London and East African ports, and then after finishing my apprenticeship on other ships in the Company's fleet, I passed my Ministry of Transport Second Mate's Certificate examinations in October 1960, and joined the B.I. *Dwarka* running between Indian and Persian Gulf ports with deck passengers and general cargo. By this time I was engaged, and by the time I took my First Mate's Certificate a year later, I was married.

We set up home in Bombay where I joined the Company's *Dumra* as Third Officer. Serving in *Dumra* as Extra Third Officer was Peter Jordan, another ex-*Chindwara* cadet. Together we hatched a plan to buy a dhow and sail it back to England, but we soon realized that the chances of selling her there were virtually nil, and that however intriguing the prospect of sailing a craft that has been virtually unchanged since the time of Sinbad, as an investment it was not a practical proposition. Our thoughts turned to building a yacht which we could use for skin-diving and underwater photography to pay our way home, and which we could sell at a profit when we reached England.

We decided to build a family cruiser suitable for ocean sailing, and studied the yachting magazines looking for a suitable craft. Agreeing on a ketch we wrote to a firm in Poole, Dorset, who advertised 'full plans and a free advisory service'.

The plans they sent us were of a completely different and more old-fashioned ketch, and although two suggested sail plans were included – one gaff and one bermudan – there was no proper rigging plan. However, with our need to catch the North-East Monsoon the following year, there was no time to start a long correspondence. The boat whose plans we had looked sturdy and seaworthy and for our purpose this was more practical than a slimmer, faster boat. We contented ourselves with writing off for the missing rigging plans, only to be told that these would be extra to the 'full plans and free advisory service'. So with time short we bought a copy of Douglas Phillips-Birt's *The Rigs and Rigging of Yachts* and using this and Eric Hiscock's *Cruising Under Sail* we designed our own rigging.

One advantage of building in India was the availability of relatively cheap Indian teak, which although not quite up to the quality of Burmese teak, is still one of the finest boat building materials known. The keelson, a 25-foot log, arrived at the Colaba Workshops' slip in November 1963 and building commenced. Indian carpenters still use traditional methods and tools, and there is a long history of wooden boat building in Bombay. Only half a mile from where our own boat was taking shape, the 2nd Rate H.M.S. *Ganges* of eighty-four guns had been built of Indian teak by Wadia's in 1819–21. Apart from its durability, teak had the advantage that it did not splinter easily, and flying splinters were the major cause of casualties on wooden fighting ships. H.M.S. *Ganges* was the last sailing ship to be a sea-going flagship of the Royal Navy, and after her honourable retirement in 1861, she became the first of the famous *Ganges* training ships, spending, incidentally, thirty-three of her years at Falmouth. She stayed in Navy service until 1929 when, by this time called *Impregnable III*, she was sold. An earlier build at the Wadia yard was the *Trincomalee* in 1817, which as the *Foudroyant* can still be seen in Portsmouth; while Sir Edward Pellew, the first captain of C. S. Forester's fictional hero, Captain Hornblower, did in reality take over the *Cornwallis* from the Honorable East India Company, who had built her at the same yard four years before.

The adze, the bow drill and other hand tools of the Indian shipwright used in the construction of the Royal Navy's

© Cassell & Co. Ltd., 1969

Sail plan and list of sails carried (showing vane arrangement of 'The Admiral')

1. 1 Spinnaker (270 sq. ft.)
2. 1 Flying Jib ('Big Fellow') (220 sq. ft.)
3. 1 Flying Jib ('Little-un') (180 sq. ft.)
4. 3 Jibs (135 sq. ft.)
5. 1 Storm jib (40 sq. ft.)
6. 2 Staysails (84 sq. ft.)
7. 2 Mains (300 sq. ft.)
8. 2 Mizzens (147 sq. ft.)

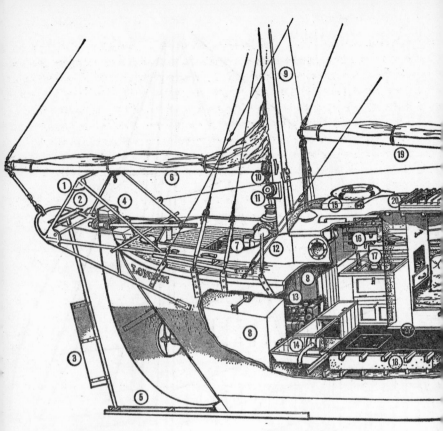

1. 'Pushpit'
2. Self-steering tiller arm
3. Self-steering rudder
4. Rudder head with tiller as finally lashed .
5. Shoe for self-steering rudder bar
6. Mizzen boom
7. Cockpit
8. Diesel fuel tanks
9. Mizzen mast
10. Gooseneck
11. Halyard winch
12. Runner as finally rigged
13. Engine-room
14. Bilge pump
15. Main hatch
16. Plate rack
17. Galley (radio and chart table opposite – see page 10)
18. Water tank
19. Main boom
20. Skylight
21. Main cabin

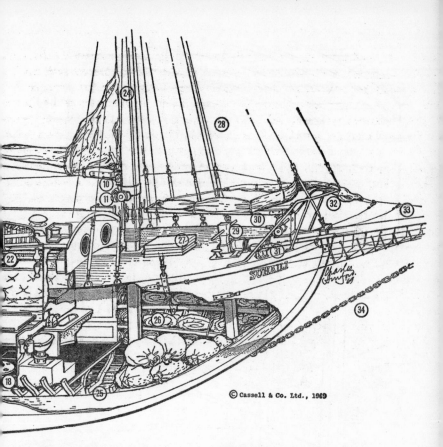

© Cassell & Co. Ltd., 1969

10. Gooseneck	*SUHAILI*
11. Halyard winch	*Official No.:* 306242
18. Water tank	*Reg:* 8–1965 *London*
22. Port outboard berth	*Burmudan Ketch*
23. Port settee berth	*Identification letters:* MHYU
24. Mainmast	*Tonnage TM:* 14
25. Floors	*Gross:* 9.72
26. Forward cabin	*Net:* 6.29
27. Forward hatch	*LOA:* 44 ft.
28. Running pole lashed to	*Hull OA:* 32 ft. 5 in.
shrouds, port and starboard	*LWL:* 28 ft.
29. Kingpost	*Beam:* 11 ft. 1 in.
30. Staysail boom	*Draft:* 5 ft. 6 in.
31. Highfield lever	*Cast iron keel:* 2¼ tons
32. Pulpit	*Built: Colaba Workshops,*
33. Bowsprit	*Bombay,* 1964–65
34. Bobstay	*Plain sail area:* 666 sq. ft.

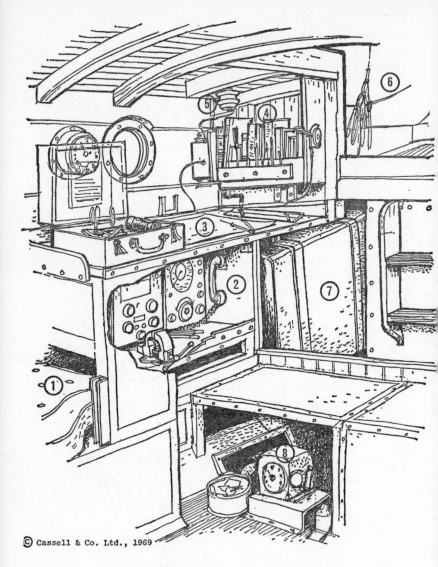

View of starboard side, main cabin, looking aft

1. Starboard settee berth, with slot for bunkboard
2. Radio
3. Chart table
4. Navigational books and instruments
5. Interior aerial connection
6. Hatchway
7. Entrance to engine-room, showing starboard Diesel fuel tank
8. Bilge pump

nineteenth century wooden ships were used to build our ketch. We would watch, fascinated, as the adze, handled almost casually by the Indian craftsmen, produced as fine a scarph as any modern plane. Teak was used for the entire construction – keel, planking, frames, deck and cabin top. To give an idea of the toughness of the boat, it is sufficient to say that the stringers, the longitudinal stiffeners, are 6 inches by 6 inches and all the planking is $1\frac{1}{4}$ inches thick. When she was launched she floated 2 inches below her designed water line.

Her masts and spars were of solid Kashmiri pine, her fittings and fastenings of galvanized steel, and the keel, cast in two sections, was $2\frac{1}{4}$ tons of iron, held by fourteen 2-inch thick keel bolts. The two water tanks of 48 and 38 gallons capacity, which were set beneath the sole, were made locally, but the engine, sails, wire and nylon rope for the rigging, toilet unit, winches and other fittings presented something of a problem. However, with the encouragement of Kenneth Campbell, the B.I. Chairman, Peter, who had returned to England on leave, was given permission to work his passage back to Bombay bringing these with him. The engine, a 38 h.p. B.M.C. Captain Diesel was chosen because we believed that if in a cruising boat you are going to have auxiliary power, you should have as much as the boat can safely take. We had two jibs, a staysail, main and mizzen, made by Jeckells of Wroxham, but later, when Mike Ledingham, another B.I. Third Officer, joined us, we found we could afford a spinnaker as well. This we ordered from Cranfields of Burnham-on-Crouch and it arrived by air in Bombay ten days after I posted the order!

Unfortunately the construction of the boat went slowly, and she was not even launched by September 1964, when we had hoped to set sail. At the same time my marriage was breaking up, and at the end of September my wife flew back to England.

I went back to the boat and on December 19th *Suhaili* – the name given by the Arab seamen in the Persian Gulf to the south-east wind – was launched by Mrs Munira Yusuf, the wife of the Kuwait Consul, who by local custom cracked a coconut on the bows whilst the men who built her chanted the traditional blessings from the scriptures.

By February 1965 the various delays meant that we had

missed the North-East Monsoon, and other problems arose. We were all short of funds, and Peter and Mike particularly had run out of time to make the trip back to England. Peter flew to Australia where he has since married and settled, and Mike eventually made his way to New Zealand. With a temporary loan from my family I bought out Peter's and Mike's shares in *Suhaili*, laid her up, and returned to England to take my Master's Certificate and do my first five month stint as an R.N.R. Officer.

I had an unfinished, half-paid-for boat 10,000 miles from where I wanted her and no crew to bring her home. I managed to raise the money to pay off the builder and while I was at it I persuaded my brother Chris, and Heinz, a Marconi radio officer who had sailed with me on the *Santhia* on the Persian Gulf run, to join me as crew. We met up in Bombay in November, and after fitting out in Mazagon Dock set sail on December 18th across the Arabian Sea to Muscat. We arrived at Durban from Muscat via Salala, Mombasa, Zanzibar, Dar-es-Salaam, Mtwara, Beira and Lourenço Marques in April 1966, but because we were too broke to buy stores even for the next leg to Cape Town, we all took jobs: Chris in an insurance office, Heinz at sea as a radio operator and I in command of a coaster. In October we were ready to sail, but our mainmast was broken in an accident and it was not until the end of November that a new hollow mast made of pine was stepped and we set off for Cape Town via East London. We sailed from Cape Town on December 24th and seventy-four days later, after a non-stop run, berthed at Gravesend.

Suhaili had proved herself a seaworthy boat, able when closehauled to sail herself for long spells without attention because of her remarkable 'balance'. There was too much weight aloft in the masts which caused her to heel over alarmingly at times but she was tough, safe, and at an average of 112 miles a day faster than we had expected.

With the voyage over, the Benfleet Yacht Club, of which I am a member, arranged a berth for *Suhaili* while I reported to B.I. It would be a month before *Kenya* arrived back in the U.K. from East Africa, so I was sent on leave. I sometimes wonder now what would have happened if the Company had been able to give me a ship immediately.

Make Do and Mend

THE sort of boat I wanted for a round-the-world voyage would have to be seaworthy and easy to handle. She would also have to be robust, and not at all complicated, and as I wanted to make a fast passage she would have to be long on the waterline, since it is upon length here that the theoretical maximum speed of a hull is dependent. She would also have to be ridiculously cheap to construct as I did not have a lot of money to spend. This, of course, is what every prospective boat owner is after: the impossible for the ridiculous. However, a large part of the cost of a boat comes in the fitting out, in building the smart interior, and I thought that if I did away with this I could get a pretty large boat comparatively cheaply.

I discussed it with an old friend, David Waterhouse, who whilst he makes no claims to being a great yachtsman, knows all there is to know in the chandlery business and has a very useful knowledge of what is going on in the world of yachting. He broadly agreed with my reasoning but suggested that we talked over the idea with a naval architect before going farther.

At the beginning of April he took me to see Colin Mudie and we put the idea to him. To Colin's everlasting credit he did not even blink when he heard how much I had to spend, but got out a drawing pad and started to sketch lines. About a week later the proposal plans arrived. Colin had designed a handsome looking boat which although made of steel and 53 feet long would weigh less than 7 tons. The system of construction was unusual to say the least. The boat was to have chines but to round these off, Colin intended putting 3-inch diameter water piping at each chine and the plating would be welded onto this. For spars and sails, to cut the costs, two 'Dragon' masts were going to be stepped, giving, I suppose, a schooner rig. Not only did this mean that the spars could be bought 'off the shelf' as if for Dragon class yachts, it also meant that fittings would be interchangeable between the masts. At my request a large square sail was drawn in to be set on the foremast instead of a spinnaker, as I felt it would be easier to handle and could be set usefully even on a fine reach.

We now had the plans, but before I could go any farther I had to get a quotation of the cost of building from a shipyard. This was almost the most interesting phase of the whole operation. Some yards refused even to quote, others when they could be persuaded to give a figure at all, went high enough, perhaps deliberately, to embarrass a millionaire. But eventually we found a yard at Woolwich on the Thames, which specialized in barges and coasters, and which not only gave me a reasonable quotation for the hull of £2,800 but appeared interested in the project. If I could build a hull at that price I could probably get the whole boat ready for sailing for less than £5,000, which was fantastic. I wasn't worried about the interior. Both Colin and I believe in tensing a hull so that it has suppressed energy within it to give back to the sea, and in order to achieve this we had a network of girders inside the boat. I intended knocking up a bunk and galley out of marine ply and making a few open lockers for food and other stores. The remaining space was going to be filled with polystyrene foam which would cut down the noise and make the boat virtually unsinkable.

But I wanted £5,000, and I might as well have wanted the moon. As far as my own resources were concerned, I had one asset, *Suhaili*, and even if I could sell her for that sum I would still be £2,000 short as I had to return the money I had borrowed to pay for her. David suggested that we look for a sponsor and started making inquiries within the trade. I put *Suhaili* into the hands of a broker just before I joined the *Kenya* and then, with the help of some passengers, wrote over fifty letters to various firms, detailing my experience and intentions. As it was obvious that if anyone else was thinking of the same voyage as myself they would accelerate their plans if they heard of mine, I kept things fairly dark. In addition to saying that I intended sailing round the world, I said that I planned first to enter for the 1968 singlehanded Transatlantic race which, in fact, was quite true, although I intended turning south the moment I crossed the finishing line, without stopping in America.

As it was a bit difficult for me to control events whilst away at sea, David undertook to look after things for me, but you cannot sell a boat if no one wants to buy, and as summer progressed with no acceptable offer for *Suhaili*, and replies to my letters to possible sponsors came dribbling in, all politely saying no, I began to get desperate.

Towards the end of the year, as a final throw, I wrote to Mr Harry Spanton, a director of B.I., and asked if the Company might consider sponsoring me. I received a phone call the next day asking me to go to Head Office for an interview, where I was grilled for an hour. I then saw the Marine Superintendent, Captain Lattin, who spent a whole morning running through the plans with me, checking costs, and advising further short cuts to save time and money. His report went to the Board and a week later I was sent for to hear their decision. It was no; money was short at the time, and they could not really justify the expenditure to the Company's shareholders. I was not particularly surprised, but I had at least been taken seriously and given a fair hearing, and Captain Lattin's advice alone made the attempt well worth while. Mr Spanton asked what I was going to do. I told him that my mind was set on going and as I had not been able to build a new boat, I'd go in the one I had, *Suhaili*. 'Well,' he said, 'whatever you do – do be careful.'

I had not made my decision on the spur of the moment. When the replies to my letters had started coming in I had begun to consider what to do if I could not get a sponsor. Everything led to the obvious answer, go in *Suhaili*. I had nothing else anyway. I had no doubts of *Suhaili*'s ability to make the voyage; the only trouble was that she is not a fast boat by modern yacht standards, just a good, sound ocean cruiser. Against this, a definite advantage of taking *Suhaili* would be that I knew her. After living in her for two years I knew her like the back of my hand. I knew her handling characteristics too. She was a boat 'in being' and there would be no need for long and extensive trials to iron out the inevitable little problems that would arise in a new boat. These had all been ironed out in the voyage from India. *Suhaili* was a proven boat and that was worth a good few hundred miles on a voyage round the world. She was still, however, laid up in her creek at Benfleet, and needed a thorough overhaul and refit before she could sail anywhere. Once again this would cost quite a lot of money and I just did not have it. I had managed to save up enough to buy a secondhand Austin Mini and pay Colin for his proposal plans during my eight months on *Kenya*, but that was all, and the Mini, if sold, would not even pay for a new suit of sails.

Suhaili needed more than that. She needed a complete scraping, caulking and painting, new rigging, ideally a new mizzen mast to cut down top weight and also to give me a mast I could manhandle about the boat in case the mainmast broke. I would need new sails, some form of self-steering, food and other stores, and the whole bill was going to run up to about £1,500. I still owed that £2,000 so I was hardly a good investment for anyone, but the money had to be raised somehow. The voyage *was* going to be made.

An obvious answer was to do all the preparation myself, but I had arranged to spend the first five months of 1968 in the Royal Navy doing more Reserve Training, and in any case I would have to support myself whilst re-fitting *Suhaili* and that required money. I decided to do my training and keep trying for a sponsor.

A week before I joined H.M.S. *Duncan* in Portsmouth, my luck changed at last. Ever since the previous voyage I had been playing around with writing a book, encouraged by George Greenfield, a literary agent who had first contacted me with the suggestion when we berthed *Suhaili* at Tower Pier. So far I had managed four chapters, but it was obvious that I was not going to have time for any more writing now that I had another voyage to plan, so I rang George and explained the difficulty.

He ignored the current book completely and started asking about the new project. When I told him of my financial difficulties he told me not to worry about them but to stand by for interviews and to get on with preparation, because he was sure that we could sell the story. I did as he said, and George was as good as his word.

I joined H.M.S. *Duncan* on January 2nd, 1968, and although busy getting to know different systems from those I was accustomed to in the Merchant Navy, I started making lists of stores and repairs necessary. Following an interview I had with David Ascoli, a literary director of Cassell, George wrote in the middle of January to tell me that he had signed a contract with them for this book. The advance payment meant that I could now afford to let a boatyard do the major re-fitting.

As time went on, George followed the Cassell contract with others from an American book publisher, Larry Hughes of William Morrow, Charles Barnard's *True* magazine in America, and finally the *Sunday Mirror*. We nearly did not sign up the *Sunday Mirror*. A meeting was arranged for lunch on a restaurant boat on the Thames and during the course of the meal a tug went past, throwing up a considerable wake. When the waves hit the restaurant it began to rock and I lost my balance and fell off my chair. An embarrassed silence followed whilst the *Sunday Mirror* top brass looked out of the portholes, at the menus, anywhere but at me, as red-faced I picked up the chair and resumed my seat. Not a word was said, but the thinking was deafening.

At this stage, early February, I knew of two others who were planning a non-stop voyage round the world: Commander Bill King and Captain John Ridgway, both of whom were having new boats provided for them by their sponsors. John Ridgway was hiding his intentions at the time and saying that he was preparing *English Rose IV* for the Transatlantic race. This told me he would be ready to leave about June 1st, roughly the time I had planned to sail. Commander King's *Galway Blazer*, a special design by Angus Primrose, would not be ready until the autumn, but as it was much longer than *Suhaili*, I could not afford to hang about until then.

In order to have any chance of beating these two, I would

have to get away early, hiding my intentions as long as possible to avoid hurrying the others; for this reason all my sponsors agreed to avoid publicizing my plans and their own part in them until nearer my departure date.

At the beginning of February, with a crew of midshipmen impressed from *Duncan*, I sailed *Suhaili* from Benfleet down to Souters' yard at Cowes, on the Isle of Wight. This was where *Galway Blazer* was being built, so as camouflage I muttered vaguely about sailing to Australia. I also took care to sneak a look at *Galway Blazer* – and came away feeling envious.

Towards the end of the month when the *Sunday Times* announced their Golden Globe trophy for the first person to circumnavigate the world non-stop singlehanded, I learned of a very formidable competitor, Bernard Moitessier of France. Moitessier in his ketch, *Joshua*, had already circumnavigated the world and rounded the Horn. He had the reputation of being a first-class seaman and I was sure that seamanship was going to count finally on this voyage.

Moitessier planned to sail in September. Allowing for his boat's speed this would enable him to clear Cape Horn before autumn in the Southern Ocean, and he could be back to Europe by May 1969. If I was going to be first round, and the voyage would take *Suhaili* ten months, I would have to leave by June 1st. I checked the weather for the route on this basis. It would be excellent for Cape Horn, which we would reach about the beginning of January, almost the best possible time; but it would also mean that I would spend part of the southern winter and all spring in the Southern Ocean – not so good. However, I could always head north if I found that the wind and seas were too much for us.

Perhaps the greatest problem in preparing *Suhaili* for a singlehanded voyage was arranging some form of self-steering. Self-steering gear is now an accepted part of the yachting scene, and indeed it was largely its development by people like Blondie Hasler and the Amateur Yacht Research Society that opened up the possibilities of singlehanded sailing over long distances. The broad principles of self-steering for yachts are fairly simple and for interested landsmen a good comparison can be made with a windmill, where a windvane, rather like a weathercock, turns the entire upper section of the windmill to head the sails into the wind. This upper section is so beautifully balanced that it needs only a slight push to move it, and to exert the force required to do this only a small windvane is required.

The action of the 'weathercock' windvane that you see on a yacht is similar, except that it is used to keep the yacht and her sails at an angle to the wind and not heading into it. And again, a principal requirement is 'balance', in that with the rudder in a central or near-central position, the sails can be so set that the yacht will sail herself, as *Suhaili* can when she is close-hauled, and needs only a slight push to turn her to one side or the other.

A self-steering gear is used not so much to keep a yacht on course as to bring her back onto it when she is thrown or wanders off. In simple terms, to achieve this the boat is 'balanced' on the required course. The windvane, doing its weathercock trick and pointing into the wind, is 'locked' by a clutch arrangement of gears or ropes to an auxiliary steering rudder or trim tab abaft the main rudder, which is 'trailing' in a fore-and-aft position.

If the yacht goes off course, the angle of the wind relative to the boat changes, and like the windmill vane or weathercock, the boat's self-steering vane follows the wind round. But now this action turns the auxiliary rudder, which gives the slight push needed to bring the boat back onto course. As the boat comes back, the windvane continues to follow the wind until the auxiliary rudder is once more amidships. The boat is now back on course and the weathercock goes back to sleep until it is required again.

Most yachts set their windvane at the stern, clear of the main boom and the disturbed air from the mainsail. I could not do this because *Suhaili*, being a ketch, had a mizzen boom extending about six feet over the stern. Unless the vane were hinged it would interfere with the boom, but in any case it would be affected by the air currents over the mizzen sail. If I removed the mizzen mast completely I would reduce the amount of sail that could be set, which would slow me down, and it would also upset *Suhaili*'s natural balance, which is remarkably good, and I did not like the thought of going on a voyage like this in an unbalanced boat. I needed self-steering, but the vane would have to go where it would be clear of sails and booms, and preferably where I could reach it easily in case repairs became necessary.

The germ of an idea finally came to me as I was watching a film I had taken in Durban of David Lewis's catamaran *Rehu Moana*. Two vanes were fitted right aft, one on each hull, and David had been able to use one or both vanes as he liked. The essence of the system was its simplicity. There were no fancy gears to jam or work loose, just the vanes connected by rope via pulleys to the rudder. I began to consider building a metal outrigger on either side of *Suhaili* level with the mizzen mast. The frame could be raised about four feet above the deck to give greater clearance, and on each outer end would be fitted a socket for a vane. To strengthen the whole fitting I planned to put in cross bars joining the outriggers together. These crossbars would get in the way on deck but would also give me something else to hang onto in the cockpit area.

The more I worked on the idea the better I liked it. True the vanes would get very close to the water and might perhaps even be immersed when the boat heeled over, but I could leave the leeward vane to trail out of gear and rely upon the windward one in those circumstances.

Fitting a small auxiliary rudder did not present many difficulties. The top end could be supported by *Suhaili*'s iron 'pushpit', and I asked Souters to build a shoe extension on the keel to support the lower end. To connect the vanes to the rudder I used a system of rope and pulleys. Each vane had a sheave bolted onto its stanchion; a spliced endless rope connected this sheave to another sheave placed two feet outside the centre line. Beneath these two inner sheaves were placed two others and round these lower ones went a rope which shackled to each side of the sideways extending tiller of the auxiliary rudder. The four inner sheaves were drilled with vertical holes and to clutch in one simply dropped a pin into a suitable position to lock a top sheave to its lower one.

The whole scheme looked like one of Heath Robinson's nightmares, and although friction was obviously going to be a problem, I saw no reason why it should not work and I looked around for someone to make it for me. Here David once again came to the rescue and introduced me to Clive Henderson, who runs a small toolmaking concern in Beckenham. Clive took some convincing to believe I was serious, but when convinced could not have been more enthusiastic. He not only made the outriggers, rudder, vanes and sheaves, he made spares as well, and when later on we set the whole thing up, he appeared on the scene to make sure that I assembled it properly.

Another idea I had was for charging the batteries by means of a propeller trailed in the water and connected by a flexible shaft to a dynamo. Clive and I did a number of experiments with high-speed propellers but had to give up eventually through lack of time, so he then made up the charger I took along with me, a small Norton-Villiers 3 h.p. petrol engine connected by a fanbelt to two dynamos. I think if we had used an alternator instead of a dynamo the propeller idea would have worked -- but the *Sunday Mirror* were relieved when I took a better-tried system.

As March came to an end, things were going along well. My stores were on order, the self-steering gear was under construction, and *Suhaili* was ready to be collected from Souters.

I went over to Cowes at the beginning of April. I spent the night with Bert Keeble at the National Sail Training Centre, and the next day collected *Suhaili* from Mike Souter and sailed to Portsmouth where I put her on the Royal Naval Sailing Association moorings off Whale Island. The work done at Souters included painting the hull after scraping and caulking, and a few other routine external jobs, but I still had to adapt the interior to take a year's supply of food and ship's stores. There was quite a lot of space available under the bunks and in lockers in the main cabin, but I should need more, so I set about ripping out the bunks in the forward cabin and building large shelves in their place. I renewed the rigging whilst in Portsmouth. The old wires were in good shape but I felt that it would be as well to get new for the coming voyage. As before I used plough steel and not stainless steel wire rope. The decayed electrical system was overhauled as well. In all these jobs I received terrific assistance from volunteers of all ranks in

H.M.S. *Duncan*'s crew, who gave up their off-duty hours to help me. I was fortunate in that *Duncan* was in dock for a month and I could paddle across to *Suhaili* most evenings.

Despite this it was becoming obvious that I was going to need more time than I had thought to get *Suhaili* ready in time to sail on June 1st, so I wrote to the Admiral Commanding Reserves and asked permission to cut short my training by one month. This was agreed to, although I received a stern reminder that I still owed eight months to the Navy. It was rather like the letters I receive from my bank manager. Still, it meant that I had May free, and on the 1st I took leave of *Duncan* after four enjoyable months, and with a crew consisting of Ken Parker, another director of Cassell's who would be 'handling your book if you make it and your log books if you don't', and Bruce Maxwell, an Australian journalist who was to be my rear link at the *Sunday Mirror*, sailed round from Portsmouth to the Surrey Commercial Docks in London. The trip round was chiefly memorable for the fierce argument between Ken and me as to our position in thick fog somewhere in the Dover Straits. Ken maintained that we were off Dungeness and I did not have a clue: Bruce, who had not sailed before, looked unhappily at the two Pommy 'old hands' who had put him into whatever position it was that he was occupying. The argument was eventually resolved when we picked up the buoy on Bullock Bank, which though off Dungeness, is twelve miles off. Within my sailing circle this is now known as the Parker Bank, and the argument as to exactly what is meant by 'off' continues.

Surrey Commercial Docks have never been fully rebuilt after the bombing raids during the last war. Their principal use now is for a dwindling timber trade and part of them has already been filled in to provide space for housing development. However, in one unused corner, Stave Dock, we berthed *Suhaili* amongst an assorted collection of craft belonging to the Sea Cadets. The big advantage was that my home at Downe lay less than ten miles away and I could get to *Suhaili* in half an hour.

My first task was in fact to take her out of the Surrey Docks and lay her alongside at Nelson Dock in the Thames at high water so that when the tide went out I could check over the hull. She had leaked a bit on the voyage round from Portsmouth and I wanted to look for the cause. To help me with this my brother Mike and his fiancée, Hazel, came down with Ken, and whilst in pouring rain they put on another coat of antifouling, I caulked the bottom seam of the boat in the vicinity of the mainmast step. This treatment seemed to do the trick, and I did not have to pump the boat out again during the rest of the stay in London.

Although half the jobs on my list were completed before I arrived at the Surrey Docks, there was still much to be done. I fitted a new roller-reefing gooseneck and halyard winches on the mainmast. Highfield levers replaced tackles on the main runners to make the job of setting these up easier. I overhauled the engine, had Green and Silley Weir caulk the deck, fitted a new twin-burner primus in the galley and remembered to order spares. A team of volunteers recruited from family and friends repainted the cabin. All the running rigging, the halyards, sheets and so on were checked and as a result I replaced all the halyards. With the exception of the mainsheet, all the others were still in good condition, but I made sure there was rope on board to replace them should this be necessary.

The old India-built mizzen mast was showing signs of wear, and after much thought and a consultation with my bank manager, I ordered a new aluminium mast to replace it. This arrived, together with two aluminium running poles, in the middle of May. I persuaded a friendly crane driver in the timber yard to remove the old mast and then stepped the new one by means of a complicated system of tackles leading from the mainmast. As I have said, one of my reasons for having this new, lighter mast was that should *Suhaili* be dismasted, I felt that I could step the mizzen on my own and carry on under jury rig. This would not have been possible with the old mast. Another advantage was that it lowered the overall centre of gravity and helped *Suhaili* to sail better.

The problem of how to remain in contact with the world whilst I was on the voyage had been exercising my mind for some time. Ideally I wanted a radio telephone so that I would be able to report my position and send messages as well as listen to the news and keep up with world events. I would not only feel less lonely, but I thought that watching my reactions would help me to spot any changes that might start appearing in my own character.

Marconi, who had loaned me one of their Kestrel I radio telephones for the last voyage, and could be relied upon to keep quiet about my plans, advised that for my requirements a High Frequency set was essential, and suggested a modified Kestrel II. Radio telephones cost a lot of money, and in their way are a luxury. I could sail without one and just take along a small transistor radio if necessary, and was quite prepared to manage like this until the *Sunday Mirror* came along in February. Part of our agreement was naturally that I should send regular reports of progress, so I now had to have an H.F. set. All along I was determined not to tie myself financially to any one manufacturer of any of the equipment I would take with me, but to buy that which suited me best or come with the best service. In this case I wrote to five firms in Britain who sold radio telephones, but as Marconi answered by telephone, and it was almost a week before I heard from anyone else, they got the order. The fitting was quick as I had not removed the wires when the last set was taken out. The only change made was in the aerials. My old arrangement had been a copper wire lead from the mainmast to the mizzen and down to the connection on the cabin top. This had been awkward and there had been a certain amount of interference from the wire backstays which affected performance. On Marconi's advice, I had two new main backstays made up with insulators fitted top and bottom, and in order to use the radio I connected up the cabin top fitment with one of the backstays. I was worried that this would reduce their strength, but neither broke during the voyage and the radio gave a far better performance than the previous set.

As May raced by, *Suhaili* began to take on the appearance of a specialized fishing boat. The main support for the self-steering vanes, a large and heavy 'bridge' constructed of 1-inch diameter tubular steel, was fitted in place and bolted to the deck. It stuck out three feet on each side of the boat and was raised four feet above the deck and looked about as decorative as a piece of scaffolding. The vane stanchions, built of stainless steel, were fitted and the large plywood vanes bolted into place. The special self-steering rudder arrived and was guided into position. We found this job more difficult than expected as the shoe was 5 feet 6 inches below the water; trying to get the rudder bar into it in the murky water of the dock was like trying to hit the bull on a dartboard blindfold. It was obvious that if I had to change the self-steering rudders at any time I would have to dive into the water to do it; but then, if the rudder did break, getting cold would be the least of my worries.

When we first roped the system up we found that the polypropylene rope slipped on the sheaves and the vanes would swing round in the wind without turning the rudder. Taking more turns on the sheaves failed to improve matters, so we had to dismantle the whole system and Clive had vertical grooves cut in each sheave to give some 'bite'. When the vanes turned the rudder turned as well now, but the whole system was very stiff and I just hoped that this would wear off before I finally set sail.

The food stores ordered from Duncan Wallet arrived at Downe on May 20th, filling a large lorry (see Appendix I). I had been immeasurably helped by the stores list Chris had drawn up for our Cape Town to London voyage. We had stocked up then for three people for 110 days. This gave food for 330 days for one person which seemed about right, so using this as a base I worked out my own requirements, adding a few 'luxuries' like sardines and dried fruit to add variety. Mainly I took canned foods, but I was given a number of dehydrated foods which turned out to be a great success when I had sufficient fresh water to add to them.

Canned foods as they come from the manufacturer are not designed for storage by yachtsmen. Apart from odd shaped tins, most are identically packed and can only be distinguished by paper labels which come loose the moment they get damp and clog the bilges with papier mâché. After a few months at sea, no tins can be distinguished and when one wants a meal one has to play a form of Russian Roulette. To avoid this I have a simple code to show what the contents of the tins are and this is painted on them at some conspicuous point. Once the tins are marked, the labels can be removed, and then I coat the tins in varnish to protect the metal from rust, which goes through the tins in a very short time. Dealing with well over 1,500 cans like this was a daunting job, but fortunately I had in Jim and Stella Friend two energetic assistants and we did the whole job in four boisterous evenings in the garage at home.

It did not look as if I would sail on June 1st, but I hoped to leave London for Falmouth on that day, and still hoped to set sail about June 7th. Only the stores remained to be put on board and with the aid of a hired van, nearly a ton of assorted tins and packets was taken down to the docks. About eight friends and some of the Sea Cadets gathered to help me with the enormous job of stowing these supplies, which had to be placed so that I could reach them easily, but more important so that they did not upset the trim of the boat and affect her sailing ability.

By the time everything was on board there was little room left inside the cabin and *Suhaili* rode a further two inches below the waterline. The appendix gives a detailed list of everything placed on board, but it is difficult to visualize the effect on the interior from a stores list. For a start, the shelves in the forward cabin were jammed with *Suhaili*'s spare sails, sea anchor, ropes, rigging wire, and so on; her requirements for the voyage if you like. Below these shelves was a space filled with tins of food. On the deckboards between the shelves were stowed nine 5-gallon drums of paraffin and Diesel fuel, and four containers of rice and sugar. I could just crawl into the forward cabin on my hands and knees over the drums. Coming aft into the main cabin, which is 12 feet by 6, both outboard bunks were packed with gear which included clothes, food, tools, the emergency liferaft and so on. The lockers behind and beneath the settee berths were full of tins as were the lockers round the galley and the radio. I had eight 5-gallon capacity polythene containers jammed together on the cabin deck between the settees, tucked as far as possible beneath the table. These contained extra drinking water, sugar, and petrol for the battery charger.

When all this was done I found that there was just no space left for my charts, so at the last minute I made a special rack inside the roof of the cabin to take them and my spare sail battens.

The two bookshelves in the cabin were packed and I had to set aside another shelf in the W.C. in order to get them all in. This was not really because I had too many books; I had to take a number of seamanship and navigation manuals, and most of the rest were lent to me by Dr Ronald Hope of the Seafarers' Education Service. He had obviously taken considerable trouble to get the sort of books I wanted and many times during the voyage I was to think gratefully of his kindness.

I took some care choosing books from home. I am a voracious book reader but I had no idea how much free time I would have, so I chose books that would take time to read and yet hold their interest all the way through. I had never really found time to read the classics, so books like *Tristram Shandy*, *Vanity Fair*, *Orley Farm*, *War and Peace*, were an obvious, and in the event wise choice. I also had about twenty-five specialist books dealing with the sea, sea-life and aspects relating to them, solely because the subject fascinates me. I did not really expect to have very much spare time on my hands, but as it was possible that I might have more than the books would fill, I took along a correspondence course for the Institute of Transport Examinations. The purpose of this was to give my mind something to concentrate on. I had no idea how ten months on my own would affect me mentally, so I decided to provide something that would help discipline my mind.

On the same lines, the *Sunday Mirror*, in an effort to try to shed some light on my mental outlook, sent me to a psychiatrist in order that he could compare my state of mind before I left with my state when I returned. I am delighted to say that on both occasions he found me 'distressingly normal'.

Of course, for a seaman, next to being actually at sea, the greatest enjoyment comes from preparing the boat for a voyage. Working on lists of food and stores had to be done, but what I really liked was poring over the Admiralty Chart Atlas and Catalogue and working out which charts and Admiralty Sailing Instructions I would need. These sailing directions, known as 'Pilots', give detailed descriptions of the world's coastlines. They also carry an almost encyclopaedic description of the climate, winds, tidal streams and currents to be expected in the area covered by each particular volume, and are invaluable to the seaman whether he sails a 200,000-ton tanker or a 4-ton yacht. I took the volumes that dealt with the areas I was expecting to pass through and I included the Antarctic Pilot in case I went to 50° South latitude, and also to give me information concerning icebergs which, as a warm water sailor, were a new and unknown threat to me.

As I expected to keep well out to sea for most of the voyage, apart from parts of Australia, New Zealand and Tierra del Fuego, I took no large-scale charts. The charts of the Oceans were quite sufficient for the greater part of the journey and I managed to make the circumnavigation on thirteen charts.* It is interesting to note that I needed seven to get from the Surrey Docks to Falmouth!

With so much food stored in the fore part of the boat I had to keep some heavy items for the stern or *Suhaili* would have sailed 'down by the head'. Apart from the engine, which weighed 500 lb., I had two 35-gallon fuel tanks which when filled added nearly 700 lb. This was still insufficient, so I stowed all my tins of beer and fruit juices, about 340 tins, in the cockpit lockers. This put *Suhaili* on an even keel. To lift the bow a little more, which makes *Suhaili* ride the seas better, I shifted four 5-gallon fuel containers from the forward cabin to the cockpit. This made hand steering a bit more difficult, but at the same time if we were ever 'pooped', that is if a wave came over the stern, there would not be so much empty space to be filled with sea water.

Despite the assistance I received – and *Suhaili* has a habit of turning spectators into helpers wherever she goes – there was still a lot of work left to be done as May drew to a close, but I did not seem to be making much progress with it and I began to think that if I did not get out of the Surrey Docks I'd never get moving at all. I decided to sail round to Falmouth, working *en route*, and finish my preparations there.

My reasons for choosing Falmouth instead of London as my port of departure were two-fold. First I did not like the idea of sailing solo through the Thames Estuary and the Downs and then past Dover and through the English Channel. I would have to keep awake for at least two days just to avoid shipping which

* For a full list of the charts and Admiralty Instructions I took with me, see Appendix II.

would leave me very tired right at the beginning and, I hoped, at the end of the voyage. Even this assumed that I had favourable easterly winds for the passage down-Channel; if I ran into westerlies, which was more likely, I could be days tacking through the Dover Straits alone, and for safety's sake I would have to pull into one of the Channel ports for a rest. If on the other hand I left from a more westerly harbour, and Falmouth was the largest in the west, I could clear the main shipping lanes almost immediately, and even if there were westerly winds, I could probably clear Cape Finisterre on one tack.

The second reason was curiosity – I had never been to Falmouth.

On Monday, June 3rd, Ken and Bruce and I met at the docks, and a fourth member of the crew, *Sunday Mirror* photographer Bill Rowntree, was introduced to me. He appeared, festooned with cameras, long-haired and sporting an outrageous moustache. Bill is a lively New Zealander who fitted immediately into the crew, but none of us could move around the boat without the cry 'Hold it there, fella' or 'That's fine, Bob' checking us, and it took a bit of time to persuade him that there were certain activities in the confined quarters of a yacht that I just would not let him photograph!

After initial engine trouble we set off down the Thames. My five-year-old daughter, Sara, had spent the last weekend with me, and as we motored past Greenwich I could see her waving from the pier. That was a bad moment for me. I had really got to know Sara during the previous year: my feelings for her are very strong and I knew that I would miss her in the year to come. I hoped that she would not be upset by my departure and I was relieved when she abruptly stopped waving and turned her full attention to a transistor radio. Children are remarkably resilient and after all she was already used to me going away to sea for quite long periods: she probably thought this was no different. I hoped so.

Suhaili was noticeably sluggish in the water, and I still had one-third of a ton of fresh water, 86 gallons, to take in the tanks. I would eat my way slowly through the cargo, but it would be some time before *Suhaili* could be expected to sail at her best. I was worried that with this heavy load, she might not ride well, but when a motor cruiser burst roughly past and *Suhaili* pitched and rolled her way through the wake without anything more than a wet deck, these fears were put to rest.

On our way to Falmouth we made one stop, at Newhaven. We groped our way through thick fog past Beachy Head and into port, using those well-known yachtsmen's navigational aids, the amber street lights on Seaford front, as our 'leading marks' to the harbour entrance. As we motored cautiously past the stubby lighthouse on the west pier a voice called out through the fog 'Glad you made it.' I thought it a nice gesture, and I hoped that it was a good omen.

At the Marina in Newhaven we were out of the public eye and were able to get on with preparations without the constant interruptions that had eventually held things up in the Surrey Docks. On the way round we had drawn up lists of jobs to be done and stores to be bought. These lists seemed to dominate our waking and sleeping hours until the minute I left, and could be found pinned up all over the boat. Just as soon as I crossed items off, others would appear to take their place. Plenty of loading lists had been published by long distance sailors but none is ever completely satisfactory for another boat and another man, whilst the time I intended to be away brought in a multiplication factor which no one had previously measured. The problem was that I had to take enough on board to keep myself and *Suhaili* going for a year, while the temptation was to add unnecessary items 'just in case' which would only add to the weight and occupy space that could be better used.

It was in Newhaven that the *Suhaili* Supporters Club came into being. Against my suggestion, Bruce was appointed Treasurer, because it was felt by the crew that having collected the subscriptions I might not return; as Bruce said darkly, 'The papers are full of stories of defaulting loan club treasurers round about Christmas.' It could also of course have been that the Treasurer was automatically in charge of the beer kitty, a natural job for any Australian. I had to content myself with the office of President, which in the Supporters Club carries responsibilities galore but no power.

Bruce left us at Newhaven to go ahead to Falmouth and

make arrangements with Vic Roberts, an ex-*Sunday Mirror* man, for our stay there. Ken, Bill and I followed in *Suhaili* on Friday, June 7th, reaching Falmouth on Sunday evening, by which time Bill had finally given up his attempts to talk me into being photographed taking a bath on deck, nude and with a bucket.

During these two days at sea I was able to experiment with the self-steering, which by then had been nicknamed 'The Admiral', for reasons which, as an R.N.R. officer, I do not intend to disclose. The vanes were quite wind conscious, although a little stiff, but the system was not transmitting orders to the rudder as well as I had hoped. The whole thing was obviously going to take time to work out, and as I knew that I would work much harder on it once I was on my way, I decided to leave it until I had set sail.

Falmouth as a port of departure was a better choice than I could have imagined. Vic managed to find us a mooring buoy in the middle of the harbour, and had booked us in at the Marine Hotel on the quayside, run by Di and Bob Drennan. If ever there was a sailor's hotel, it is the Marine. In the Chain Locker bar, ruled then by Bob's father, Jock, there are mementoes of ships and seamen stretching back beyond the great days of the Falmouth Packets, when crews were paid off in the bar and passengers stayed in the rooms that ramble down the hill to the water's edge. Di and Bob took us completely under their wing. We would wander in and out at all hours of the day or night, dirty and tired, and always they or Nigel Andrews, the chef, would produce meals or something hot to drink as if it were the most natural thing in the world. Before I left I booked a room for my return, promising to give Di and Bob a date from off Australia.

The last few days in Falmouth were chaotic. *Suhaili* had still leaked a bit on the way down to Falmouth, so I decided to take one last look at the hull before setting off. Bill and I took her round to Mylor and tied up alongside the jetty and let her dry out as the tide fell. I checked the seams yet again but they appeared tight and I did not want to force too much cotton in as it might strain the planking. Having dried out, we put on another coat of anti-fouling paint as the weed-killing properties are lost if the paint hardens.

Marconi sent a radio engineer, Ron Stringer, down to give the set a last-minute check, and before long he too found himself learning something of the practical side of boat maintenance.

A number of small metal fittings had also to be made and Vic introduced us to Pat Flux, a large, gruff and big-hearted engineer who 'hadn't the time to spare' but overnight made a peg board for the tiller, a spare tiller, counterweights for the windvanes – and then came down at dawn to make sure we fitted them without ruining his work.

I decided to leave on Friday June 14th, thirteen days after Ridgway and six behind Chay Blyth who had rowed across the Atlantic with Ridgway and was a late entry in *Dytiscus III*. My parents arrived the day before with Mike and Hazel, followed by George Greenfield. That night Bob and Di threw a party for us which lasted until 5 a.m. I got up three hours later with that sinking feeling that I always associate with those moments before entering the boxing ring as a schoolboy when I was up against a bigger and stronger opponent. I also had a slight hangover.

There seemed even now so much to be done and at the last moment I realized that I could not just set off for a year and ignore my ties. Whatever one may wish, it is really no more possible to 'drop out' from a modern society to make the sort of voyage I planned than it is to drop out in 'protest'; we depend on the continued support of others even to try. So whilst my family and friends rushed round Falmouth making last minute purchases, I spent the morning dealing with mundane and un-heroic things like annual subscriptions and insurance premiums.

We brought *Suhaili* alongside to fill up the fresh water tanks and whilst this was going on I received an unexpected but welcome last visit from David Roberts, the Port Chaplain. In my rush from home I had forgotten to bring along my Bible and David whisked me off into town and bought and inscribed for me a new one.

Her water tanks full, we put *Suhaili* back on the mooring and then all gathered ashore for a final beer and 'Oggie' with Di and Bob, Jock and Nigel. I put some money on the bar, but Bob shook his head. 'No,' he said. 'You pay when you come back.'

Out on the mooring I hoisted the sails and started the engine; there was no wind and I would have to motor clear of the harbour. This was the worst moment of all, the one I had been dreading. Mother and Father had come alongside in Robin Vinnicombe's *Huntress* and we had to say goodbye. They have backed me wholeheartedly all my life in everything I have chosen to do and made endless sacrifices for all their children. They, more than anyone, understood what impelled me to make the voyage, and they would bear the brunt of the worry and waiting until I returned. As I looked at their faces I almost decided not to go; it was too unfair.

I patted Gus, the family Labrador, went forward to cast off, and found Ken and Bill still busily bolting down a Highfield lever for the jibstay.

'O.K., I'll finish that,' I said. 'I'm off.'

Falmouth to the Forties

June 14th, 1968–September 10th, 1968 (Day 88)

SIX miles out of Falmouth, *Huntress* gave a farewell blast on her foghorn; Mother and Father, Mike and Hazel and my friends waved, and then they turned back. It was a rather shattering moment as the first feelings of true loneliness came to me. I began to wonder what I should be like in a week's time if I felt like this now, and I wished I knew how I would react to being alone for long periods. To take my mind off the problem, I set up the aerial and made my scheduled contact with the *Sunday Mirror* office. This was really to give everyone confidence in the radio and check our system before I had gone too far to make any rearrangements. All went well and we arranged for another chat the next day. This completed, I got out a chart of the world, had a long look at the route and started working out the best course to steer in order to take the fullest advantage of the winds and currents. It may seem to be one hell of a time to be doing this, but there was no need for such detail before. The route down the Atlantic is fairly obvious but would depend on the winds I encountered. You can plan an exact route for a sailing vessel but you cannot expect to keep to it. What I was now doing was to work out a few points to aim for as nearly as the winds would allow and when I came up close to the first I would plan the next stage. The first point was 150 miles west of Cape Finisterre, the next 50 miles west of Madeira Island and the last before the Equator was the Cape Verde Islands, which I intended sighting to check my navigation and take a departure for the next part of the voyage to my landfall in Australia. From a psychological point of view this planning was the best thing I could have done. I became thoroughly absorbed in it and by the time darkness fell, I was keen to get on and start crossing off the miles.

Suhaili steered herself all the first night without need of the self-steering. The wind was from the west-south-west, so we were close-hauled and she did not want much attention from me. However, I slept huddled fully clothed in the cockpit with a hand flare and foghorn handy just in case any ships came too close. At one point after I had dropped off for an hour I awoke to find we were heading back towards Cornwall with the Lizard light well in view; the wind had come round, but I was able to adjust the course slightly and this carried us through the rest of the night.

The most important job facing me was making the self-steering system work, so as soon as it was light, I fried up some bacon and eggs and then tackled the Admiral. The vanes were too stiff so I poured metal polish into the bearing and then spent some time spinning the vanes round. This action, I discovered, loosened the connecting lines, which had to be taken out and respliced. That done, the system worked – to a certain extent. I wanted to steer westwards for a few days in order to get well clear of the Bay of Biscay, and with the light north-east wind, *Suhaili* would never have held that course without the Admiral. I did find, though, that we had to yaw a bit off course before the wind on the vane built enough pressure to turn it.

Apart from trying to get the Admiral loosened up, I spent the first few days settling myself in for a long stay. Having spent something like two years using *Suhaili* as a home in port and at sea, I had grown familiar with her and felt at home after even months away. What I was now doing was shifting things around to make myself more comfortable and making sure that the items I might need in a rush were accessible. I had intended keeping both the settee-berths clear so that I could choose which-ever one was the most comfortable. It makes quite a difference to the comfort of sleeping in *Suhaili*'s settee-berths if you can manage without a bunkboard, the plank that slots in an upright position at the side of the berth to stop you being thrown out.

With the bunkboards in place, the berths are rather like coffins. So, if the boat is heeled over, I like to sleep in the lower bunk as one can then discard the bunkboard and rest against the padded back of the settee; unless the boat rolls violently, gravity stops you being tumbled onto the deck. Unfortunately I found that I had so much equipment that I wanted at hand that I had to sacrifice the starboard bunk for use as storage space; so, in practice, when *Suhaili* was on a port tack I had to sleep in the port hand coffin.

My first week's sailing was disappointing as far as speed and distance were concerned – 77 miles in the first day, then 80, 52, 38, 62, 87 and 100 – which left me about a hundred miles north-west of Cape Finisterre. The winds were light and I did not get as far west as I wanted. However, when the winds began to freshen I decided to head south rather than west as I wanted to get a move on, and I hoped that I would manage to work sufficiently clear of Cape Finisterre. When I passed it on June 22nd we were 60 miles to the west, which wasn't half as far as I would have liked but was at least well clear of the shipping lanes. We sailed due south from there until meeting the North-East Trades, when I set a course to clear Madeira Island.

During the first week I made several attempts to contact Alec Rose who, in his *Lively Lady*, was heading towards Portsmouth after his non-stop singlehanded run from New Zealand. Bruce had told me to try calling at 6 a.m. G.M.T. but I never received a reply. I'm not surprised, because nobody had told Alec to listen out for me in particular and he must have had plenty of other things to think about at that stage in his voyage. However, three weeks later on July 11th, 'had 14 mins. conversation with Bruce and received best wishes from Alec Rose. He also warns me to watch out in the Southern Ocean. He should know!'

My concern was to put the opposition behind me as soon as I could, and on Thursdays when I spoke to Bruce on my regular schedule he gave me the latest positions of John Ridgway and Chay Blyth, together with progress reports on the competitors who had yet to start. I plotted this information carefully so that I could get some idea of how I was doing. It was soon obvious that I was gaining steadily on Ridgway and Blyth without having to push myself to the point where I was using up energy faster than it could be replaced by food and rest. Naturally this gave me a boost and I calculated that I should be in the lead by the time we reached the Southern Ocean. Despite this it was not until June 28th, my fourteenth day out, when I was due west of the Straits of Gibraltar and running down to leave Madeira and the Canaries to the east, that I had a day's run exceeding a hundred miles, and even then I had two more poor days before picking up the North-East Trades.

This was an important milestone. For the first time since leaving Falmouth we were running before the winds, as we would be for five months in the Southern Ocean, and apart from the extra speed we should get, it gave me an opportunity to test the Admiral on this point of sailing and iron out any difficulties that arose. The vanes were still a little stiff, but to my great relief the system worked without any adjustment.

July 1st, 1968   *Day 17*
The big thing is that she is running nearly right before the wind and sailing herself. As I sat watching her it was quite amazing the way she recovered from surfing down a wave so that when the next wave arrived the stern was pointing straight at it. She managed it far better than a helmsman could have done.

It had taken me sixteen days to complete less than 1,200 miles, but for a good bit of this distance we had been in the 'Horse Latitudes', the area of generally light and variable winds between the south-westerly wind belt covering the region that includes the British Isles, and the North-East Trades farther south. From now on our speed began to increase. The North-East Trades blow at an average speed of about twelve knots and are as dependable as the sun.

I had settled in by this time, and was working to a daily routine which I had developed on my previous voyage but which, obviously, had had to be adapted to lone sailing. I tried to get to sleep at 10 p.m., if the sailing conditions allowed, and apart from a check at 2 a.m. (more frequently in the shipping lanes or bad weather) I slept through until 6 a.m. when I got up and made my rounds of the deck, setting what adjustments seemed necessary to the rudder, Admiral and sails. Breakfast followed, usually fried eggs and something else, followed by a mug of coffee and the first cigarette of the day. If it was fine enough I always sat on deck for this. Nothing can compare with the freshness of the early morning at sea. My favourite watch on a ship is the 4 to 8 because one gets the sunrise and the delicious feeling of newness that comes with it. Whilst smoking I would plan my day. If the Admiral was feeling gouty I would steer, but if not, I would get on with the numberless little jobs that have to be done to keep a boat seaworthy.

June 24th, 1968   *Day 10*
Once the charger was at work I cleaned out the engine bilge, finding a spanner, an old fan belt, some rubber pipe and an assortment of rags. These latter I put on a rope and towed o'side to clean them as I always run short. Next I took some of the caulking compound and rammed it into holes in the forward hatch and round the king-post where water has been entering the boat. I finished up the tin of compound in odd places around the deck. After lunch of cheese and Marmite sandwiches I refilled the charger and continued boosting the batteries. . . . By this time it was beautifully hot so I went over the rigging with a mixture of white lead and tallow and then brought clothing and bedding out to air. I finished up a tin of Teepol giving the cabin a good scrub out and went for a swim, my first since leaving the U.K. Much to my disgust a wash removed most of what I had assumed to be suntan! . . . The log does not seem to want to work. I overhauled it but this made it even less enthusiastic. [Later I handed it and did not use it again.]

When the battery charger was working on deck the cockpit became untenable, and as the exhaust fumes seemed to find their way below, I had to find something to do on the fore part of the boat. If there was no work to be done, I used to take a book up there and read. Towards midday, before taking my noon sunshot, I would, if the day was warm, dive overside for a swim. Before doing this I paid out one of the sheets so that it trailed astern and acted as a safety line. Diving ahead of the boat, usually from the bowsprit, I would swim as hard as I could until the stern came level when I would grab the safety line and haul myself back on board. Then I would have a good scrub with salt water soap before diving over again for a rinse. This kept me cleanly fit!

I was free of one daily chore. The morning we left Ken asked me if I had enough razor blades; I said I had, and Ken went off to buy some for me. Two days out I was looking for a razor blade to sharpen a pencil, but I could not find my packets and had to do with one left over from the last voyage. Ken returned to London with his year's supply of razor blades still in his pocket, and I grew a beard.

A sedate lunch followed my swim, usually consisting of biscuits and cheese or the like, with a pickled onion on special occasions as a treat. The afternoon would be spent just like the morning, working or reading, until 5 p.m. when, if I felt like it, I dropped everything for a beer or a whisky. Whilst I had this I used to write up my log book, or later, after I had decided that the log was giving insufficient detail and I started keeping a diary as well, I used to write that up. Dinner, usually a largish meal, followed. This was more often than not a stew, which is easy to make; and if one makes too much, it is a simple matter to add a few more ingredients to change the flavour for the next meal. Coming back from Cape Town we had developed a *Suhaili* stew, constructed of bully beef, tinned peas, soup powder and beef cubes. When thin, this was a good stew; when it thickened up it went well with chips. A tin of a different vegetable alters the character completely, and by constantly adding new bits and pieces, one always has a mature basic meal ready. When after a few days one grows tired of it, I recommend throwing a spoonful of curry powder into the mixture to finish it up.

June 25th, 1968   *Day 11*
I think I shall set myself up as a curry cook when I get home. 'R K-J entertained the Ladies Guild to a lecture which was followed by one of his celebrated curries. 37 people were later detained. . . .'

Before it got dark I would make a final round of the deck, checking the sails and rigging. Shackles can work loose and I used to have a shackle check every day, walking round with a marline-spike and checking that the pins were tight. In the voyage I only had three shackles work loose, but one was the bronze shackle on the jib clew, and the sail had thrashed to pieces before I could refix the sheet. This sort of thing is expensive, hence regular checks.

Before climbing into my sleeping-bag, or onto it if the night was warm, I took a last look at the weather and gauged whether to set more sail or reduce sail for the next four hours, and that would complete an average day. I have mentioned little of the actual sailing but then one constantly watches the sails and adjusts as necessary, and if conditions warranted it, I could be at the helm all day.

The most alarming factor in the first few weeks was that the bilges kept filling with water and I was having to pump them out twice a day, more often if the sea was rough.

June 30th, 1968   *Day 16*
... she is taking in more water than she should. I have a feeling it's coming in about the garboard strake [the strake or plank next to the keel] as I noticed yesterday that the anti-fouling had flaked off thereabouts. It does not appear to be coming in forward anyway, which is some consolation, if one can console oneself over any leak.

Whilst we were in the North-East Trade Winds I could do little about this as the only way to find the cause was to go overside and check the hull below water. To do this properly the boat has to be stopped and moving around as little as possible, conditions which I could not expect until we got into the Doldrums, when we could expect warm days and calms. The warmth is important as if one stays immersed for long, even in the Tropics, one loses a great deal of body heat, and the best way of warming up is to lie in the sun.

On July 9th we closed the Cape Verde Islands and ...

July 10th, 1968   *Day 26*
The alarm woke me at 0120 and I went up to take a look for land. I was about to go below again when I saw Fontes Pereira de Melo light about half a degree above the horizon. I altered course to the south in order to pass between the islands of Santo Antão and São Vicente as I thought I might be able to report myself on the way through. The wind was N.E. but backed to the north as I came up to

land. By 0430 P. de Melo light bore west and I could see the lights of São Vicente. I was quite pleased with my landfall. I was in fact a couple of miles out in my reckoning but this was along my position line and so excusable. The land had that barren, rocky appearance that I find so attractive and in ordinary circumstances I would have anchored and gone ashore for a climb. As I rather expected, once into the channel between the Islands the wind force increased considerably, although because there was little fetch, the waves broke but did not get big. *Suhaili* raced along. I had the spinnaker, staysail and mizzen up and was doing a good 7 knots. The log jammed – there are about 6 ballbearings missing in the bearing – and so did not show my true speed. I thought about reducing my sail a bit, but decided the thrill was too good to miss. I have not had racing like that since the last voyage when running before the S.E. Trades. Halfway through the channel, with São Vicente clearly showing abeam I passed a large cargo ship. I tried calling him up but could not aim the light properly as well as steer and all I got from him was a succession of W's [in International Code 'I am unable to read your message owing to light not being properly trained or light burning badly']. He passed about 3 cables to port. I was beginning to feel tired by this time so I brought out the J. Walker still ¼ full and finished it off. It had a far more potent effect than usual, due to the fact that I have not been drinking much for about 4 months, I expect [I had had jaundice], and made me quite light headed. I think it was this that caused me to discover an island in my path soon afterwards. I had no chart of the Islands and no Pilot either, so I had to rely upon the Atlantic–Eastern Portion chart which shows São Vicente the size of a matchend, hence I thought it possible that an island existed. There was a full moon and ahead I saw a black shape. For some time I pondered which side to leave it; at first it seemed close to land but as I progressed it moved farther out from São Vicente and eventually I decided to go between it and the land. I altered course and it soon dawned on me that my 'Island' had moved farther out – it was showing no lights so I had ruled out a ship at first sight, but it was obviously something large moving. It was not until just before sunrise that I was able to recognize it as a pall of heavy black smoke which completely hid the boat making it. I threw the whisky bottle at the moon! By sunrise the end of São Vicente Island was abeam and I set to work on the Admiral.

Two days past the Cape Verde Islands we ran into a calm patch and I reduced sail. Donning a mask and snorkle, I dived overside and went straight to the spot level with the mainmast about a foot above the keel where we had had trouble on the previous voyage. The trouble was there all right and a large gap was showing along the seam for about eight feet. I swam under the keel and checked the other side. It was the same, and as *Suhaili* pitched and rolled easily in the water I could see the gap opening and closing slightly. I swam to the surface, hauled myself on board, lit a cigarette and started to think the problem over. What really worried me was the thought that maybe all the floors, the brackets that join the frames to the keel, were working loose and that this was just the beginning of real trouble. It would be suicidal to carry on with the voyage if this were the case but at the same time it was very difficult to see if the danger was serious, as the floors were for the most part hidden by the water tanks which were built into the boat. Those I could see I checked and they seemed firm enough, so I convinced myself that they were all basically strong and the trouble was just a continuation of the old problem and could be put right by caulking. If I was wrong in this, I just had to hope that not all the floors would go at once and I would be able to manage to make a port before *Suhaili* broke up.

It was not until after the voyage, when *Suhaili* was on show at Holborn Circus in London and I saw her dried out properly for the first time, that I really saw the extent of this weakness and how strained she was. Right along this seam, water from the bilges within the boat had seeped out, and the stains on the hull were very noticeable.

Having decided that caulking was the answer, I had to think of some way of doing it five feet below water. Normally dry twisted raw cotton is hammered into the seam, stopped with filling compound and painted over, but I could not do that. I decided to try and do the job with cotton anyway and hope that the fact that it would be wet would not make too much difference. We had had to do just the same thing when in the middle of the Arabian Sea, but it had not been easy, and at least I had had two other people helping me and keeping a lookout for sharks. This time I would have to do the job on my own and hope that I would notice any sharks whilst they were still circling.

I got out the cotton and twisted up some pieces in 18-inch lengths, a convenient length to handle although ideally I should have done the whole job with one piece. Next I put a long length of line on a hammer and lowered it overside near where I had to work. Finally I dressed myself in a blue shirt and jeans to hide the whiteness of my body, something that sharks, great scavengers, always associate with refuse, and strapped my knife to my leg. I put the cotton on deck where I could reach it from the water and taking my largest screwdriver as the most convenient caulking instrument, I went overside.

The job was impossible from the start. In the first place I would run out of breath before I had hammered enough cotton in place to hold it whilst I surfaced, and each time I came up for air I lost all the work done. Secondly the cotton was just not going in properly, and even when I changed the screwdriver for a proper caulking iron I made no progress. After half an hour of fruitless effort I climbed back on board and tried to think of some other way of doing the job.

A while later I was busily engaged in sewing the cotton onto a strip of canvas $1\frac{1}{2}$ inches wide. When the whole strip, about seven feet of it, was completed I gave it a coating of Stockholm Tar and then forced copper tacks through the canvas about six inches apart. I went into the water again and placed the cotton in the seam so that the canvas was on the outside; I then started knocking the tacks into the hull to hold the whole thing in place. The finished job did not look too bad but it was a bit ragged at the edges and I thought that it might be ripped off when *Suhaili* got moving again, so I decided to tack a copper strip over the canvas to tidy it up. The copper strip was, in fact, left on board by the Marconi engineers when they fitted the new radio, and I am afraid that I had not drawn their attention to it when they finished.

So far, although I had kept glancing nervously about me whilst I was in the water, I had seen no fish at all. But whilst I was having a coffee break, having prepared the copper strip and made holes for the tacks so that I would have an easier job under water, I suddenly noticed a lean grey shape moving sinuously past the boat. The sharks had found us at last. I watched this one for ten minutes hoping it would go away as I did not want to have to kill it. I was not being kind to the shark; if I killed it, there would be quite a bit of blood in the water and the death convulsions would be picked up by any other sharks near at hand who would immediately rush in, and I would not be able to get the job finished. After ten minutes, though, during which the shark kept circling the boat and showing no signs of leaving, I got out my rifle and, throwing some sheets of lavatory paper into the water, waited for the shark to come and investigate. On its first run round the shark passed about three feet below the paper, but then he turned and, rising slowly, came in again. I aimed the rifle at the shape and with finger on the trigger, followed it as it came in. Three feet short of the paper the top of the head broke surface and I squeezed the trigger. There was an explosion in the water as the shark's body threshed around but within half a minute the threshing ceased and the lifeless body began slowly to plane down until it disappeared into the blue. For the next half hour I watched carefully to see if any other sharks would appear, but apart from two pilot fish, which, having followed their previous protector down until they realized he would never feed them again, now decided to join a larger and apparently stronger master, *Suhaili* and I had the sea to ourselves. I went overside and in an hour and a half had the copper tacked over the canvas on the port side. A light wind getting up forced me to leave the starboard side until we were next becalmed. But in any case I was quite chilled from four hours immersion, and also a little tense from constantly glancing around expecting to see a shark coming in behind me, and I was quite glad to give the job a rest for a while.

Two days later, when becalmed again, I went overside and repeated the job on the starboard side without incident. The leaking into the boat almost stopped completely, and I never had to pump out the bilges so often again. I still worried about the floors, but no more than I worried about the keel bolts or hull fastenings, none of which gave the slightest trouble.

By the middle of July we were coming into the Doldrums,

which at this time of the year lie north of the Equator. The sea was a Mediterranean blue and usually fairly calm.

I rigged up an awning over the cockpit with my sleeping-bag to provide shelter from the sun, brought a mattress up from below and reclined like an Oriental Potentate. When I felt too hot I dropped overside and swam lazily alongside the boat in the rather warm water. The gentle tenor of my ways was occasionally interrupted by the rain squalls, which although they led to a hurried dismantling of my palace, cooled the air wonderfully:

July 17th, 1968   *Day 33*

At 1800 a large rain squall struck. I handed the spinnaker and set the jib at 1730 as I could see it coming, then, just before it arrived I struck the staysail and reefed the main and mizzen and put buckets beneath the goosenecks. It was glorious. I had a bath and it was all I could do to stop myself dancing – beautiful cold water, and of course the atmosphere cooled at once. The height of the squall, which lasted for about 2 minutes, brought the rain pelting down whitening the whole sea, which was otherwise dark as the sky was hidden by black cloud. There was a wonderful sunset soon afterwards. The clouds were all tinted blue . . . except for one which was golden. A beautiful sight – I wish I could paint.

I usually managed to collect some of the water in a bucket hung beneath the goosenecks, and this I used for drinking purposes. To anyone who had never collected rain water and drunk it either fresh or in tea or coffee, my advice is try it. Tea was rather a treat as I had only taken two pounds of it because it is so difficult to keep properly in a damp atmosphere. As well as that, a certain amount of water is wasted in the pot and I was watching my consumption of drinking water down to the last drop.

The U.K. Radio Telephone station at Baldock was becoming rather weak now, and on July 19th I had my last direct contact with Bruce. Although the range was nearly 3,000 miles, he came through clearly and we chatted for half an hour during which time he brought me up to date with the race:

Bruce hopes to be in Melbourne when I pass which will be

splendid. Of Ridgway and Blyth there is no news – I'm keeping a good lookout for them! King and Moitessier plan to start in about a fortnight. Those two worry me as both have longer boats than *Suhaili* and I will have a bare seven weeks start so I cannot afford to hang about.

After the radio contact, my last with the U.K., I turned in again until 0700 when I got a chronometer time check. I then had breakfast – eggs and potato bread, the latter a bit mouldy now – and as the sky seemed clear I set the spinnaker in place of the jib. I would have preferred to set the large flying jib but the last two times I have had to take it in when it has been blowing as the brake has failed to lock with the result that the sail has gone into the water.

This winch was giving me a lot of trouble at this time. On July 23rd:

The winch did not work, of course, or rather its brake failed to brake and I ended up with a mass of sail in the oggin. Fortunately we were not going very fast so I was able to haul it out without damage, but it is alarming and I do not see what I can do about it – short of rigging a purchase in place of the winch. For £58 I would have expected reliability. They are made for the Yacht Fittings Manufacturer's Yachtsman, of course, the man who thinks nothing of spending a couple of thousand each season. I feel this is a very short-sighted policy as there can be only a very small percentage of the yachtsmen in this bracket, and a reliable and cheap winch would sell well – instead one gets unreliable and tarty fittings, fine on a Gin Palace.

Another hate I have developed is for bronze shackles, simply because they don't seize up. I have lost two so far which have worked loose during the night. This is in spite of my diurnal shackle and chafe checks. They are no doubt ideal for weekend sailing, but a disadvantage for long distance cruising. The disadvantage of requiring pliers to open a shackle is outweighed by the advantage of knowing it will remain done up, especially when singlehanded.

This was actually the last time a bronze shackle gave me trouble as I took to getting them as tight as I could with pliers and then putting a piece of seizing wire round the eye of the pin and the shackle itself.

The fine calm weather gave me an excellent opportunity to do some work on the boat and I spent some time making a canvas bandage which wrapped round the fore hatch and prevented water getting in through the gap between hatch lid and base. I also put some flexible seam stopper round the skylight where water seemed to have found a way in.

As when running a race you divide it up into laps, so I had divided the voyage up into seven sections. None of these was of the same distance and their borders were only geographical positions that had little importance apart from the psychological value of having completed a lap. Basically they were Falmouth – Equator; Equator – 40°S 0°E (west-south-west of Cape Town); 40°S 0°E – Perth; Perth – Bluff; Bluff – Cape Horn; Cape Horn – Equator; Equator – Falmouth. We had almost completed the first lap when we met southerly winds just north of the Equator. There is a strong west-moving equatorial current in this area, which can carry a boat as much as forty miles in a day and in order to reduce its effect on my course I took *Suhaili* over nearer to the African coast than is normally recommended. I think this paid off because when the variable light winds of the Doldrums steadied in southerlies about four degrees north of the Equator, we were in 15° West longitude, and I was able to sail *Suhaili* rather freer than normal which gave us some terrific days' runs.

July 27th, 1968   *Day 43*

I did not get to sleep until 1 a.m. this morning, due mainly to a feeling of unease due to the rising wind. Eventually I took a turn in the main boom [a reef] and then dropped quickly off. I was awakened at 6 a.m. by a squall and I took a couple of turns in the mizzen. *Suhaili* was screaming along when I got on deck, throwing the waves aside contemptuously and appearing to jump from wave top to wave top. It was exhilarating and frightening at the same time. Later I was able to tie the time of this squall in with the crossing of the Equator, which on average took place at 0700. At noon I calculated that we had covered 170 miles during the past twenty-four hours!!!

The two sights run up crossed perfectly with the Meridian Altitude, so I don't doubt the position. This is quite fantastic, and even allowing for the current, say 40 miles to the west, is an unheard of speed for *Suhaili* close-hauled. . . .

There was a most interesting cloud formation this morning. Tufts of cirro-cumulus which slowly expanded and merged into a vast sheet of cloud with clearly defined edges. At one time it was possible to see the cloud forming at the south-west edge. This sheet passed to the north-east and then another identical one came up from the south-west.

This was my forty-third day at sea and so far I seemed to be mentally and physically fit. I had had no illusions or anything to make me think that loneliness was having an adverse effect on me. I had heard voices only once, and that had been a very eerie experience. I was in the 'engine-room' at the time reconnecting the batteries to the radio after a day's charging, when suddenly and unmistakably I heard voices. My hair started to bristle on the back of my neck at this. I knew there were no ships about and no humans for hundreds of miles and my immediate thought was that 'there must be something to supernatural occurrences after all'. I am not a superstitious person; I feel that most things have an explanation if you look hard enough for it, but voices, when I knew that there should not be voices, unnerved me a bit. I came out of the engine-room pretty fast and at once discovered the cause. I had left my small tape recorder connected up with a tape on it, and what I heard was the spoken introduction to a concert! That evening I noted:

Whilst working on the batteries I had reconnected it. On thinking over the incident later, I felt that my reactions had been perfectly normal, in fact I drew quite a bit of comfort from the fact that the sound unnerved me, not because there were voices, but because there were voices when I *knew* there couldn't be any. Voices are a perfectly natural background usually, but I realized that they were not natural in my environment, and that is what disturbed me. I thus convinced myself of my own sanity, or, more correctly, I reassured myself that I am still as sane as I ever was. There is a subtle difference. So far, therefore, no visions or voices.

My food seemed to be lasting well, but the onions were going bad rather quickly, mainly because they had got wet in the forward cabin and it did not look as if they were going to last very long.

The two fo'c's'le bunks were removed and replaced with racks for the bulky foods, sails, heavy warps and the like

◀ *Overleaf: Suhaili* under storm jib and reefed mizzen—our 'working suit' when running before a gale

I did much of *Suhaili*'s fitting-out in the comparative peace of London's Surrey Commercial Docks

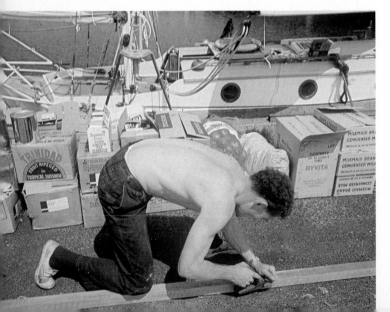

One man, 30,000 miles, 10½ months = 1,500 tins, 250 lb. onions, 350 lb. potatoes, etc. . . . In Surrey Commercial Docks before sailing to Falmouth

At Mylor, near Falmouth, Bill Rowntree (with time off to take photographs) and I slapped on a last coat of anti-fouling the day before *Suhaili* and I sailed. The Admiral's gantry and rudder show up clearly here

Saying goodbye to Mother and Father was the worst part of leaving Falmouth

Overleaf: The Admiral's gear consisted of an outrigged vane set on a freely ▶
rotating pulley wheel on each side of *Suhaili.* From each of these pulley wheels
a spliced 'endless rope' ran inboard to link it to the top one of two pulleys set
one above the other on the 'bridge'. The windward set of two pulleys would
be locked by a pin, and a 'steering rope' (which ran from the one arm of the
self-steering trim rudder round both lower pulleys and back to the other arm)
operated the arm and consequently the rudder

30,000 miles to go. This photograph, taken from *Huntress* as my family and 'Supporters Club' turned back to Falmouth, shows the Admiral's leeward vane out of gear and swinging freely, which was how I left it in the early stages of the voyage.

The smell of decaying onions has been offending me for some time so I took 3 bags out onto the deck and sorted them out – I was left with about 1 bagful. All had shoots and many were mushy. This is a bitter blow as I rely on onions for fresh food. I should have made sure of really hard ones before I left.

It was a great disappointment because I am fond of onions and consider them to be good for one. The eggs were going off as well. The last time I had tried to make an omelette I had broken four and all had that slight smell people of my age associate with the powdered egg of the wartime and immediate post-war days. I made the omelette anyway, but it was not very enjoyable.

Cooking had its hazards though, and on a small boat there always seems to be a shortage of space to put things down. The day before we crossed the Equator I had produced a stew in the pressure cooker, and having stewed it up, removed the cooker from the stove and put it on the bench step at the after end of the cabin. I turned to get some cutlery, put the kettle on the stove, and sat down – on the pressure cooker! As I was not wearing any clothes at the time I leapt up with a yelp of pain. There was no *important* damage but it was about three days before I could sit down comfortably again.

Cape Town radio, which had been trying to get through to us ever since the last contact with Baldock, started coming over quite strongly on July 27th, and I was able to speak to my new contact, Natie Ferreira, and receive the latest news of the other boats. Ridgway and Blyth were still thought to be ahead, and no one else had yet started. I had not expected to overtake the first two just yet, and in the South-East Trades which we were all in now, I could not expect *Suhaili* to gain much as we would be close-hauled, not her best point of sailing. *Suhaili* never has sailed close to the wind. I was actually getting within 65° of it, which wasn't good, but was average for her. A more modern design would get within 45°, which means an extra ten miles made good in a day's run of 100 miles, and in the comparatively low-speed areas in which yachts operate, that is a considerable gain.

The news that no one else had yet started was good. It meant that we had at least seven weeks start and the longer that the fast boats delayed the better my chances. I have learned since that the opinion of some was that the younger men set out rather too early, and Blyth, Ridgway and I were described as rash in one newspaper. The truth was that we had smaller boats that would not go as fast as the older competitors in their larger boats. If we wanted to win we had to set off early, and although this meant we would reach the Southern Ocean rather too soon in the year, we would arrive at Cape Horn during the best possible time, January. We could have played safe and sailed in August but then there would have been no point in going at all as we would have stood no chance of winning. Still, whatever you do in life there are always people who take a delight in telling you you're wrong, who raise a difficulty for every solution; happily this sort of advice more often than not comes from those least qualified to comment.

As usual after a radio contact I felt the loneliness of my situation and sought comfort in my books:

I had a most unsatisfactory day. I always do when I have been in radio contact. I get excited by getting through and then the feeling of anti-climax follows, and I feel depressed. I spent a lot of time lying on a bunk reading and finished *Erewhon and Erewhon Revisited* by Samuel Butler. I cannot think why I have never heard of this book before.

and on another occasion

Finished *War and Peace* by Tolstoy today. I know that good books like good wine should be taken of sparingly, but I could not stop myself in this case.

But in the evenings I could put my tape recorder on and soon cheer up:

I repaired the Gilbert and Sullivan tape cassette ... and had a wonderful evening. I joined in sitting at the table in the homely light of the cabin light. It is not cold enough yet for clothes, just pleasant. ... I think I'll have a nip of Grant's. I can think of no one with whom I'd trade my lot at present. Intelligent, attractive and interesting female company is all that I require to make the situation quite perfect. Not that I am feeling romantic at present, but if I had female company I expect I would!

Some of the problems associated with loneliness and having to do absolutely everything for oneself were beginning to appear. Normally, when I have a number of jobs that need to be done, I take the one that most suits my mood at the time. This just would not do now; I had to do things at once or when the weather was favourable regardless of my mood. Then, too, if there was nothing urgent to be done, and no job that could occupy my time, I found myself getting bored and books would act only as a temporary stopgap. I would get restless and long for the voyage to be over, and it was not until October that I found I had come to accept at all philosophically that I was to spend perhaps a year of my life in this way.

Cooking was becoming a chore, and as for thinking up new menus from the limited selection of food available, my imagination was running dry.

I had some difficulty deciding what to have for dinner. If one had to put as much mental effort and imagination into the reproduction of the human race, it would have died out long ago. Eventually I decided on an omelette, but the four eggs I broke were all bad so then I made a cheese sauce and threw a tin of carrots and some parsley into it. Not bad; too much flour in the sauce, though.

This, I think, was the second period of my adjustment. When I had got over the initial problems and doubts, a short period of acceptance of the new environment arrived. This was followed by a second, longer stage of deeper and more serious doubts. Surviving this, I had my second wind, and was able to settle down to things. I got through it by forcing myself to do some mental as well as physical work. For example, one evening I began to write out a description of the Admiral. The self-steering seemed simple enough, but trying to write out a description was far from easy. Anyway the effort shook me out of my depression.

I also tried my hand at an epic blank verse saga. It began:

Suhaili turns her head south once more
Bound for the Southern Sea,
Where no ship may appear for most of the year
And there's nothing on your lee.

> Where the horizon's unfouled, apart from waves and cloud,
> Or a 'berg floating solitary.
> And the winds roar their hate, put the waves in like state
> At Intruders' Impertinency.

and seemed pretty deathless at the time.

By July 29th the wind had backed round from the south and was coming from the south-east, and it stayed steady from that direction until August 6th, by which time we had reached latitude 18° South, longitude 26° West and covered 920 miles in the meantime. This was a better speed than I had anticipated and I put it down to three things: The new aluminium mast which reduced the top weight and allowed the boat to sail more upright; the cut of the new sails which set beautifully; the improvement of my own technique.

The wind now started to vary and although mainly from the north which was fine, we occasionally had to put up with adverse winds and squalls.

Ennui has set in with a vengeance; part of this is due to the fact that we are being thrown about a great deal and I cannot hold much steady. The present weather beats me it is so unexpected – squall, calm, squall, calm, steady for an hour – squall, calm, etc. It's quite hopeless setting more sail as I would have to reef again immediately. I cannot stand to do anything that requires two hands and writing like this is only possible if one hand steadies the book and I wedge myself in a bunk. Waves are constantly breaking over the boat sending water cascading everywhere. I have the chart table jammed out to protect the radio and canvas thrown over it as well. My sleeping-bag is damp and there is no chance of drying it, which coupled with my lack of any real exercise makes sleeping difficult, hence I lie awake until late and oversleep and wake up tired. The answer is to force myself to some hard work – but what? Anything physical means certain bruises and cuts and any writing is exceedingly difficult – hence I take the easy way out and read. A reaction to this laziness will set in shortly, the sooner the better.

One thing about these squalls is that you know when they are coming. Whenever there is a patch of cumulo-nimbus there is sure to be a squall preceding it. There may then be rain and then follows a calm. . . .

The staysail definitely pulls the boat more than its proportion of the sail area would lead one to think. Speed has dropped between one-third and a half, whereas the staysail at 84 sq. ft. is only about one-sixth of the sail I have set at the moment. I think it must fill the gap between the jib and mainsail creating a slot on each side of itself, which doesn't exist otherwise as the sails are too far apart. The obvious way of decreasing the wind pressure on the boat would therefore seem to be to reduce sail in some other way. This is not practical, however, because it would leave a disproportionate amount of sail forward. There would appear to be no answer to this. I don't like to reduce speed but I cannot afford to push the boat too far, we have worse to come yet. If this were the last leg it would be different, but sailing to Australia non-stop is old hat; I want to make the circumnavigation!

The squalls brought a certain amount of rain and as I was able to collect regularly I decided to start trying to grow the mustard and cress seed that I had brought along with me to supplement my daily dosages of vitamin tablets, yeast tablets and calcium tablets. I spread a piece of newspaper out on the shelf in the loo, soaked it with fresh water, carefully poured out the seed evenly all over and hoped for the best. The seed and newspaper developed an unquenchable thirst which I eventually decided was too extravagant for my slender resources and my quest for fresh salad brought in the end only speckled papier mâché. I still kept the ten packets of seed in the hope that at some future date I might be able to try again, because by this time my onions had all gone and in future my salads were made from pickled onions with some of the vinegar from the jar mixed with salad oil as a dressing.

I had other troubles:

August 6th, 1968   *Day 53*

This was the first day I thought about giving up and heading for Cape Town. The reason being that apart from the leaks round the cabin . . . as I was taking a reef in the mainsail owing to a squall, the whole sail suddenly dropped round my ears. The brake failed, the same trouble I get with the other one with the 'Big Fellow' [the 220 sq. ft. flying jib]. When I think that I have hoisted people aloft and relied on that brake I shudder. I eventually got it to grip by feeding it Plus Gas. The trouble appears to be grease on the drum so I shall have to strip it and clean it, but as this is a delicate job I shall have await a calm.

Having got over this I discovered that the 'Y' piece on the main gooseneck is loose, the stem is coming adrift from the jaws. This is really serious and when I first noticed it I was put right into the dumps as I have no spare and nothing from which to manufacture a replacement. I am terrified that it will go any minute, and then I shall be without a mainsail until I can rig up a jury arrangement. One possibility that has come to mind is to drill vertically down through the jaw and stem and put a bolt through. I don't have any taps so the bolt will have to go right through. It will of course be much weaker but it might hold. The main difficulty here is drilling it; I'll have to do it by hand and this will take the best part of a day. Still, if it works it should be worthwhile. But the point that is at present worrying me is whether I should go on knowing this and other weaknesses. None of them is disastrous taken by itself but the combination could be, and if the mainsail dropped, or the gooseneck gave at the wrong moment I could be in real trouble. I won't make any decision as yet, I'll wait until I get the opportunity to have a closer look at everything, and I don't think I'll mention any of these troubles in my report . . . as there is no point in alarming people. If I make Australia O.K. then all this will, upon reflection, just appear as a localized panic. If I decide to pull in, the reasons will be obvious to all. I don't fancy pulling in somehow, not having come this far. . . .

1830. I have wedged the tape recorder and have G. & S. on again; it always cheers me up, but I would have liked a tape of stirring patriotic stuff – the thought of generations of Britons and their achievements always encourages me, a reminder of traditions which spurred them on. Most nations have a bookful of heroes but, and of course I'm prejudiced, I always feel that Britain has a greater share than most. After all, in my circumstances would a Drake, Frobisher, Grenville, Anson, Nelson, Scott or Vian (note – all sea-men!) have thought of giving up? It's a great encouragement to think of countrymen like these looking down on one, even if this little voyage can never come close to their achievements. In its own small way, though, it is a continuation of the same traditions – and notice how it is mostly Britons who have responded to the challenge. . . .

On August 8th, when we were roughly midway between Rio de Janeiro and the island of St Helena, I had another contact with Natie Ferreira in Cape Town and learned that John Ridgway had been forced to retire into Recife, in Brazil. No new starters, so Chay Blyth and I were the only two in it for the time being. Natie and I were fast becoming friends and this schedule went on rather longer than expected, running down the batteries, so as soon as it was finished I got out the charger. For some time I tried to get it going but the magneto did not appear to be doing its job and there was no spark. I stripped down the engine, removed the flywheel and took the whole thing to pieces. The trouble appeared to be grease on the points although how it got there I don't know. Anyhow, I cleaned it with ether and began to reassemble the engine. Only at this stage did I realize that I had no means of setting the spark gap again; I had forgotten to bring along a feeler gauge.

. . . I eventually got round this by counting the pages of this book – there are two hundred to the inch, therefore one page equals 5/thousandths. I wanted a gap of between 12-15/1000 thus three thicknesses of paper. (I took it from the bottom of these pages.) . . .

and it worked again! I celebrated by listening to Lourenço Marques radio but this had a depressing effect.

I feel lonely tonight. Listening to L.M. has brought back memories of South Africa, and although human nature being what it is one always remembers the good times and forgets the bad, on the whole we had many more good memories in S.A. It's Saturday night and I can remember the parties all too well. People were much more social and seemed to enjoy themselves more there than in the U.K. I still regret not settling there at times. This sudden contact with a world that I have missed for two years is not the most settling of sensations. Still it's pleasant here, the sea is flat calm and the sheets are rattling in unison with the sound of water lapping the hull. The moon has just risen and it's not yet got cold. I have just made a mug of cocoa and am sitting drinking it as I write this. A short while back I was shaking to Little Richard who has apparently come back into fashion with the re-emergence of Rock'n'Roll. It's as well I am on my own as my 'Shaking' is very graceless.

Despite what I have written I do not allow myself to get maudlin over being alone. Ah that's better – Ella Fitzgerald – from Paraguay. This music is making me romantic, or rather long to be romantic. There is nothing to beat dancing under a tropical moon, Latin American music for preference.

I now made a serious error in my navigation, one that I estimate must have cost me nearly two weeks. We were about 500 miles east-south-east of Ilha de Trinidade on August 12th and the winds, though variable, were more from the south-east than anywhere else. I decided that instead of continuing south and slightly west, I would head east and slightly south, straight for Cape Town, taking a more direct route and thereby, I hoped, saving time. The mistake lay in that this meant we remained within the Variables. Had I continued south we would have run into the westerly winds in the Southern Ocean in about a week to ten days and then had favourable winds. As it was it took us another twenty-two days to reach the Southern Ocean. I can be wise about it now, and I realized the danger then, but as we kept making progress towards Cape Town, and as the wind kept changing direction, it always held out the hope that any day it was going to steady from the west. The general strength of the wind at any time began to reach higher forces as well. Force 6 was the highest we had ever reached in the South-East Trades, and then only on two occasions; now the wind would get up to that force on nearly every change of direction.

The Admiral was still playing up; the vanes were stiff and it took a fresh breeze to get the system to operate properly. As we had sufficient wind for this less than half the time, I took to steering for long periods. The real trouble was that the nylon bearings for the vane stanchions seemed to have swollen somehow, if this is possible. I tried everything to get the vanes to swing more easily. Oil went in first, but that made things worse. Penetrating oil followed but made no difference. I also tried meths, paraffin, detergent, and soap, and when all these failed I tried Brasso thinking it might wear things slightly, but it didn't. Things only began to work efficiently later, when in desperation I removed the vanes and took a rasp to the nylon bushes.

On August 14th I celebrated two months at sea:

August 14th, 1968   *Day 61*
                        2 months at sea
and I don't know where we are! I caught the sun early this morning for a longitude but have not seen it since. Every time I awoke last night we were steering a different course so a D[ead] R[eckoning] would be a guess.

I have just made a currant duff to celebrate and it's turned out rather well. I used six tablespoons sugar, two handfuls flour, a bit of yeast and a handful of currants. Put it in a mug, wrapped it in a tea towel and steamed it in a pressure cooker. It really is good, I never realized this sort of cooking was possible; it's a pity I have so little flour. I find, having consumed half of it, that it is a little sweet, and although the yeast has lightened it a bit, it has the consistency of a dumpling.

Later – I am suffering for my gluttony.

From August 16th–21st we made 590 miles in all, but in a zig-zag so that the actual distance covered towards Australia was considerably less, and I was still some 1,500 miles to the north and west of Cape Town on latitude 33° South. We had the wind all right but from the wrong direction, the south-east.

August 19th, 1968   *Day 66*
Up at 0600 after a comfortable, if uneasy, night's sleep. I had to reef first thing as the wind was getting up despite a rising glass. Everything is damp below and there are waves frequently breaking over the whole boat. The skylight still drips and my sleeping-bag is damp – tough! As I was climbing out to take a sight a wave caught me and soaked the sextant; it seems to be O.K. but I cannot dry it properly and am a bit worried about the mirrors. The boat's motion is not at all comfortable and cooking is very difficult. Yesterday I had seven pieces of Ryvita all day, today so far I have had a Vesta Risotto, but I'll try to make a stew this evening. I think the wind will ease and back soon, the glass has remained high all day. The trouble is that the swell lags behind the wind so although the wind is not far off the beam, if I put her as close to the

wind as she will steer we get stopped dead. The most worrying leak is the main hatchway where the water pours in when the waves break over us and it all spills over the chart table and radio. I have both covered with towels, dishcloths and rags.

I have done nothing all day except sit in full foul weather gear reading *Vanity Fair*. I don't find it possible to relax or concentrate when we are being thrown about like this.

On the 22nd, Natie Ferreira had exciting news for me. Moitessier had sailed from Plymouth on the 21st and King hoped to set out from the same harbour that day.

The faster boats had started at last, giving me a two month start – little enough, in fact not enough in theory. Still, that made it all the more interesting; after all, it's human nature to try harder if you are only the second in anything, and I know that I get very lackadaisical if I am the favourite. Now the pressure was really on Chay Blyth and me. We were racing time as well as each other now and could not afford to miss any opportunity. I realized that from my own point of view it would not be sufficient just to overtake Blyth, I had to average at least a hundred miles a day to keep a theoretical chance of winning. At this stage in the voyage my average speed was just short of this figure, but I hoped to put it up once we reached the Southern Ocean.

The weather was getting noticeably colder and the wind more boisterous though still variable. We were getting close to the Roaring Forties and I started to prepare *Suhaili* as well as I could for what I expected to come. I removed any unnecessary gear from the deck such as running poles and spare sheets and stowed these below. I sealed off every opening such as the engine control box and the forward hatchway, and also put more seam stopper round the skylight, which was still leaking. August in the Southern Hemisphere is equivalent to February in the north. I could expect some pretty rough weather and I wanted *Suhaili* as ready as possible to take it. I went through all the stores, giving priority now to storm sails, spare lashing for emergencies, the sea anchor and warp and anything that I might need in a hurry. I put all my tropical clothing at the bottom of the sail bag I used as a wardrobe, and put sweaters, jeans, shirts and socks at the top. Finally I topped up my ready-use polythene containers in the main cabin with petrol and paraffin from forward.

A couple of days later, on the 27th, my preparations were put to the test when we ran into the first real gale of the voyage, unfortunately from the south-east. As it was some time since I had last ridden a gale at sea in *Suhaili*, and as I expected gales to be a part of the natural order of things for the next few months, I studied this one closely and experimented a good deal with various rigs. The problem of how to allow *Suhaili* to lie was of course different in this gale, when I wanted to sail as close-hauled as I could, from the Southern Ocean where I expected to run, but my main concern was to keep the boat riding comfortably either way.

Just before dusk I handed the staysail and took three more rolls in the mizzen. The course fell off 30° to the north, we had been heading about 70° True, but the speed was negligible and she rode much more comfortably. I want to try and get a full uninterrupted night's sleep if I can as I feel very tired.

All well apart from water getting into the engine-room, and this morning I was having to pump it out every two hours. Since I have reduced sail it's eased though, so I think the leak is via the cockpit lockers.

I could have taken sights this morning but was too occupied with the sails. It would not have been easy as the horizon was often hidden by spray from the waves, and I would probably have soaked the sextant. There is no particular worry as to position at the moment anyway, there is plenty of sea-room and until the wind eases or backs there is nothing I can do. I know where I want to go but can't go that way. There is no point in straining her, and a few extra days on the voyage are better than having to head for Cape Town. I thought of doing this this morning when at one time I felt very depressed, but there is no physical reason why I should give up, and I hope that after a good night's sleep I will have less trouble with the mental aspect.

The wind continued between Force 8 and 9 for a whole day, building up a steep, breaking sea; however, if I had not noticed it before, my boat was proving herself now.

Suhaili is behaving beautifully. She is riding the waves well, although lurching about a great deal. She pounds occasionally. If the wind eased even slightly I could let out some sail and head due south which would be splendid. As it is I should imagine, what with leeway, we are probably heading just south of west.

There is water everywhere and when a wave breaks over us a torrent comes in via the hatchway swamping the chart table, book rack and radio. Where the sea is not getting in condensation has formed. I have managed to keep my sleeping-bag reasonably dry by placing a piece of canvas over it, but it has got damp like everything else. I have taken to wearing my foul weather clothing inside the cabin, but the benefits from this are questionable as there is no ventilation and my clothing gets damp from my body heat.

The only damage received during the whole time was that the hook I used to hold the starboard runner to the deck lead, sheared off. It just was not strong enough to take the whip of the mast when we pitched. I rigged up a different system for the two runners which replaced the hook with a shackle and hoped it would now prove strong enough.

My sextant was causing worry by this time. It had received repeated soakings with salt water and the mirrors were tarnishing round the edges. During the latter part of the gale I had tried for a position, but an unexpected lurch had toppled me off balance. I had protected the sextant with my arm as I fell to the deck, receiving a nasty bruise, but when I next checked the instrument I found it had a considerable error. Fortunately September 2nd was a fine and reasonably calm day so I spent it taking sights every half hour and plotting the resulting position lines on a chart. Making allowances for *Suhaili*'s progress, the end result was like a multi-spoked wheel without a rim. The small but definite hub in the centre showed me that the sextant was still working accurately: a large, open hub formed by the crossing of the position lines would have indicated a fault. This was a relief, but just the same, next time I had some decent rain I left the sextant out to wash the salt off it.

The Roaring Forties

September 11th, 1968 (Day 89)–November 8th, 1968 (Day 147)

WE sailed into the Southern Ocean on September 3rd with three weeks of winter left. That night, perhaps a portent, the spinnaker split. There was, of course, no reason why I should suddenly feel that the weather would get more violent just because we had crossed the parallel of 40° South, but just the same it had a psychological effect on me, and I found myself half wanting the first storm to break so that I could see what I might expect during the next four months.

For two days we had very good weather, but there were obvious signs in the sky that a cold front was coming and the barometer's falling needle confirmed this. I had intended sailing along the 40° parallel right the way to Australia, but, naturally enough, the course zigzagged a good deal, depending upon the prevailing winds. To start with we went south and were about 42° South when the cold front arrived. This was my first experience of a Southern Ocean depression and it was quite an experience. As the cold front passed, the barometer suddenly jumped up two millibars and the wind backed in minutes from north to west-south-west and rose to gale force. I reefed right down on the mainsail and mizzen and replaced the jib with the storm jib. These last jobs were done in a vicious hailstorm and I was glad to get below to examine the level in the brandy bottle.

Suhaili was sailing along quite fast, and the Admiral seemed to like the stronger winds and was reacting well. The wind soon

61

built up the sea, and as the old sea, left after the wind backed and coming from the north, was still quite large, we soon had a confused cross sea which was uncomfortable and potentially dangerous. I stayed in my wet weather gear that evening, lying on a piece of canvas on my bunk so that I could rush up immediately if anything went wrong. For an hour or so I made a tape of my feelings and tried to describe the scene, intending to send the tape home from Australia, but then as things seemed safe I dropped off to sleep with the wind howling a lullaby in the rigging, and the sound of the water rushing past the hull coming through the planking quite clearly where I lay. The next thing I remember is being jerked awake by a combination of a mass of heavy objects falling on me and the knowledge that my world had turned on its side. I lay for a moment trying to gather my wits to see what was wrong, but as it was pitch black outside and the lantern I kept hanging in the cabin had gone out, I had to rely on my senses to tell me what had happened. I started to try to climb out of my bunk, but the canvas which I had pulled over me for warmth was so weighted down that this was far from easy.

As I got clear *Suhaili* lurched upright and I was thrown off balance and cannoned over to the other side of the cabin, accompanied by a mass of boxes, tools, tins and clothing which seemed to think it was their duty to stay close to me. I got up again and climbed through the debris and out onto the deck, half expecting that the masts would be missing and that I should have to spend the rest of the night fighting to keep the boat afloat. So convinced was I that this would be the case that I had to look twice before I could believe that the masts were still in place. It was then that I came across the first serious damage. The Admiral's port vane had been forced right over, so far in fact that when I tried to move it I found that the stanchion was completely buckled and the ⅜-inch marine ply-wood of the vane had been split down about 10 inches on the mizzen cap shroud. The whole thing was completely jammed. Fortunately I was using the starboard vane at the time, be-cause I could not hope to try and effect repairs until I could see, and the time was 2.50 a.m. It would not be light for another four hours. *Suhaili* was back on course and seemed to be comfortable and I could not make out anything else wrong; however, I worked my way carefully forward, feeling for each piece of rigging and checking it was still there and tight. I had almost gone completely round the boat when another wave came smashing in and I had to hang on for my life whilst the water boiled over me. This is what must have happened before. Although the whole surface of the sea was confused as a result of the cross-sea, now and again a larger than ordinary wave would break through and knock my poor little boat right over. I decided to alter course slightly so that the seas would be coming from each quarter and we would no longer have one coming in from the side, and went aft to adjust the Admiral accordingly.

Having checked round the deck and rigging, and set *Suhaili* steering more comfortably, I went below and lit the lantern again. The cabin was in an indescribable mess. Almost the entire contents of the two starboard bunks had been thrown across onto the port side and the deck was hidden by stores that had fallen back when the boat came upright. Water seemed to be everywhere. I was sloshing around in it between the galley and the radio as I surveyed the mess and I could hear it crashing around in the engine-room each time *Suhaili* rolled. That seemed to give me my first job and I rigged up the pump and pumped out the bilges. Over forty gallons had found its way into the engine-room and about fifteen more were in the main bilge, although how it had all got in I did not know at the time. Doing a familiar and necessary job helped to settle me again. Ever since I had got up I had been in that nervous state when you never know if in the next minute you are going to be hit hard for a second time. I could not really believe that the boat was still in one piece and, as far as I could see, undamaged. It's rather similar to when you uncover an ant nest. The exposed ants immediately wash their faces and this familiar task reassures them and prevents them panicking. Pumping the bilges was a familiar task to me and when it was completed I felt that I had the situation under control and set about tidying up quite calmly. The only real decision I had to make was where to start. I couldn't shift everything out of the cabin as there was nowhere else to put things, so I had to search for some

5ᵗʰ September 1968   DAY 83.

Quite calm from 0200 onwards and at daybreak I set more sail. It looks as if the cold front of a depression is approaching so we can expect some foul weather.   The glass is getting really low.

Through to Capetown at 1200 a very clear circuit. No news from London still.   The South African Airforce are unwilling to fly out to look at me, which is a pity as I would have been pleased to see them, however, I expect that they have more important things to do.

The wind rose during the afternoon and suddenly backed at 1700 and came on with a vengeance.   I have reefed right down on the main and mizzen and taken in the jib, leaving the storm jib in its place.   We don't appear to be going dangerously fast so I won't stream a warp.   I am frightened of it damaging the steering fin and will only do it as a last resort. There is a bit of a cross sea which might be dangerous.

I have just made a tape for the people at home and think I'll try and sleep. Its 2300 and hailing

6ᵗʰ September 1968   DAY 84.

Awoken by a fantastic broach or knock down at 0240. I was lying in the port bunk when we suddenly lurched over and the contents of both starboard bunks that were not firmly jammed landed on top of me.   I scrambled up out of it and went on deck and the first thing that caught my eye was the Admirals Port Vane. It had been bent over about 50° and the plywood had been cut down about 1 foot by the Mizzen Mast Shroud.   The force required to do this damage must have been tremendous.   Otherwise, apart from a broken main boom guy all seemed O.K. on deck and I went below.   My first job was to pump out the Engine Room which had taken about 40 gallons of water.   Whilst doing this I discovered that the port side of the battery shelf had come loose and the batteries had shifted.   Fortunately it was the port side as the fuel tank checked the batteries after they had moved a couple of inches. I then sorted out the galley and discovered the pliers in the saucer rack. They had flown across from the Radio Table and miraculously missed the saucers. The cabin heater was firmly jammed in the vice and so did not move at all. On my bunk I found books, stationary, clothes, Oranges and lemons and all the Medical Stores plus some packets of films. The Battery charger had moved about 6" but the force was sufficient to break off the exhaust close to the engine. Everything stowed in the W.C. had shifted, and the Bosuns bag was on my pillow. In the foreward cabin everything seemed O.K. apart from one empty polythene container. It took me until 0500 to tidy up and then I wrapped myself in a piece of canvas and went to sleep on the jib until 0830. I managed to make some porridge for breakfast which made me feel a lot better and after a cup of coffee and a cigarette I had cheered up considerably. I reckon I can repair the Admiral given the right weather, I wont attempt it to-day it's much too rough and windy. I wish the wind would back further to the South as we are still heading South of East. and I want to get North where it will be a bit warmer and also the weather should be better. The wind is from the S.W at present. I decided not to risk the sextant to-day, but in any case the horizon is all but indistinguishable on account of the waves.

The stain at the side of the page is caused by Brandy. These new fangled metal tops are a bloody waste of time. In this case the top worked loose and I lost the entire contents of a new bottle opened to-day. This was very annoying as I do not have unlimited quantities of the stuff, about enough for half a bottle a week so I have lost two weeks supply. The only consolation is that I had taken to-days ration from it.

The wind seems to be easing this evening. I'll turn in fully clothed just in case. We are rolling rather heavily and threatening to broach the whole time. Its bitterly cold. below 40°F large object amongst the mess, stow it away and then use the space vacated as a base. It was two hours before my bunk was cleared. I found books, films, stationery, clothes, fruit and tools all expertly mixed with my medical stores, and for days afterwards odd items kept appearing in the most out of the way places.

Working aft I started on the galley and put that straight, finding the pliers, which I had last seen on the radio shelf, tucked away behind a pile of saucers in their rack. It must have missed them by millimetres. The radio seemed all right, although it had got very wet. I mopped up what I could see, intending to do the job properly after daylight.

Whilst doing this I noticed a lot of water dripping down from the chart table immediately above the radio, and on following this up I discovered that water was pouring into the cabin round the edge each time a wave broke aboard. Tracing this back, I discovered that there were ominous cracks all round the edge of the cabin, and that the interior bulkheads had been shifted slightly by the force of the wave breaking over the boat. The sight of this, and the realization that if we took many more waves over the boat the weakened cabin top might be washed away, gave me a sick feeling in the pit of my stomach. If the cabin top went it would leave a gaping hole 6 feet by 12 in the deck; I was 700 miles south-west of Cape Town and the Southern Ocean is no place for what would virtually be an open boat. Just then another wave hit and I could feel the whole structure wince at the blow, but it did not appear to shift. Well, there would not be time to put extra fastenings in if it was going. I would just have to put lashings over it if things got worse and hope that the weather would ease and allow repairs to be made the next day.

The cabin was now clear so I found the torch and checked the engine-room for sources of leaks as water was already sloshing about in the bilges again. The first thing I noticed was that all the batteries were at a crazy angle and were fetched up against the port fuel tank. The side of the battery shelf had been knocked out by the weight of the batteries when the boat lurched and only the fact that the port fuel tank was in the way stopped the batteries from falling and being ruined. This would have meant no more radio and an end to getting the engine going. My two spare batteries were old, and could only be relied upon to work the Aldis signalling lamp and my tape recorder. I pushed the batteries back onto their shelf and lashed them in place, so that even if the other side of the shelf carried away they would not move again.

There was nothing else I could do until daylight, so I took a tot, folded the jib on the cabin deck, wrapped myself in a piece of canvas and fell asleep. Canvas may seem an odd covering, but it does keep the water out to a certain extent and once my own whisky induced heat had spread, the canvas kept me quite warm.

When I awoke three hours later and poked my head outside, the waves seemed less ferocious, but occasional squalls, usually accompanied by hail, were whipping across the surface and turning the dull grey sea into a milky white. After quickly checking that all was well on deck, I dived below again and started cooking up some porridge. By the time I had put this inside me and followed it with a mug of coffee and a cigarette, I was feeling quite happy. I obviously could not repair the Admiral in the present wind, as the vane would be blown away the moment I tried to unfasten it, so I decided to try and strengthen the cabin.

I got out my box of odd nuts and screws and selected the longest bolts and heaviest screws in order to try to reinforce the cabin top fastenings. The job kept me busy all day, but I slept a lot better knowing it was done.

That evening one of those infuriating little accidents occurred which, although it did not affect my ability to go on, nevertheless left me feeling rankled because it was so unnecessary. I had just opened a new bottle of brandy for my evening drink, and having poured out a good measure I put the bottle on the spare bunk, jammed by the sextant box. About an hour later a strong smell of brandy began to invade the cabin and I eventually traced it to the newly opened bottle. The bottle was sealed by one of these metal screw caps, and as the boat rolled in the sea, the movement had slowly loosened the top until the contents could escape. I was furious about this. As my allowance was half a bottle of spirits a week I had lost two weeks' supply, but I consoled myself with the thought that I had at least taken that day's ration from it!

On September 7th, two days after the knock down, the seas had eased sufficiently to allow me to tackle the Admiral. I had to do the job anyway as the wind direction had changed and I now needed to gybe round and use the port vane. The whole job was easier than I expected. I had two spare stanchions for the self-steering vanes so I decided to take the plywood fin out of the buckled stanchion and rebolt it into a new one. The job was complicated by the heavy rolls *Suhaili* was making and more than once I found myself completely immersed in the sea, which was most uncomfortable as no wet weather gear is completely waterproof and none is designed for swimming.

Until we reached the Southern Ocean we had met only one gale. The average had now changed dramatically, and five gales passed us in ten days. It was no good taking all sail in and letting *Suhaili* ride them out quietly, as we lost too much distance like that. The winds were from the west and I wanted to go east, and I was racing against time anyway. If I wanted to win I had to keep pushing the boat as much as I dared, but the frequency of the gales appalled me and I began to appreciate what Alec Rose had meant in his message.

Keeping the boat pressed left me on tenterhooks all day in case I was overdoing things, and it was even harder to stop myself from reducing sail at night when the wind always appeared stronger. I slept fully clothed, usually rolled up in the canvas on top of the polythene containers in the cabin. As I would quickly get cramp in that position, I would then try sleeping sitting up. This would be all right for a bit, but sooner or later the boat would give a lurch and I would be picked up and thrown across the cabin. If I tried wedging myself in the bunk I could not get out so quickly in an emergency, and if the boat received a really big bang I would get thrown out of the bunk and across the cabin anyway.

I became rather tired and irritable through lack of proper sleep; an idea of my feelings at this time can be seen in my diary for September 9th.

September 9th, 1968   *Day 87*

I finally awoke at 1100 having had three hours uninterrupted sleep in the bunk. The wind was down so I got up and set more sail. We were rolling very heavily and it was difficult to stand inside the cabin, but I managed to heat up some soup and in the afternoon, a superhuman effort, I made a prune duff, which was a great treat. I also made a new drink. Brandy, honey, hot water, sugar and a lemon, which tasted wonderful and bucked me up. I needed it. I felt very depressed on getting up. I cannot do anything in these conditions. (I am writing this late at night and the rolling has eased a bit.) The real trouble is I am so far from achieving anything at the moment. I used up a lot of nervous energy last night by leaving the jib up, for what – maybe an extra 20 miles if we're lucky – and what difference does 20 miles make when I have about 20,000 to go?

The future does not look particularly bright, but sitting here being thrown about for the next 150 days, at least with constant soakings as I have to take in or let out sail, is not an exciting prospect. After four gales my hands are worn and cut about badly and I am aware of my fingers on account of the pain from skin tears and broken fingernails. I have bruises all over from being thrown about. My skin itches from constant chafing with wet clothes, and I forget when I last had a proper wash so I feel dirty. I feel altogether mentally and physically exhausted and I've been in the Southern Ocean only a week. It seems years since I gybed to turn east and yet it was only last Tuesday night, not six days, and I have another 150 days of it yet. I shall be a Zombie in that time. I feel that I have had enough of sailing for the time being; it's about time I made a port, had a long hot bath, a steak with eggs, peas and new potatoes, followed by lemon meringue pie, coffee, Drambuie and a cigar and then a nice long uninterrupted sleep, although, come to think of it, to round it off properly. . . . Here, in a nutshell, is my problem; I have all this to look forward to, but it's so far ahead. I really want something in the more immediate future to look forward to. Australia possibly, and yet that is eight weeks ahead at least and will only be a brief contact with a boat, not something special I can look forward to, and even then I am only halfway; I still have a slightly greater distance to go. It's all a great prospect; why couldn't I be satisfied with big ships?

The life may be monotonous but at least one gets into port occasionally which provides some variety. A prisoner at Dartmoor doesn't get hard labour like this; the public wouldn't stand for it and he has company, however uncongenial. In addition he gets dry clothing and undisturbed sleep. I wonder how the crime rate would be affected if people were sentenced to sail round the world alone, instead of going to prison. It's ten months solitary confinement with hard labour.

Rather an interesting sight this evening. I was adjusting the Admiral at 2000 so that we would run better when I thought I saw a light ahead. I went forward and saw it again quite clearly low down on the surface. It rapidly drew close dividing into two as it did so and we passed between it. It, or rather they, were two wedge shaped lumps of luminescence, about 2 ft. 6 ins. long and about 8 ins. square at the thick end, narrowing down to about 4 ins. square at the other end. Possibly a leptocephalus but if so an unusual shape.

It's quiet just now, although I have one foot on the galley to hold myself steady, as we are rolling heavily. Note that the pressure has remained steady for over twenty-four hours. The wind seems to be veering which is good news.

The 10th was a bad day, and once again the diary carries the mood.

September 10th, 1968   *Day 88*
It is perhaps as well that I am more of an optimist, or perhaps fatalist would be a better word, than a realist, as if I were to be the latter I could give up after today. On thinking about it though, perhaps I am a realistic optimist – it's all speculative anyway. First, it was not too bad today; the weather on waking was reasonably fine and I managed to get sights. At noon we had covered a fantastic 314 miles in two days and were due south of Cape Town. Obviously leaving the sails up and hanging on gave us this terrific mileage – if only I could maintain it but, on account of the occurrence about to be related, I am going to limit the speed from now on.

I was just creating a bully beef and Ryvita sandwich, having plotted noon, when I noticed that we had yawed more off course than usual. I went up to investigate and discovered that the self-steering rudder had broken. It was blowing about Force 3 at the time and we were moving quite fast on a dead run so I took down the main and mizzen, and just left the headsails to steady her.

After a difficult tussle I salvaged the bits and set about getting the spare ready to ship. This was not at all easy as although the bolts that held the rudder to the bar came undone, the female socket that takes the tiller securing bolt was rusted up and I had to scrape it out with a fork. This done I tried to ship the spare from aft, but only succeeded in bending the bar so, as this will weaken it, I hauled it out, stripped off, took a slug of brandy, and dived in and fitted the bar in its shoe. All well so far, except this description covers three hours' work. Having set the Admiral to work again, I hoisted the mizzen and went to hoist the main but the brake wouldn't work so I had to strip that. The main at last hoisted, I went back to check the course and knocked the lid off the binnacle. I fixed that; the hinge had broken. As I appeared to be accident prone I decided that the safest place for me was below and I made a mug of Barmene and had, I think, a well-earned cigarette.

The self-steering rudders gave me cause for concern. If one could break after about 8,000 miles, less than a thousand of which were in the Southern Ocean, how soon would the spare go? The cause of the trouble was obviously that the vertical bars on which the rudders were mounted were not strong enough, and the strain was too much for them. The last two days' fast going had been more than the first rudder could take and the spare was built the same way, so I would obviously have to reduce speed if I was going to keep any self-steering.

I lay in the next morning and spent the whole day reading Trollope's *Orley Farm*. There was a bit of psychology here, as I was feeling tired and not very enthusiastic and I knew that if I kept myself from doing anything but essential work, I would shortly get interested again. By the evening I was quite restless but I kept myself away from work, and sure enough the next day awoke raring to get on with repairing the rudder.

The repairs took me three days. The old rudder blade was hopelessly split, so I made a new one out of one of the teak bunkboards. The bar had broken by the middle of the blade, and to rejoin it I cut the handle of a pipe wrench and then filed it down until it fitted inside the bar, like an internal splint.

I put the two broken ends of the bar together and then drilled through the bar and wrench handle, riveting them together with pieces of a 6-inch nail, heated on the primus stove. The final job looked pretty strong, but to make sure of it, I bound it with glass fibre.

Whilst I was working on the rudder the potentially most serious damage as a result of the knockdown came to light. I had left Falmouth with 15 gallons of fresh water stowed in polythene containers, and whilst passing through the Doldrums and Variables I had managed to catch quite a lot of rainwater and had not had to touch the fresh water tanks at all. Having watched *Suhaili*'s behaviour in the Southern Ocean, I decided that she would probably sail better if I could lift the bow a bit, so I decided to start using the forward fresh water tank. I connected the feed pipe to the pump and began to suck up water, but the pale brown and rather unpleasant smelling liquid that came out bore no resemblance to clean water. I kept pumping for a while, hoping that I might find that the bad water was just the contents of the pipe, but it stayed discoloured. Feeling throughly alarmed I uncovered the tank and took off the inspection cover. The putrid smell of bilgewater told me that I did not have to look farther to know that the water was contaminated and undrinkable. I tried the other tank but it was little better – I would poison myself if I tried drinking from either.

I lit a cigarette and sat down to consider the situation. Firstly, there was no immediate panic. I had well over ten gallons of water in the polythene containers, enough for forty days without discomfort. The Cape was 400 miles north of me so I was in no danger. Next, could I go on? I thought of the rain and hail that had accompanied the depressions of the last few days. There was obviously plenty of rain about in the Southern Ocean, so I should be able to collect enough to keep me going. Lastly, should I go on knowing that I would have to depend upon the rain to support my life? Well, there was a good forty days' supply in the containers to start with, and I had three hundred tins of fruit juices and beer to supplement this. If the worst came to the worst, I could distil drinking water by boiling sea water on the stove and condensing the steam, so long as my paraffin lasted out. Australia was about fifty days away and it looked as if I could manage that length of time without catching any rain at all, so obviously the thing to do was carry on and see how things went.

But now the radio began giving cause for concern. I failed to make a scheduled contact with Cape Town, as although I could hear them they couldn't hear me. This worried me as I had not failed to make a schedule so far. I waited until after dark when radio conditions are generally better and then tried calling on the distress frequency. Much to my relief, Port Elizabeth radio came through straight away and I was able to send a message to Natie Ferreira letting him know that we had received damage but were safe and that I was going to try to head north a few degrees to find some better weather and give the boat a thorough check. Port Elizabeth wanted me to report every eight hours just in case anything went wrong, but I managed to reduce this to twice a day in order to conserve my batteries. To improve morale I listened to the South African Radio for a while that evening, and picked up a magazine programme dealing with the year 1947. At one point they mentioned that in Britain that winter was the coldest on record, which I found amusing, as I remembered it clearly as an excellent winter for tobogganing.

A day later I heard that Chay Blyth had been forced to pull into East London. The last news I had had gave him as being off Tristan da Cunha three weeks before and I had wondered how close we were to each other in the Big Gale. I now knew he must have been about two days ahead of me. We had been racing against each other for three months and I had only closed the gap by four days. For my own sake I was sorry to lose the competition.

Suhaili headed north-east for a few days and the weather got noticeably better. I was able to tidy her up properly and restow stores so that they would not fall out so easily again. The boat itself was as good as I could make her and I decided to start repairing the spinnaker as I should need it if the weather continued fine. It had split completely down one side and two corners were torn so I thought the best thing I could do was sew rope along the edge all the way round. This was quite an

73

enjoyable task and I got on with it quickly considering the difficulties of holding myself steady whilst I sewed.

It was whilst I was in the middle of the job and halfway along the rope, which I had tied to opposite ends of the cabin to keep it taut and out of the way, that one of those silly incidents occurred which seem funny now but was far from being so at the time. I was standing braced in the middle of the cabin using one hand to steady myself and the other to sew. Coming to the end of a length of twine, I used my teeth to help tie a knot, and then tried to stand up. I had not moved more than three inches when I felt a painful wrench at my moustache. I tried to move again, very slowly, but as the spinnaker began to rise with me I decided not to continue the movement. With my free hand I groped around to discover the cause of the trouble and found that my moustache was firmly tied to the spinnaker. I thought for a moment and then tried to stretch to the nearest point where the rope was made fast, but I was a good foot short. I rolled my eyes round looking for the knife but it was tantalizingly out of reach. This was quite a problem. Here I was, hopelessly entangled. I could not undo or cut the knot that held me and it was getting on towards beer time. There was only one way out of it. I closed my eyes, gritted my teeth and jerked my head sharply back, tearing myself free. It hurt like hell and tears filled my eyes, but it soon passed off and at least, as I rushed to the mirror to reassure myself, the symmetry of the moustache was not badly upset. I gave it a trim with my surgical scissors, and while I was at it gave myself a haircut.

On the Admiralty weather charts that accompany *Ocean Passages of the World*, a book that not only gives the best routes to follow between ports, but also shows alternatives for the different seasons, we were heading out of the area round the Cape of Good Hope where for up to ten days in a month the winds will blow at gale force. The frequency of gales began to diminish; we even had some really fine weather which made my spirits rise and allowed me to air my sleeping-bag and a sailbag full of wet clothing which had accumulated whilst we rounded the Cape.

The radio batteries had been run very low and I got out the charger as soon as it was safe to do so. After removing the cylinder head to clear the valves, both of which were stuck, I left the motor going right through the night. The exhaust pipe and silencer had been broken when the boat was knocked down and the noise of the engine was frightful. The wind began to rise during the night but as I wanted to get the batteries up I left the charger at work, even though it made sleep impossible. During the night I went into the engine-room to check the batteries' strength with a hydrometer, and whilst I was doing this *Suhaili* broached before a wave, lurched, and I fell over. The hydrometer was in my hand and some acid from it was flicked over my face and into my left eye. I struggled out of the engine-room as fast as I could, and rushed on deck. The cockpit was awash and I scooped up a handful of water and threw it into the eye. I kept doing this for about five minutes, then went below again and washed it with fresh water.

The eye had begun to sting before I splashed water into it, and now it throbbed painfully. I found the medical box and took out the antiseptic eye drops. I could not see anything wrong with the eye in the mirror, but according to the *Ship Captain's Medical Guide* the eye should be rested after such an accident. One thing I had not thought of when checking my medical stores was an eye patch, so I had to put a bandage round my head at an awkward angle in order to leave my right eye free. The result was very piratical but not at all practical, and in fact I only left the bandage on for one night as it got in my way. It was not a pleasant night; I did not know the extent of the damage and having a fertile imagination I considered the possibility that I might lose the use of the eye. I debated turning back for Durban, but Commander King and Bernard Moitessier were in the race, I was in the lead and stood a slight chance of winning, and I felt that this would be worth giving an eye for, so I carried on. As it turned out, the eye was not damaged much and by the end of a week had ceased throbbing and has given no trouble since then.

When *Suhaili* broached, the charger was swamped and knocked over in the cockpit, so I decided to call it a day and took the unit below. I had to dry it out and clean the generators before it worked again. The other loss was my distilled water for replenishing the batteries. The top was off the container when we heeled over, and the container went flying. In my rush to wash my eye I had not noticed it, and by the time I found it all the contents had disappeared into the bilges. From this point on I had to use rain water in the batteries.

The next day, my one-hundredth out, found me some 1,400 miles east of Cape Town:

September 22nd, 1968   *Day 100*
Last Day of Southern Winter.

Awoke to find us heading north so got up and gybed. I banged my elbow badly during the night and what with that, numerous other bruises and an eye that throbbed, I felt as if I had just gone through ten rounds with Cassius Clay. As the wind was down I let out some sail and then went back to bed. It's warm and reasonably dry there and I feel very tired. I awoke at 1400 to another gale building up, this time from the S.W. so I had to start taking in sail again. Reefing is no longer an easy business. My hands are very sore and covered with blisters and whirling the handle is sheer hell. I noticed today over seven sail slides [the slides on the sail which run up a track on the mainmast] loose or missing on the mainsail so there's the first job when the wind goes down. I got up at 2000 and made a risotto which I followed with a tin of fruit to celebrate our 100th day, then I turned in again. This may seem very lazy, but I wanted to rest my eye as much as possible; also to give some idea of how tired I have become, each time I turned in I fell asleep at once and it was the alarm that woke me. We should get calmer weather shortly as the glass is rising steadily. Well, with this rest behind me I should feel energetic enough to get on with some of the jobs that need doing. I have set the alarm for just after midnight; it might be possible to set more sail then.

I was obviously trying to encourage myself with my headings. The one hundred and first day, September 23rd, begins '*The First Day of Spring Tra-La!*' and continues:

Up just after midnight to find it a lot calmer so I let out sail and turned in. Up again just after 0700 to find us virtually becalmed and the wind looking as if it was going to box the compass again. After a quick breakfast of coffee, Ryvita and damson jam, I took a sight and then I lowered the mainsail; for the first time since sailing, the sail came off the mast. I spent all morning retying sail slides and replacing missing ones – seven were missing, two of which are at the top of the mast. I used one strand of the nylon Portuguese fishing line I bought in Lourenço Marques when on the *Congella*. It's better quality than British man-made fibre. I just hope they stay on. This was completed in time to take a Meridian Altitude. We have covered 243 miles in two days, not too bad considering we had light winds twice. I made a curry for lunch. I'm getting better at them, but onions are needed for best results. I wish I knew how to cook rice; Chris had it taped last voyage. After this I pottered – new halyard on staysail as the old one has chafed; tightened the port mizzen topmast shroud, went round with the oil can and grease tin and also whipped the thimble in the port storm jib sheet eye. The starboard one needs doing as well as the thimbles keep popping out, but it was wet so I left it for now. I set the charger to work; bless it, despite Saturday's knock over, it went. The batteries are coming up very slowly, there is something wrong somewhere but I cannot discover it. I have given up listening to the radio in the evenings to conserve power. I have just filled [the charger] again, the third fill today; none of the batteries has reached 1200 yet but they are getting close at last. I will run it as long as I dare but there will be no repeat of Saturday's performance. That was like a scene from the 'Twilight of the Gods', with the boat rushing through the sea, which was breaking over the bow, the wind howling in the sails and rigging almost drowning the sound of the unsilenced charger.

I decided to turn the engine today as it has not had any use for over two months. I tried to turn it by hand first, and even bent the handle of the pipe wrench which gives some idea of the force I was exerting on it, but it seems to have seized up. I checked all the cylinders, but the oil I put in is still there. I also checked the gearbox but that was clean. I'll take the starter motor off during the next calm spell and see if that is the cause of the trouble. Whatever the trouble it's my own fault for not turning it daily. Now I have a lot of work on my hands to get it free, even if I manage that – a stitch in time etc!

As expected, the wind has boxed the compass, and if everything goes according to pattern the wind will get up to another gale tonight – still I had today to get some work done for which I am very thankful. I would like to get working on some letters now, but writing when it is blowing is not easy and although my eye seems O.K. – it feels as if there is something in it at the moment – I don't want to take any risks for a while by reading or writing by oil lamp.

I seem to have got quite chatty about this time:

September 25th, 1968   *Day 103*

Awoke at 0800 to find us heading N.W. I don't know when the wind backed or veered to the S.S.E. as I slept or rather was unconscious most of the night. I did not sleep well and kept waking but was unaware of my whereabouts whilst awake. I gybed round and let out some sail; the motion is very uncomfortable. It poured with rain this morning but I was unable to catch any of it because the sail is rolled on the boom and the motion throws most of the water off the sail. In order to trap rainwater the booms must be rolled so that the sails are drawn down the lee side of the booms. The mizzen can only be reefed one way and so will only catch water when we are on the port tack. The main happens to be rolled the same way as the mizzen at present.

I held the sextant out in the rain for ten minutes to wash it off and then took out a cotton shirt to wipe it with. The shirt has miraculously remained dry and has a beautiful smell of soap about it. I conjure up memories of a life I have almost completely forgotten, where people daily immerse themselves in special containers filled with hot fresh water – a strange habit which cannot be healthy – sleep in sprung beds with clean white sheets and have special clothes to wear in their beds, and where, most peculiar of all, they transfer their food from the cooking pot to a plate before eating!

I remember reading an article once in an Insurance Company's House Magazine about people's 'off' days. This must be one of mine. *Suhaili* quietly gybed in the afternoon, so as we were hardly moving I held on to the port tack to gather water. As soon as the bucket was full I untied it and it dropped from my hand onto the deck. I caught it just before it went overside. As I have only two buckets left I gave this up and gybed back. The wind was about non-existent and one needed to be a Burmese Goddess to hang on [as *Suhaili* pitched and rolled in the swell], let alone do anything! I next decided to have a cup of coffee and of course everything played up. First I put methylated spirits into the primus to heat it up, but it failed to get hot enough and I had to add more meths. As I was pouring the boat lurched and I lost my balance. The meths spilt out of the can over the stove and my hand. Immediately the whole lot went up in flames which I managed to smother before any damage was done, but of course whilst I was doing that the meths in the stove went out and I was back to square one again. I started off again, got the stove alight this time and put the kettle on. Up to this moment the stove had not been rocking too badly; now for some reason it lurched and the kettle toppled over extinguishing the flame and wasting two pints of fresh water. I really lost my temper at this and gave the stove a good swipe with the pressure cooker which did not do either of them any good but made me feel a lot better, and I started again. I think I must have scared everything, because this time all went well and I got my coffee. I feel I have established the principle between the stove and myself that if I want it to work, it's bloody well going to work, and it will save itself a lot of bother by co-operating to start with!

Whilst on deck I noticed a seam going in the mainsail. In order to stop it going further until I can do a proper job on it, I got out needle and sailtwine. After half an hour I had made four stitches, and the rolling of the boat made this an achievement.

Suhaili will steer between north and west at present, and I'm damned if I'm hoisting more sail to try to improve things; the glass is still falling and you can bet your last shilling that the moment I have more sail up the wind will arrive with a rush and using a spanner it takes an age to reef the mainsail.

The remark about reefing with a spanner refers to the fact that I had lost my main reefing handle overside a few days before when I had slipped on the wet deck going forward. Reefing down using a spanner was a very slow business so I decided to see if I could make a new handle. All sorts of ideas occurred to me but I eventually decided to try and square a rigging screw whose internal circumference was the same as the circumference of the reefing gear lug. I cut the bottle part of the screw in half and then heated it on the primus until it was red hot. Then I hammered it until it cooled and repeated the process until I had the right shape. I had to file out the corners a bit which took time but I ended up with a snug fit. The problem of a handle was solved by bending the screw and securing a bolt to the end, and presto! I had a reefing handle. I derived great satisfaction from the job and it put me in a thoroughly good mood.

By the end of September we had covered over 3,000 miles of the Southern Ocean and I had lost contact with Cape Town radio. As far as I could make out, my transmitter had packed up soon after the knockdown. I had been meant to contact Perth Radio Station in Western Australia, but had been unable to get through, and when I tried to meet my last schedule with Cape Town, I could hear them calling me for over half an hour but they obviously could not hear me. Cape Town had been most helpful and co-operative throughout my passage through their area, and I did not like leaving things in the present unsatisfactory state.

During the next spell of fine weather I stripped down the transmitter, cleaned out the encrusted salt and tried to find the fault, but I might as well have tried to sort out a railway time-table: in the first place the circuit diagram looked like a plan of Clapham Junction, and in the second, I am no electrician. I changed the valves and tried the transmitter again, but the fuses blew before the power started to come through. I spent two days trying to find out what was wrong and eventually had to admit defeat.

As I could not get the radio to work in the easier conditions clear of the Cape of Good Hope I decided to have another attempt at turning the engine. I stripped off the electric starter motor and exerted pressure directly on the flywheel. I calculated that I had to exert a turning moment of at least half a ton before the flywheel moved at all, and this was by means of a complicated system of levers that would have filled Emmett with awe. The main difficulty was finding bearing points and at one stage the lot slipped and my right forefinger was gashed down to the bone. I swabbed out the cut with Swarfega and then wiped it clean. Plaster would not stick to the skin and I had a terrible job covering the cut. Eventually I found a pair of heavy duty leather gloves and put these on before going back to try again. This time the flywheel moved, which gave me a terrific feeling of relief as I had been wondering what I should do if I could not shift it. Stripping the whole engine down in the middle of a heaving sea would have been next to impossible:

It took me forty minutes to turn it one revolution, but then it began to ease and I felt it was worth trying the self-starter. I ran the disconnected starter for a minute on the spare batteries just to make sure it was O.K. and give it a chance to clear any 'cobwebs', and then fitted it. It worked! It turned. Tra-La! Not fast, not easily, but it turned. I had removed the heater plugs so that the starter would not have to overcome the compression and the diesel oil I put in a few days ago came out as a thick mist. Rather rapidly I evacuated the engine-room and spliced the mainbrace. If it is still calm tomorrow I'll try to get it going and give it a run for an hour or so. There'll be a mammoth air lock to overcome and these always give me trouble.

I don't feel in the least tired this evening. I have the tape recorder running and feel very happy. I'm trying not to think about the lack of progress. I threw over an empty paper sack which had contained potatoes, the first of three empty, and an hour and a half later it was 20 yards away!

This was a trying period in some ways. The winds were generally light, but the gales round the Cape of Good Hope were fresh in my memory and I was still wary.

October 1st, 1968   *Day 109*

Calm all day. The diurnal variation in the barometric pressure gave me a few qualms, the wind builds up so quickly, but despite gusts in the morning which gybed her, there was very little wind and the day's run of 81 miles reflects this.

At midnight tonight it will be four weeks since we crossed the Greenwich Meridian and we should be 66° E [approximately 600 miles west of St Paul's Island], an average of 16½° of longitude or in this latitude 740 miles a week. The last ten days have knocked the average down badly. At this rate we'll be off Melbourne on November 6th. I set the 'Big Fellow' this evening goosewinged out to port; it has made a little difference but I'll be glad when the spinnaker is ready. I worked on it, when allowed, all day.

I had a terrible job getting to sleep last night; I was feeling frustrated by our slow progress and this sort of thing causes me to

81   T–D

tense up. I usually notice it in my legs; they feel as if they want exercise, rather like they do when you have been climbing all week; your legs get used to the work and want to go on doing it. I eventually dropped off at 0300 and awoke when we gybed just after 0900. There was so little wind that even with full sail set she drifted round. . . .

I have her with the sails, apart from the 'Big Fellow', boomed out to starboard at present, although I ought to be heading south a bit. The reason for this is that the port vane works better than the starboard one which sticks a bit, and I cannot afford to have the rudder stick with 890 sq. ft. of sail set.

The port halyard winch, the one I use for the storm jib and 'Big Fellow' caught it today. I put my foot on it so that I could reach the running boom slide and it spun round despite the fact that the brake was on. I was given a nasty jerk and found myself on the deck. Picking myself up, and commenting quietly upon the halyard winch's ancestors, I collected a screwdriver and attacked it. The brake now works!

We appear to be slightly down by the head again. I don't know why, as I have added no weight forward. Tomorrow I'll decant some petrol from the tins in the foc's'le into my polythene containers. I am going to have to watch the petrol consumption, I have just over 20 gallons left and if I don't fix the main engine there is no reserve for charging. I have ceased to listen to commercial broadcasts to conserve power, but I think we'll have to miss a couple of weeks if the radio is to last all the way home.

It's a fine night, the wind has freshened slightly and we are making about 4 knots at the moment, increasing to 5 now and again. There is a bright gibbous moon. By this time next month we should be within a few days of Melbourne with any luck. At least there'll be plenty of moonlight so we should show up if there is any shipping around.

People talk about the empty sea and sky, but in my experience, more often than not, some form of life is in view. There are many varieties of seabirds which spend their whole lives, apart from the breeding season, living miles away from land. Most common during my voyage were petrels and albatross. The stormy petrels seem far too fluffy and delicate to live in such a merciless environment, yet even in the roughest weathers they are to be seen skitting low across the water, reacting instantly to the changing airflow caused by the waves inches below and extending one tiny, fragile leg beneath them to gauge their height above the waves. The old seamen watching them following in the wake of their ships for scraps of food used to call them Mother Carey's Chickens, a name which probably came from *madre cara* or *mater cara*, the Dear Mother or Virgin Mary.

The albatross is one of the most graceful of birds. I watched them in strong winds leisurely flapping their wings as they moved up wind, and then turning to glide down close to the waves across the wind. Until you see them close up, you just cannot appreciate their size. Wing spans of 6 to 8 feet were quite common. I had a trolling line out most of the voyage with a hook and lure on the end and this proved so irresistible to the albatross that I had to take the hook off to avoid injuring them, but I left the lure out because the birds gave me so much amusement. They did not seem to realize that the lure was moving, because they would land on the water, peck at the lure, usually missing, and then rise up on the water with their wings half extended, running along the surface uttering an irritated '*Squark! Squark!*' The whole picture was so reminiscent of Donald Duck in a temper that I often burst out laughing at their antics. What puzzled me, was why they ignored bully beef when I threw it to them!

When sitting on the water an albatross looks exactly like a dodo. They often sleep on the water, and more than once in the voyage there was a sudden commotion under the bow where some albatross had suddenly woken up as *Suhaili* came up to it. I think that on one occasion one of these birds must even have been dozing in the air because it flew straight into the mast. The impact shook the whole boat and brought me up on deck with a rush just in time to see the albatross recover itself a few feet above the water and fly on unconcernedly as if nothing had happened.

There are all sorts of superstitions concerning albatross, one of which is that seamen must never kill them. But this must be fairly new, because one of the names given to a species found in the Southern Ocean is Cape Sheep, a name that comes from the days when the seamen used to make jackets decorated with their feathers.

Albatross need a run along the surface before they can take off, and look like a heavily laden Lancaster bomber trundling along a runway as they struggle up into the air. In the days of the great steel-hulled barques running out to India, China, Australia and back, it used to be a favourite pastime amongst seamen to capture an albatross as a pet. It could be let loose on the deck as the bulwarks prevented it taking off, but as a pet its bad temper and snapping beak gave it marked disadvantages.

I never caught an albatross; I never tried to kill one either. I think being alone in a vast and hostile environment gave me a feeling of comradeship with any fellow animal – although I would certainly have killed them had I run short of food.

Regular visitors to us were dolphins and whales. I always welcomed the dolphins, as apart from the feeling of affinity with any warm-blooded creature of such a high intelligence, I have never grown tired of watching them race past a boat, manoeuvring with such agility that although the sea seems full of them, they never appear to touch each other. Whales I was frightened of. I saw many different species, most larger than *Suhaili*, and I had to trust that they would not decide to come too close to investigate. A large blue whale would not have to exert itself to turn over a boat of *Suhaili*'s size. But as with the birds and mammals, I always felt a little lonely when the whales left; even if we could not communicate, I felt that we shared the same difficulties.

I was still worried about the accuracy of my sextant. Despite the fact that I seldom had to make an adjustment, the feeling persisted that there was a slight error, which although it did not show at low altitudes, gradually increased as the observed altitude increased. Roughly halfway between the Cape of Good Hope and Australia lie two small, isolated islands, Amsterdam and St Paul's. I decided to make a check by heading in the direction of the islands and seeing if I made them when expected. No sooner had I made this decision than the wind, which had been light for a few days, freshened from the north, and in order to get the maximum speed I had to steer a course that took me well south of the islands. It did not really matter as I would find out if there was an error when I got near Melbourne anyway, and I think that the slight disappointment I felt was due to the fact that I rather wanted to see two completely uninhabited islands.

For four days we sailed fast. I left the large flying jib, the Big Fellow, set as long as I dared, in fact longer than I should, as it took me well over half an hour to get it in when I eventually decided the wind had risen high enough. It's not an easy sail to take in at the best of times as it is made fast at the end of the bowsprit, and that end has to be let go before one can start lowering the sail. In strong winds, once the sail is let go, it billows out, clear of the boat and out of reach. I took to putting a small length of rope on this end so that I could draw the sail in again, but if the boat yawed off course, and the sail filled, this rope would be torn from my hands. On one particular occasion I was further handicapped by the gash on my hand, which I was trying to protect; however, the rope ripped this wound open early on which gave me something less to worry about. The sail was ballooning right out of reach by this time and I did not have the strength to haul it in, so I just let go the halyard and tried to haul the sail in before it went into the water. I wasn't quite quick enough, and even the small part that remained in the water proved too heavy for me and dragged the whole sail from my hands.

My arms felt like lead by this time, and I was panting with the exertion, but the sail had to be brought in or be let go and lost. *Suhaili* could not be left dragging this huge sea anchor or something would be sure to break. I hauled in one corner of the sail and unshackled it and let it go again. This reduced the drag as that end now flowed out astern. Once again I threw my weight onto the main bulk of the sail and inch by inch I hauled it in. My fingers were no longer gripping by this time; all the strength had gone from them so I was having to use my hands like claws. The wind frequently caught the salvaged part of the sail on deck, blowing it up and enveloping me and I had to sit on it to hold it down. When the sail was inboard at last I bundled it up and sank down wearily on top of it. I must have stayed there for five minutes. I was completely exhausted and just did not have the strength, now the danger was over, to gather up the sail and take it below.

The wind stayed fresh, which made life difficult; however I was learning how to keep morale high:

October 5th, 1968   *Day 113*
We are moving about a lot; it took me over an hour to make some porridge this morning, during which the kettle fell over and I spilled sugar all over the radio. Fortunately this last accident made me lose my temper, so I got porridge.

I have had the tape recorder going most of the day; with it going the cabin seems more homely and less empty. It's a pity there was not time to make more tapes before I sailed – I know the words of all the songs now. One thing frustrates me. I cannot make out the first verse of 'I am a Pirate King'; I hope that Ken knows this one as we can add it to our selection on the way from Falmouth to London. Boy, am I looking forward to that trip. We'll load up with beer and set a course for Parker Bank south of Dungeness. That will keep us well clear of the shipping.

I wish the sea would ease just a bit. I would like to get shifting. Every time I look at the wake I think of the other boats and how much bigger their wakes will be. I'll be lucky to make Melbourne by November 7th at this rate, not good enough.

But the next night I was lying in my bunk when there was a terrific bang on the coach roof. I looked up at the skylight and saw the main boom much lower than usual. With a sinking feeling I climbed on deck and discovered what I had feared most – the main gooseneck had broken.

October 6th, 1968   *Day 114*
0130. Well this may be the end of it all. I don't know yet; I need time to think it out. The main gooseneck jaw has sheared as I rather feared it would. I've just come below from lashing the end of the boom to the mast end taking three reefs using the reefing points. We can still sail alright but under a further handicap in that the smallest I can make the mainsail is now three reefs; after that it has all to come in. I don't feel particularly depressed or angry even. I suppose I felt that this was inevitable; anyway I accept it as such. I shall fix something up I suppose, but what I don't know at the

moment. I wish I had left some of the junk from last voyage on board; a bit comes to mind that would have been a perfect replacement. Well, I am having some brandy and then I'm going to bed, praying we don't gybe. The glass is falling to add to the fun. If the saying 'things happen in threes' is true, we're O.K. as this is the third thing to break.

Slept until 0830. It was too rough to think of unlashing the boom all morning so I spent the time rummaging for bolts and bits and pieces that might come in handy fixing the job. The simplest thing to do seems to be to drill out the old jaw and bolt it to the mast fitting. It could still swivel like that. Conditions eased for a while after lunch and I was able to remove the jaw. The stem of the jaw broke where pinned. I have been drilling out the remains of the stem all afternoon. I have given up now as I cannot see properly and I only have three drill bits left. The stem socket goes to within $\frac{1}{4}$ in. of the end of the metal which makes my job easier as the jaw appears to be hardened. My largest drill is $\frac{1}{4}$ in. so I am going to have to file out the last bit. It's going to take some time to do all this. I'm not helped by the weather. The wind is still strong and with the glass still falling is likely to increase if anything. The sea and swell are nasty and we are lurching heavily. *Suhaili* is yawing between east and south. It's a miracle I have not broken any bits so far. We are taking continuous bangs from the sea and all day at an average of five minute intervals a wave has broken right over the boat.

This is the second day I have been unable to see the sun so God knows where we are. Anyway we should be well south of the Islands.

I feel tired and a bit depressed this evening. This constant pounding worries me too; she's a good boat but there must be a limit. Things are beginning to go now; last night I fell against the mizzen and my elbow landed on a seam which broke the stitches. I don't seem able to keep up with the work at present, I wish I was fresh and had a few days of decent weather.

To add to my worries the wind kept up so I could not make repairs.

October 7th, 1968   *Day 115*
Awoke at 0600 and checked the course [which was SE] before rolling over again. I was dozing at 0635 when the wind increased and the

boat's movement became bumpy. Feeling tired and a bit confused, it was a minute before I convinced myself that I had not just checked the course. I looked at the compass and got up in a hurry. We were heading north so obviously the cold front had just passed. I climbed on deck and looked around. The sea was already white with spray and appeared to be still getting up. I could feel the wind increasing. I quickly took in the staysail and most of the mizzen and then gybed, being as careful with the main boom as possible. It was freezing cold on deck; the temperature was actually 38°F but with a Force 10 wind it felt a lot colder. I nipped below and took a quarter of a bottle of brandy which made me feel better and then went back on deck. The mainsail was beginning to come apart along the leech so I took it down and she rode much more comfortably, but was still going a bit too fast for my liking especially as we had a rather vicious cross sea. I took in the rest of the mizzen, just leaving the storm jib set and then put out the orange warp as a bight, both ends fastened on board. The orange line floats anyway, but now it flew! I put a figure of eight knot in the main sheet and streamed that, and then did the same with the mizzen, jib and storm jib sheets. You could almost walk on the ropes astern! The glass had by this time started to rise. At 0640 it had been 1008, by 0900 it was 1010 which was comforting. She seemed quite comfortable so I went below and made a cup of coffee from the Thermos. The water was lukewarm so I heated it with the remains of the brandy. I ate half a packet of dates, three handfuls of peanuts and six digestive biscuits and was about to turn in where it was at least warm, when a cross wave caught us. We went over to about 90° and came up again immediately. Quite a lot of stuff shifted, but nothing like as much as on the previous occasion. I checked on deck but all was well, so I tidied up and climbed into my sleeping bag. There was nothing I could do but pray anyway. I got up at 1130 by which time the wind had eased quite a bit, down to about Force 7, so I reset the staysail and let out a bit of mizzen. She no longer needed the lines astern so they came in too. I could not work on the mainsail as it was much too wet on deck so I carried on with the gooseneck jaw. I was lucky enough to find another drill bit, a sharp one, and I soon discovered that the jaw was not hardened; the trouble had been blunt bits. By 1700 I had the job done, so I fitted it and put the main boom back in its proper position. Only one of its teeth had got damaged by banging against the mast and I soon had that filed down.

The only bolts I have that can do the job are not long enough to pass through both lugs on the mast, so I'll just have to hope that the one lug will take the strain. The bolts I am using, I have three left, were given me in Falmouth by Dad. Jim [Friend] had found them at home and sent them down. I would have been in trouble without them.

This done I started stitching up the sail. I managed to get both ends of the tear and the centre of it sewn up before the light failed, but as I did not want to waste twelve hours sailing I hoisted the sail anyway. This was quite a job, and a shackle I had put on the swivel piece jammed the boom guy. Whilst I was clearing this, the inevitable happened. A wave caught us and over we went. I was drenched and lucky not to be swept away. I went back to hoist having got the shackle off and the handle on the halyard winch flew back and cracked my wrist. The bloody brake had failed again. I was in agony, it hurt like hell. I moved my fingers to see if the wrist was broken; they moved O.K. but before going on I went below and put a bandage round the wrist, which was already swelling. The force of the blow, which was direct and not glancing, had cut the skin. I said a few polite things about halyard winches and their ancestors, and as soon as the pain was bearable went up and finished hoisting the sail, treating the winch with a great deal of respect.

It was 2030 by this time and I was cold, wet and hungry so I went below and got the heater going and changed my clothes. I then made one of the Vesta Risottos which tasted terrific. I wish I had brought more of that type of meal. It's so convenient. Having eaten, I thought about having a whisky, but decided that Horlicks was more what I needed, so after a strong cup of that I turned in.

A good night's sleep worked wonders, and by the next day I was quite light-hearted again:

October 8th, 1968   *Day 116*
I, today, discovered the magnetic properties of cheese! I do not expect the scientific world to gasp at this discovery which I will not put on quite the same plane as Newton's discovery of gravity. Nevertheless, it is a most important and interesting discovery. In

order that posterity will not lose the record of how it came about, I give the details below. (*Alarums off! Commence soft guitar strumming!*) I was getting out some fresh tins for the ready use lockers round the galley, and as usual placed the butter and cheese in the locker above the galley (which Ken says is too hot for fats and which point I acknowledge but ignore, because I have always kept fats there!). My task completed I checked the course on the cabin compass. To my astonishment (*fast beat on guitars*) it was reading 60° off course. I checked the sun – it had not moved, noticeably anyway, so, being a quick thinker, I realized that the tins just placed in the locker, which is immediately behind the compass as I should have explained before, must have caused this elevation. I removed the butter – no change – so I removed the cheese (*guitars reach crescendo*) it swung back its full 60°. I next experimented with the jam, Ryvita, coffee, salt, Vit. Tabs., and others but they had no effect. Thus cheese is magnetic – Q.E.D.

I'm G & S'ing again this evening, at present walking my flowery way down Piccadilly with a Poppy or a Lily in my needy, evil hand!

On the 13th I thought we'd had it. The wind was blowing a good Force 10 and we were running under the storm jib when really big waves started to come up from the south and hit *Suhaili* with stunning force. This was by far the worst weather I had ever encountered and the terrifying shudders and cracks every time a wave hit the hull convinced me that the boat would not last long. I did not see how anything could stand up to this sort of continual punishment. Water was coming into the boat as if out of a tap from leaks all round the coachhouse I had never known before.

It is amazing how one's mind works in times like this. I can remember thinking that the boat might go any moment so I'd better get the liferaft out: Australia was a couple of thousand miles away, but the winds and currents would push a raft that way and I would stagger ashore eventually. I would put a couple of tins of dried fruit in the liferaft with anything else I could manage, and I would take the dinghy so that I could row myself north a bit to make sure of reaching land, and not miss Australia and carry on round the world in the Southern

Ocean. For some irrational reason I also thought of poetry and the words of Robert Service's ballad 'The Quitter' came to mind.

> When you're lost in the Wild and you're scared as a child,
>> And Death looks you bang in the eye,
> And you're sore as a boil it's according to Hoyle
>> To cock your revolver . . . and die.
> But the Code of a Man says: 'Fight all you can,'
>> And self-dissolution is barred.
> In hunger and woe, oh, it's easy to blow . . .
>> It's the hell-served-for-breakfast that's hard.*

I think that saved me. It brought me up with a jolt. What was I doing getting the liferaft out? The boat hadn't gone yet; I had not really tried everything. I went back on deck and stood watching the sea for a while. Its character was slowly changing. The huge south-west seas were dominating now and the old northerly seas had been knocked flat by the wind. *Suhaili* was lying beam on to this large sea, and if I could get her round to lie with the sea she might be all right.

The decision facing me was this. Whether to put out more warps astern, or bring her round and put out the sea-anchor forward. She was lying nearly beam-on which was why the waves were hitting so heavily. I decided against the sea anchor because *Suhaili*'s bow is not really suitable, the bowsprit and attendant rigging gets in the way, so I got out the blue polypropylene line and put the whole coil out astern, both ends made fast to the kingpost forward and led aft. The bight seemed to be on the horizon but it dragged the stern up to the wind. Like this she yawed a bit with the result that the storm jib was being thrown from side to side with terrific bangs so I hardened up both sheets and this, in fact, helped keep the bow down wind nicely. I was a bit worried about the two rudders, but although the seas were very heavy and moving past quite fast, the rudders seemed O.K. The orange warp, the bight of which was fairly close, seemed to break the crests up slightly. It was quite amazing the difference the blue warp made. From rolling beam on to the seas without it, and being terribly battered, we were suddenly lying very quietly stern to seas, which were occasionally breaking over the

* From Robert Service, *Collected Verse*, Ernest Benn Ltd., London, and Dodd, Mead, New York; Ryerson Press, Toronto.

decks. We were pooped twice but not heavily. I had been having to pump the bilges frequently, about every two hours, but ceased this as soon as we were round. In the morning I tried to seal up the port cockpit locker as water was pouring from there into the engine-room. Each time she rolled about a gallon would get below which explains why I was pumping so often. The four Diesel fuel drums are still in the cockpit. One is empty and serves only to jam the others in place. Another was filled up with water which has forced the diesel oil out. The cap was no good. I threw this drum overside to give myself room – it sank immediately – and refixed the rag in the lower water hole. But this was only half the problem, as most of the water gets in via the locker lid, so I screwed that down and caulked it. It helped a bit.

Quite why I got so depressed about the middle of the day I don't know. It was after I had put out the orange warp but before I put out the blue one, so I had not exhausted all the possibilities. I think it may be due to the fact that I am feeling very weary, and the low glass is not encouraging. Also the blows the boat was taking were very heavy. After one of them I was convinced she had stove in the hull. It was cold on deck and I was wet, and I have not been eating properly the last few days.

Tonight I feel better; I've just eaten a curry, but terribly tired. She seems to be riding comfortably and the wind appears to be easing a bit. I've just been on deck, the foredeck is dry!! I'm going to hope for the best and turn in. It tells on your nerves this sort of thing – you never know when she just might get hit by a big one, and it's so dark that you can only see the waves when they are on top of you. Can't hear 'em, too much noise from the wind.

Next morning I awoke with a stiff back and a bruise the size of a cricket ball at the base of my spine. I don't know how I came by the bruise, but I had been knocked about a good deal the day before, and when one is occupied one doesn't notice bangs. I had a strenuous task hauling the tangle of warps in again; 120 fathoms of 2-inch polypropylene being dragged at three knots weighs a good deal, and it took me twenty minutes to haul that in alone.

The self-steering began to give trouble again. It was stiff and operated slowly and then only in jerks. This meant I had to do a lot of steering myself. My diary entries became shorter because I was tired and when I did get below all I wanted to do was collapse into my bunk. Eating was another problem. I did not feel hungry, and the thought of the effort required to make a meal put me right off food. The succession of gales continued, and eventually I headed north to find better weather. The shearing of the main gooseneck worried me; I thought that if that could break then so could other things and this made me jittery. I wanted a rest and time to check everything. I also wanted to report to a passing ship if I could, and as the steamship routes are north of the sailing ship routes I hoped to kill two birds with one stone by heading northwards.

We were about 500 miles from Australia by this time; although the weather had been rough and uncomfortable, progress had been excellent, and I was beginning to pick up local radio stations in Western Australia. This kept me abreast of the news and the Albany wool sales; every time I tuned in, it seemed, I picked up the latest market report, and after a few days I could have given anyone a full run down on every aspect of them.

Despite kinder conditions the self-steering rudder broke again on October 23rd, after we were well into the Australian Bight. What was worse, I lost most of it and was left with no bits and pieces that could somehow be put together again. The weather was too rough to put in the now repaired original rudder, so I steered for a day myself. To add to my troubles, one of my primus burners developed a leak and I had to blank it off. This left one burner which had to last if I was going to have hot meals and coffee for the rest of the voyage. I could manage without hot food but not without coffee. I have a reputation for being ill-tempered before I get my coffee in the mornings!

The next day I managed to fit the last self-steering rudder. I did not try getting it into its slot from the deck but dived overside and connected it that way. It was much simpler and quicker, but the water was freezing cold, and took my breath away when I first entered. As usual I rushed to check the brandy bottle level on getting out. The rudder vibrated badly, and to ease it I put rope lashings around its bar to support it. This rather stiffened it, but it worked, though I wondered for how long. To reduce the strain I did not sail the boat as fast as I could have done, but even so, the rudder was not going to last. I wondered what I should do when it gave, but the thought was a bit depressing so I thought about other things.

The diary for the next day, October 25th, when I was 450 miles east-south-east of Cape Leeuwin, begins with:

YIPPEE!!

Sighted a ship – the *Kooringa* of Melbourne at 1730 today. I had just finished writing a letter and glanced through the forward porthole and saw the superstructure. I rushed on deck and there she was about three miles away. I had reckoned on reaching the shipping lane at 1700 and was going to stay up all night if necessary, but to sight a ship within thirty minutes of getting there is phenomenal luck. I dashed below and grabbed the rifle, loaded a clip and fired three shots. I had hoisted *MIK* [the International Code for 'Please report me by radio to Lloyd's'] at lunchtime and I cleared these flags. For a while nothing happened, then as I fired off the remaining two rounds she turned towards me. As she came close she sounded one blast and then hoisted the answering pennant, so they saw my signal. At last people at home will know I'm safe. I got out the fog horn and sent 'All Well', which I hope they received. They came within a cable's length and then turned and came back for a look. The fact that they did this rather indicates that they realized who we are, so I hope the news gets out quickly. *Suhaili* was not looking very tidy I'm afraid. I should have spent the day on deck but I fiddled with the radio instead. I did screw a couple of bits of wood to the deck where the Highfield levers are wearing a bit. I also turned off the W.C. inlet valve as I don't use the W.C. and it has rather a lot of pipes on it.

In fact, I used a bucket instead of the W.C. It was much more convenient, although one had to be careful not to upset it.

Melbourne to Otago

November 10th, 1968 (Day 148)–November 20th, 1968 (Day 159)

For some perverse reason the weather now became very warm and calm; we drifted along for a couple of days and I was able to repair the ravages so far. I also began to get a suntan again; the Southern Ocean had bleached my previous tan away.

One morning I awoke and smelt the unmistakable aroma of land, or as people ashore call it, the smell of the sea. In fact, it's the smell of the sea shore so both seamen and shore people are right in a way. There were also a large number of insects in the air that day, including many butterflies, and I immediately began to worry about my navigation. The sighting of the *Kooringa* right where I thought I was on the shipping lane had given me confidence in the sextant, but I now began to wonder if I had reached the shipping lane where I thought I had. Maybe I was a hundred miles farther along it. I eventually traced the sea shore aroma to the weed growing on *Suhaili*; the warm weather had dried it out and was causing the smell, but the insects still worried me. Insects are often found at seemingly impossible distances out at sea. Charles Darwin in his voyage round the world in H.M.S. *Beagle* found spiders all over the rigging when hundreds of miles off the South American coast. He theorized that they were blown out to sea by the offshore winds. That was all very well; they were small spiders, but I was sixty miles off the Australian coast and had a large butterfly. I took extra and very careful sights that day but they all put me where I supposed I was, and I came to the conclusion that the butterfly was wrong, not me.

That same evening I noticed some porpoises swimming by the bow and I rushed up with the camera to try to take a photograph of them when they leapt clear. In the Duke of Edinburgh's book *Birds from Britannia* there is one shot of a porpoise's tail disappearing under water with the caption 'Missed it'. Since reading the book, I have had a burning ambition to photograph a porpoise in mid-leap and smugly to send him a copy. I missed the porpoises this time, but on turning to go aft I found three whales following closely in *Suhaili*'s wake. The photographs of these just show empty ocean!

I was beginning to get excited at the thought of reaching Melbourne, seeing Bruce again and receiving some mail with news from home. But so far, although I had listened regularly to the news broadcasts, there had been no mention of the *Kooringa* sighting me. The obvious reason for this was that it was not a newsworthy item, but it worried me in case I had not been reported, in which case I would not be met at Melbourne. I sighted another ship a few days later, and although I set off a hand flare, burning my hand in the process, it did not show any interest, and a feeling of anti-climax began to descend as a result. This was not helped the next day when the tiller broke.

November 2nd, 1968   *Day 141*
0330. Barely turned in, had not dropped off, when we started really pitching heavily. I got up to try another adjustment and found the tiller loose; it had sheared off where threaded at the rudder head. I had a lot of difficulty getting the head off and lost a hammer in the process. It's not on properly now but I'm scared of banging it too much. I don't know what will go next. Of course the fact that I could not control direction did not help and I had waves breaking over me the whole time. It was over forty minutes before I got the spare fitted. I have taken in sail now and she is easier but I have little control over direction. As I feel at the moment I think I'll give up at Melbourne. I've had enough. I'm tired, exhausted would be nearer the truth, frustrated because nothing I do seems to make any difference to the course, and scared to think what will

break next. I still have the engine in pieces and water is getting at it, but I cannot raise the energy to do anything about it.

1930. We are now becalmed. Come on God, give me a bloody break, it's been nothing but calms or gales for weeks; how about some steady winds for a change.

I tried to rest this afternoon but couldn't because we kept yawing. We still are. I'm going to get half drunk tonight and make sure of some real rest. Whilst I have written this she's yawed 120°. The *Admiral* waving around responding to nothing as far as I can see; mind you there's no wind and a heavy swell.

I fixed up an electric lamp within the oil boat-lamp last night as the flame kept going out. I do not have one reliable oil lamp. This beer is wonderful, I wish I'd brought another twenty cases of beer, I could have used it. As it is I shall have to go on brandy after this one can as I have to ration myself. It was a false economy only having five cases of beer. Brandy does not have a very intoxicating effect on me, not as great as, say, whisky.

She's stubbornly steering due east at the moment, whereas I want to go 120° to avoid hitting land. Still I expect there is a slight southerly current here.

The self-steering rudder packed up for the third and last time the very next day, November 3rd, when I was still about 300 miles from Melbourne. The metal shaft sheared again, but in a different place; the bottom section was lost, so I had no chance of making repairs. I took the vanes off and lashed them to the cabin top.

Here I was, not yet even halfway round the world and with no self-steering. I could draw little encouragement to continue the voyage without it from the state of the boat. Although I had managed to fit the spare tiller it was not a very good job. I had not dared hammer it home because the rudder bearings were showing signs of wear and I did not want to strain them. As a precautionary measure I had put lashings on the rudder to relieve the strains on it and also to hold it if the pintles went. I was out of touch with the world as my transmitter had packed up six weeks before and I had been unable to discover the fault. This did not worry me too much as the receiver still worked and I was able to get the news and time signals, but I knew it would be causing concern to my family and friends. The engine had seized up and I could hardly blame it after the bashing the boat had received south of the Cape of Good Hope. Water had been coming in all over the place and the engine-room was not the easiest place to keep dry.

These were the physical reasons for heading for Melbourne and giving up, and the more I considered them the more I felt that it would be foolish to go on, particularly as I still had Cape Horn ahead of me. I was not very fresh now either and nothing like as fit and strong as when I set out. And yet I was in the lead. Ridgway and Blyth had retired and I was way ahead of my nearest competitor. Sure, I had not done badly; *Suhaili* was the smallest boat ever to make the voyage to Australia non-stop, but wouldn't it be a much finer thing to be the first man round the world non-stop? After all I was nearly halfway; it would be a pity to waste all the work so far.

How would any man act in the circumstances? I don't think there would be any disagreement on this score and I only did what millions of others would have done. I decided to carry on for the time being, at least as far as New Zealand, and see if I could manage without the self-steering. My immediate concern, then, was to try to balance the sails and rudder on all points of the wind so that the boat would steer herself in roughly the right direction.

Now I am not an expert yachtsman. It has been said that seamanship in the days of sail consisted of manipulating the yards, sails and cordage to manoeuvre a sailing ship by applying, in a rough and ready manner, the principle of mechanics to the propulsion of the wind-driven ship. That's about as far as I have ever progressed. I've sat in yacht clubs listening to people arguing in detail about how to get the most efficient 'slot' and things like that, and frankly I do not understand half of it. I have not sailed a wide variety of boats and my experience, apart from the dinghy sailing that Bertie gave us, has all been picked up from *Suhaili*.

I suppose that by the time the self-steering packed up I had covered about 32,000 miles in her and you would have to be pretty thick not to learn how your boat handles in that time. I knew that if I lashed the helm and hauled all the sheets tight she would sail close-hauled without further attention; what I had to do now was find a way of getting her to run before the wind like that, as until some time after Cape Horn I could expect following winds.

If I could not manage it, well, I had two good arms, and I would steer for about sixteen hours each day and then heave-to to eat and sleep. The actual work did not frighten me; it's not too bad once you get stuck into it and you rarely have to exert yourself full time. What oppressed me was the thought of sitting for two and a half months with nothing but steering every day. I doubted if I could think of sufficient subjects to keep my mind occupied all that time, and the time drags if you have not some absorbing subject to think about. Still, I could worry about that when the time came.

When the rudder broke the wind was northerly and I wanted to go east, so I lashed the helm amidships and slackened all the sheets and sat down to watch what happened. I comforted myself with the thought that Joshua Slocum had managed to set *Spray* on almost any course he wanted by adjusting the sheets and tiller, and *Spray* was a sloop, which I felt would not be as easy to balance as *Suhaili*, who as a ketch, had more sails to play with. But I did not get very far with my experiments that day as the wind soon died away leaving us becalmed.

The weather in the Southern Ocean is fairly predictable. It is governed by the succession of depressions that are continually forming where warm tropical and cold polar air streams meet, at about 40° South latitude. The air pressure had been high but was beginning to fall and a cold front had passed a day before. I could therefore expect northerly winds for a while anyway and during the night north-north-east winds arose. This was fine as it meant I could leave *Suhaili* close-hauled, and I went below for some sleep. The winds lasted all the next day and it was not until November 6th that the next cold front arrived and the wind swung round to the south-west.

By this time my sun sights were putting us close to King Island, which lies at the western end of the Bass Strait, between Tasmania and the Australian mainland. I had last seen land four months previously when we passed the Cape Verde Islands, and as I did not like to put too much trust in my sextant, which had taken a bashing since then, I turned north to clear the island. All day I kept a lookout for land, or any signs of land such as land birds or orographic clouds, but I could see nothing. The most foolish doubts came to me. How did I know I was anywhere near Australia? Maybe my navigation was hopelessly out. Then I thought of the radio stations I had been listening to for the past fortnight. At first I had picked up Perth, then Albany and its wool sales, then Adelaide, and now I was getting Melbourne, Sydney and Devonport, whilst Perth was fading – I could not be far out.

All this time I had been steering north and I was finding that *Suhaili* would steer herself for quite long periods with the wind on the quarter. Eventually she would swing one way or the other and I would have to bring her back on course, but I felt that this was encouraging.

As soon as it got dark I climbed onto the Admiral and looked for lights, but it was not until 2230 that I detected a flicker to the east. It was too distant to make out its identification characteristic, so it did not help much as it could have been either King Island or Cape Otway on the mainland, depending upon the current we had experienced from noon. If it was Cape Otway it was time to alter course to the east, whilst if it was King Island, we needed to go farther north. I altered course to the east to get closer and find out just where I was. Quite a rough sea was running by this time and it was nearly an hour before I was able to get a complete characteristic of the light as I kept losing sight of it and this upset my counting. But it was Cape Otway. We had come farther north than I expected and I had to steer south-east now in order to clear the headland.

I felt pretty happy as I sat steering through the rather choppy sea that had built up off the Cape. Here I was, just about halfway round the world, the third and smallest boat to make the voyage (Chichester's *Gipsy Moth III* was 53 feet long; Alec Rose's *Lively Lady* 36 feet; *Suhaili* 32 feet). I began to wonder if I was expected and if perhaps I'd get some news from home. Maybe the *Kooringa* had reported me. Anyway, civilization was just over the horizon, and I began to be tempted by the thought of a sound sleep in a soft, unmoving bed, a large steak, and company, despite my resolutions of a couple of days before.

I kept thinking that no one had got farther than this, so why not pull in, there were plenty of reasons over and above the self-steering packing up. But I knew this wouldn't do, and I'd never forgive myself if I did not try to go on.

By half-past two the next morning we were abeam of Cape Otway. I steered for three more hours and then lashed the helm and went to sleep. Before going below I reduced sail and guyed out the booms, leaving *Suhaili* running dead before the wind, which was still blowing from the south-west. Port Phillip Heads, the entrance to Melbourne, lay to the north-east, and I knew that if *Suhaili* gybed she would come to no immediate harm with guys on the booms, and the wind pressure on the other side of the sails would heel the boat over and throw me out of my bunk and I could then readjust the course. It was a drastic warning system, but there was no doubt that it would work.

When I awoke at 0830, land was clearly in sight to the north-west, a wonderful sight. I knocked up a quick breakfast and then let out sail and took the helm. I had never been to Australia, and I still have not, but I knew that there must be a pilot vessel and I hoped to meet up with it or with some small craft off Port Phillip Heads, and throw over some mail which could be forwarded to London.

Shortly after lunch I picked up the lighthouse which marks the Heads, and soon afterwards I did indeed see the pilot vessel. As I came closer it turned and made towards the port, and I let off a flare to attract attention. The farther out I could meet him the better, as with a south-west wind, Port Phillip was on a lee shore and I was going to have some hard tacking to do to get out into the Bass Strait again. I don't think my flare was seen, but just then a ship came up from the south-east and the pilot vessel came out again to meet it. By the time the pilot had been transferred I was close enough to hail the small pilot launch The coxswain of the launch looked round, waved me away and carried on back to his mother ship. Obviously no one was expecting me. I sailed in pursuit, still yelling at him, and then a figure appeared on the bridge of the pilot vessel and I shouted to him that I was non-stop from the U.K. and would he please take my mail. I received a wave of acknowledgement and on rounding the stern I saw the launch, which was halfway out of the water, begin to be lowered again. As I sailed round the stern of the *Wyuna*, a seaman appeared and leaned on the taffrail watching me. I yelled across that I had been on my own for 147 days, and I asked him what the other fifty per cent of the human race looked like. He caught my meaning, and moving his hands to describe the shape, replied, 'Something like that!'

I gybed *Suhaili* round and then, of course, the wind got up and she gathered way. Now the launch was chasing frantically after *us* for about two minutes whilst I was still sorting out sheets and guys, and only when I luffed up could they catch me. I had all the letters and articles I had written, together with films taken on the voyage and some charts showing my progress, stowed in a waterproof rocket box, and when the launch came close it was an easy matter to throw it across. I also gave the coxswain a message to radio to the U.K. for my family and friends. The box safely transferred, the launch turned back, and after a final wave I adjusted sail to get as close to the wind as possible to clear Cape Shank to the south-east.

It was 1610 when I set course again. My log book, normally kept in the rather staid manner affected by ships' officers, blossoms out with 'Homeward Bound' underlined numerous times. In fact, of course, I was not halfway yet, and because in things like this I find I encourage myself by making the first part as difficult as possible and reward myself with an easy second half, I looked upon the International Date Line, east of New Zealand, as my personal halfway mark.

For three and a half hours we had rough going, and then as Cape Shank at last drew abeam, the wind and sea eased and I was able to lash the helm, make a cup of coffee and have a cigarette. We appeared to be inshore of the shipping lane, but having hung out a lantern, I set my alarm clock at two hourly intervals through the night so that I could keep a check on our position, and also to be ready in case the wind changed.

At daybreak I could see hills in the distance to the east, but otherwise I had the world to myself. The sea had gone down and for the first time in two months there was no south-west to west swell. It was too good an opportunity for climbing the mast to be missed and I got out a tackle and the bosun's chair. Over the last month some more sail slides had come off the mainsail, mainly the upper ones, and slowly a collection had built up at the top of the mast. I had been unable to oil the track so the slides had stuck there, and as I had now used my spares, I had been awaiting a favourable opportunity to go up and pull them all down. This sort of job is quite out of the question when there is a sea or swell, as both one's hands are needed for hauling. I have found that I cannot rely upon my legs to hold me if the boat rolls, and swinging around thirty or forty feet above the deck with no hands free is not recommended.

Just as I had made all ready and was about to climb into the chair, an aircraft swooped down on us. At first I thought it was just a pilot out for some fun, but it kept circling round and I realized that it must have come out looking for me. This was good news, as it told me that my mail and messages had been passed on, and that Mother and Father and the rest of my family must know that I was safe.

The plane circled for about half an hour, but after the first ten minutes the novelty had worn off and in any case I wanted to get the job in hand completed while I could, so I hauled myself aloft and sent the slides down.

We sailed slowly south all day. I was heading for Banks Strait at the north-east corner of Tasmania, as this was the shortest way to the south of New Zealand. Once I had recovered the slides, I did a few repairs on the mainsail and then, as it was warm and sunny, I decided to sunbathe. I had been stripped off about ten minutes when the aircraft returned; I don't know if the pilot was trying to catch me out, but he was pretty close when I first heard him. I dived for my trousers. Twice more this happened during the afternoon, when first a helicopter appeared and then another aircraft. I gave up sunbathing after the last, and as I might have expected, was left on my own for the rest of the day.

Having not had an uninterrupted night's sleep for three nights, I turned in early. The wind was light, the sea calm, we were well clear of any navigational dangers, and also off any shipping routes. I had twelve beautiful hours sleep and awoke ready for anything.

Land was in sight to the south at daybreak and I turned due east towards Banks Strait, which I hoped to reach before nightfall. The Strait is about seven miles wide, but there is a bend in it and only one light to guide shipping and it is as well not to take risks. As the day developed, however, even though I pressed *Suhaili* with as much sail as I could set, I realized that we were not going to make it. The tidal stream turned against us at the crucial moment and at dusk, when the tide turned in our favour, I was still trying to pick out some conspicuous landmark to guide us into the Strait. Many hills were in sight, but when you are not sure where you are it is easy to mistake these and confidently put yourself many miles from your actual position, and many a ship has been lost because of a Master's over-confidence.

I waited impatiently for it to get dark. As I could not tell where I was in daylight, my hoped rested in seeing the loom of Swan Island light, which had a good range. I decided that if I did not see it within three hours I would heave-to until daybreak. I was about to take star sights to help fix my position when I saw a flicker of a light ahead. I climbed onto the Admiral and watched the horizon intently. There it was again. All was well, and on we pressed.

We cleared the Strait soon after midnight and after lashing the helm, I turned in. The wind must have died during the night, because when I awoke soon after daybreak we were still in sight of the Swan Island lighthouse. I let out all sail again and set a course straight across the Tasman Sea for the port of Bluff, over nine hundred miles away on the south coast of South Island, New Zealand, where I had suggested any messages and mail could be handed over to me.

For the first two days the wind was such that *Suhaili* was close-hauled and I had no problem sailing her, but when it changed and came round to the north-west I had to start playing with the sails again. First I tried putting them all out on the same side and leaving the helm lashed so that the boat would run on a broad reach. This was quite hopeless as she kept bringing her head up into the wind. I hauled her back on course and gave her a bit more weather helm and continued this until she ceased luffing up, but now she tended to gybe if left alone. I would have probably continued fiddling about had not a rising wind forced me to take in sail, and under the reduced sail she became far more balanced.

For some time after this I continued making minor adjustments, and once the boat seemed balanced I carefully marked the position of the tiller and left her to it.

That night I was awoken by the crashing of the sails as *Suhaili* gybed. I rushed on deck to find that the wind had freshened, upsetting the balance. All the sails were aback and the boom guys looked as if they would give way at any minute. I leapt for the tiller throwing all my strength on it to hold it hard over. *Suhaili* started to come round, but as soon as I eased the helm she went back. Once again I put my weight on the tiller only to be almost jerked overside as it came away in my hand. It had broken off at the rudder head, just like its predecessor. I swore fluently, threw the tiller into the cockpit and took in the mainsail and most of the mizzen, so that with a jib set forward *Suhaili* tended to run off before the wind. For the next hour I was kept fully occupied lashing the tiller to the bucking rudder head. It meant the tiller was now about one foot shorter which with the lessened leverage would make steering harder work, but at least I could steer.

I lashed the jury tiller amidships and watched the course. To my great satisfaction and considerable surprise, *Suhaili* seemed to like the sail arrangement and was heading the right way. However, I could not remain satisfied with that state of affairs for long, so I started to give her more mizzen to see if she would still sail as well, only faster. I finished up with all the mizzen set and the mainsail fully reefed with the booms guyed down again, and *Suhaili* belting along comfortably at five knots. It was worry at first when the mainsail started to gybe, but I soon discovered that if left alone, the mizzen would push the boat back onto course.

We were well into the Tasman Sea by this time, and it was beginning to look as if it might be possible to continue the voyage. I was not too tired and the days' runs were good, as good as before the Admiral had packed up, in fact. Thinking of continuing the voyage made my spirits rise immediately. Up until this point I had not really thought about it since leaving Australia, mainly because if you don't get too excited about a thing, you don't feel so let down if it doesn't work out. But *Suhaili* was balancing so well that the long stretch across the Southern Pacific no longer seemed quite so formidable.

For the next two days I continued experimenting with different arrangements of sails and I probably learned as much again about *Suhaili* during this time as I had known before I left England. Necessity is the mother of invention and I am always quite happy to leave things until I have to cope with them, and then throw myself happily into the problem. This is what happened now and at the end of the two days I had not only discovered that *Suhaili* would run quite well under reduced canvas but I had also found out how to make her reach quite well. Of course these abilities had been there ever since *Suhaili* was built, but I had been too lazy ever to work them out before.

I was now getting close to New Zealand and on Sunday November 17th, at 9.00 p.m. as usual, I switched on the radio to listen to the weather report. New Zealand's weather is governed by the depressions that build up in the Tasman Sea. The advantage of this sort of condition is that you can predict fairly accurately what the weather is going to be like for the next day or so, and as the weather changes quite quickly, the New Zealand weather reports are detailed and lengthy and up to the standard of shipping forecasts elsewhere. Judging by the detail in the reports it appeared to me that most New Zealanders followed the weather bulletins as closely as we follow a daily serial at home.

The weather had been fair and settled for a couple of days and my barometer was rising, so I hoped that these conditions would last until I had passed clear of the Foveaux Strait. The weather report forecast unsettled conditions for the next twenty-four hours which suited me, but it also mentioned that a very deep low was forming south of Tasmania, and I did not like the sound of that. However, the previous deep low had passed well to the south and I hoped that this would do the same, in which case I could expect a half gale or even a gale, but we could navigate Foveaux Strait in that.

It was my usual practice to switch the radio off the moment the weather forecast had been broadcast, but this evening for some reason I left it on for a few minutes. Maybe I was lighting a cigarette, but whatever the cause it was indirectly responsible for giving me the most harrowing experience in the whole voyage. This was not apparent until later, of course, and at the time I blessed the chance that kept my hand from the switch as the next words that came over were 'Master, *Suhaili*'. I switched on the transmitter and reached for the microphone which was wrapped up in my sleeping bag. I did not really expect it to work but at least I could try. Usually when a station has a message for a ship, it calls the ship concerned and then waits for an answer before reading out the text of the message. It was essential, therefore, for me to get through in reply. However, even as I was connecting up, the announcer began to read out the text, not waiting to know if I was listening: '*Imperative we rendezvous outside Bluff Harbour in daylight. Signature: Bruce Maxwell.*'

This was splendid news. Apart from assuring me that my letters must have reached home safely, it meant I might receive some mail and I was anxious to know how things were at home. It would be nice to see a familiar face as well. I blessed the radio station. Obviously they thought that I might be listening in and on the chance of it they were reading the message out every day.

I now had to calculate when I expected to reach Bluff Harbour. At noon we had been 160 miles away so with a decent wind I might get there before sunset the next day. We were sailing well at present under the Big Fellow and mizzen, running nice and steadily before the wind and making about five knots. I decided to leave her like that for the night and get up early in the morning, by which time land should be in sight, and decide then whether to press on or idle for a day and make Bluff on Tuesday at daybreak.

When the alarm woke me at 0500 on Monday morning I found land in sight to the north, and even better from the point of view of finding my position, away to the east I could see Solander Island, a steep rocky outcrop seventy-two miles from Bluff. I estimated that Bluff was still about ninety miles away and it was unlikely that I could make it before sunset, so I reduced sail and hove to about six miles short of Solander

Island. The barometer had begun to fall during the morning, but I felt no alarm, since I expected to be clear of Bluff before the cold front arrived.

At midday I set sail again to clear Solander Island, as we had drifted slowly down onto it during the morning. It looked very appealing to me, as I think an uninhabited island will appeal to anyone, but this was rather more interesting as there was something grand in the vertical sweep of the rock, which was nevertheless covered in greenery although I could not make out what the plants were holding on to.

By the time we were clear of Solander, the wind had begun to freshen and sea was choppy and confused. I had to steer all afternoon as it was quite hopeless trying to effect a balance when the boat was being thrown about.

After a rapid fall all morning, the barometer steadied in the late afternoon at 980 millibars. It had read 996 twelve hours before and it was obvious that the depression had moved very quickly across the Tasman Sea and that the front was not very far away. I was by now too close to Foveaux Strait to hope to change course and steer south of Stewart Island, which would give me a clear sea. If the front arrived before I had got clear, I would be left too close to a lee shore for comfort. There was no alternative but to keep heading for the Strait and hope that I could steer the boat clear of the dangers there, particularly the line of islands and shallows across the far end.

I cleared away the warps so that I could stream them quickly and I also got out the sea anchor and coiled it down in the cockpit. For some time I tried to think of a way of lashing the self-steering vanes securely to the boat, but wherever I put them, a part always overlapped the cabin top and it only wanted one good wave under the protruding part and they would tear loose. The thought of the damage those two heavy pieces of plywood could cause decided me, and I threw them overside.

Dark cloud was beginning to form to the west by this time, hiding the sun, so that I was unable to get a last check on the compass. Well, too bad, I thought; I'll just hope to pick out the lighthouse on Centre Island at the entrance to the Strait before rain obscures everything. With the last gleams of daylight I handed the mainsail and lashed it firmly to its boom and then set up both runners, giving the mainmast all the support I could. I glanced round the deck to check that everything was secure and then climbed out along the bowsprit to check the storm jib tack and clew. There was nothing more I could do now. We were running under the storm jib and a scrap of mizzen and *Suhaili* appeared comfortable in the light wind and ominous stillness.

Glancing at my watch, I realized that I had just time to switch on the radio for the weather report, so I went below. The announcer's voice sounded as calm as usual. I suppose he had read out the same sort of thing many times before, rather like a judge reading out a sentence. The only person who appreciates the awfulness of the words is the unhappy prisoner. As the verbal picture unfolded, I began to feel more and more like that prisoner. The cold front was about eighty miles away, moving at 40 knots. Winds of Force 9 were expected and these would reach a peak of Force 10 the next day. Very heavy rain and poor visibility were also prophesied. I believed him; all the signs pointed to it.

I listened to the announcer reading out the message from Bruce again and wished I had not heard it. I could have been past Bluff by now and clear of the islands by the time the front arrived. Still, that's the way fortune plays with one, I thought, and the Lord's will be done; I just hoped that His will and mine were the same.

I put the kettle on; it was still quiet outside, although as black as pitch, and I thought of Bruce sitting in a comfortable hotel lounge with a large beer in front of him. Perhaps we'd be drinking together within twenty-four hours. This last thought stuck with me, and I had even begun to welcome the idea when it struck me how disloyal I was being to *Suhaili*. We had come a long way together and here was I idly dreaming of giving her up in order to have a few creature comforts. She had brought me through some pretty awful weather, but now, when I was absolutely necessary, unlike the previous occasions when she only had need of me as a navigator, I was thinking of giving up. I felt very ashamed of myself.

Determined to make amends, I made a cup of coffee, added a large dash of brandy and then sat down in the cabin with the

Chart, Pilot, and Light list to memorize the characteristics of the lights and the courses I needed to steer safely through the Strait. I also have another aide which I find very useful at times and that is to work out how far I am away from a light when it appears to be one finger's width above the horizon. A finger held horizontally at arm's length subtends an angle of about $1\frac{1}{2}°$. It gives me a rough guide and when it is not possible to get the sextant out for an accurate angle, serves quite well. I could do no more. My Pacific Tide Tables had gone soggy a long time before so I would have to watch for the current and keep two logs going in my mind to work out the greatest and least distances we could have gone, and make sure I didn't go too far on any course and miss a conspicuous mark.

I was standing in the hatchway smoking when the rain began to fall, and the wind to rise. About twenty minutes previously in the eerie stillness and quiet that prevailed, I had caught a glimpse of a light ahead, which I identified as Centre Island lighthouse. I took a bearing on it and so had my first course to steer. This was fortunate as I had only had a rough idea of my position up until then and once the rain began to fall everything was blotted out for the next three hours.

So far so good. Round one to us.

The wind, which had been from the north-north-west, changed abruptly when the rain arrived and began to freshen from the west. I climbed on deck and paid out the big blue warp and then streamed the sea anchor. I wanted to go as slowly as possible whilst it was impossible to see any lights. I stayed mainly in the hatchway; I could not see farther than the bow because of the rain so there was little point in keeping a lookout, and I could keep warmer that way.

Suhaili was riding the waves beautifully as usual and very little water was coming on board, most of the waves being parted at the stern and rushing in a flurry of foam down each side.

By 0230 the wind was blowing a gale and I handed the mizzen and sheeted the storm jib hard amidships. The rain was easing now and I could occasionally get glimpses of the stars through the broken sky. Fortifying myself with a quick look at the level in the brandy bottle, I climbed onto the Admiral's bridge to keep a lookout. All I could hope for was a glimpse of the Centre

Island light. If in the darkness we had passed it, I would just have to hope we were in the centre of the Strait and clear of the hazards each side. I felt we had come slightly north of due east, so if I saw breakers ahead I intended setting the mainsail and fighting the boat south. For half an hour I clung to the rigging as the wind howled through it and looked in vain. What rain was left was mixing with the spray and I found it difficult and painful to look astern, where the waves were now tumbling over each other in their headlong rush before the wind, throwing clouds of spray into the air, which were immediately seized and thrown along the surface like hail. Then the darkness began to whiten at intervals to the north. I could see no light but only a bright patch covering an area of the horizon. I counted the seconds and worked out the characteristic. It was Centre Island and it looked close. I leapt down from my perch, pulled the tiller about one inch to port and relashed it. This was all that was necessary to bring the boat's head round 30° to starboard, which was needed to clear a cluster of rocks south-east of the lighthouse. Still she ran on, rolling a bit now and occasionally putting the deck under each side, but no waves were sweeping over her.

For an hour longer I stayed standing on the Admiral. I hung on with one hand only, changing hands every few minutes so that they would not grow numb. All this time I peered ahead, watching out for breakers, although it would have been difficult to distinguish them in the broken water which filled the sea all round us. Still, it was better to be up looking for them than doing nothing.

Eventually, when I could no longer see any sign of the Centre Island light, I decided we must be past the rocks, and went below for Irish coffee and a cigarette.

The boat's movement was surprisingly easy below. We were now into the Strait, of course, and the great swell that is a characteristic of the Southern Ocean was unable to exert its full effect. The main disturbance was due to the waves which had quickly built up and were racing along with the wind.

By the time I had warmed through it was getting light and I climbed out onto my perch to continue watching for land. Slowly the sky brightened, but it did not help much as visibility was reduced to less than a mile by all the water in suspension.

I checked the course. We appeared to be running down the middle of the Strait which in this visibility would mean I should not see the Bluff and I could sail straight on into the trap of shoals and islands completely unawares. I brought the tiller back amidships to bring her back onto an easterly course and we began to close the land, although we could not see it.

As time passed and I saw nothing, I began to get seriously worried. Suppose the current was stronger than I expected – I could be past the Bluff by now. Alternatively I could have been pushed back to Centre Island again. The wind was still rising and visibility was if anything getting worse. Some kelp floated into view. Was it fixed? No, all well, it was a broken piece torn off from its stem somewhere to windward by the force of the waves.

The longer we were without sight of land, the more I worried and eventually I began to make out shapes in the atmosphere around us. This was easy enough as the swirling air was constantly changing colour and it was a simple matter to see a misty headland suddenly forming near by. This went on for some time until at 0730 a shape ahead of us began to harden, its edges and loom drawing steadily closer. I could pick out nothing distinctive in the blurred outline, nothing to tell me what piece of the coast this was. But no matter where it was in relation to Bluff, it was dead to leeward of us and we would have to alter course at once if we were not going to finish the voyage at its feet.

We were still under storm jib alone, but the way this land was hardening to the south, putting the tiller over as before was not going to get us clear. My heart sank; I would have to set the mainsail and I did not know if the mast would take the strain or if it did, how long it would be before the sail was reduced to shreds. Well, better to run ashore without sails or a mast than do nothing to try to get her off. I worked my way along the boom throwing off the ties that held the sail down and once at the mast shipped the winch handle and hoisted the sail. I could feel *Suhaili* straining immediately; there was too much drag from the sea anchor and warp. But before I could attend to that I must put her on a safe course, so I set the mizzen fully reefed to hold the bow up. Now we really began to notice the seas. Whilst *Suhaili* bravely rode up over the large waves, she could do little with the smaller ones which flung themselves viciously at her, broke against the hull and sent walls of water over the boat. Well, we'd have to take it; anything was better than running ashore, and if I strained the boat coming through this, at least I would still have a boat and I could get repairs done to her in New Zealand. In order that nothing should check our progress towards safety, I set to work to reduce the drag by hauling in the sea anchor. I had not got two fathoms in when I realized that both the painter and tripping line were hopelessly entangled around each other and the warp. We were making about 4 knots by this time and in normal circumstances I doubt if I could have hauled the anchor and warp inboard. However, desperation lent me strength and using the boat's motion to help, I slowly began to haul the tangle on board. I was sitting in the cockpit facing aft with my legs braced against the washboard. Each time the bow came up and the boat lost way, I threw my weight against the warp and then hung on so as not to lose my gain as the boat made another rush forward. At first it came in about six inches at a time and I wondered how long 720 feet was going to take, but the work became easier and once I had the sea anchor in I had little difficulty. There had been no chance to sort the tangle out as I hauled in and the cockpit was now a mass of twisted rope. I jammed as much of it as I could into the cockpit and lashed the rest down to prevent it being washed overside by the waves which were sweeping over us.

Up till now I had been too busy to pay any attention to the land, my efforts being entirely taken up with putting the boat on a safe course, but now I looked to leeward to see how we were doing. The land appeared much closer and I could even see the spray rising at its foot where the waves were breaking; however, its end appeared in sight about 45 degrees on the bow, so we still had a chance of clearing it.

I began to wonder if this was, in fact, Bluff. It bore a strong resemblance to the Bluff at Durban and it ended very abruptly. However, I could see nothing on it, no lights, houses or radio

T–E

masts that would help me identify it and as it could be just one headland with more land hidden in the mist beyond I decided to keep heading clear of it for a while yet.

We were doing all we could now. *Suhaili* was smashing into the waves and the lee side was under water most of the time, but we were slowly beginning to draw clear. My spirits suddenly rose. For the first time I began to think that we might get through. I had never thought that we would not make it, but my thoughts had been neutral; they now began to become positive.

I suddenly realized how cold and wet I was, and tired. My back and arms were beginning to ache from the effort to haul in the warp and my hands were that rich red colour which meant they were going to make their presence felt for a few days. I carefully checked the horizon for any more shapes and then, seeing nothing, went below for a cup of coffee. How I blessed my foresight in filling the Thermos with hot water earlier. Boiling a kettle would have been quite impossible now. I lit a cigarette and sat down on the polythene containers, the hot cup cradled in my hands and slowly beginning to thaw them out. I suppose it was reaction now that the immediate danger was passed, but I began to feel extraordinarily content. *Suhaili* was behaving splendidly; we must, I thought, be halfway through the Strait so if we missed Bluff we should pass through the islands during daylight and I could head up coast to Dunedin and meet Bruce there. Best of all, the glass had begun to rise so it was unlikely that things would get much worse, even though they might not improve for some time yet.

All this was encouraging, and in quite a refreshed state of mind I climbed back on deck to keep a lookout. The first thing I noticed was that the sea was down although the wind was still blowing a full gale. The waves were nowhere near as large as before and this pointed to a reduced fetch on them. The only possible barrier to windward was Stewart Island itself, so it looked as if we were almost on the southern side of the strait. I decided to go on for a bit and see if, when we sighted land, there was anything distinguishable showing. Even if there wasn't, though, it would give me a point of departure for making the northern shore.

At 0900 an island came into view; soon another appeared and

I tacked round, and once steady went below to work out where this put us. As far as I could tell we appeared to be due south of Bluff so maybe that was the land we had nearly run on to. Well, I'd head north and see what we could find.

A few minutes later I received an unexpected navigational aide. Coming out of the mist ahead of me I made out a small ferry. It was being thrown all over the place and I honestly felt that I was having the easier time of things; it is often the case that a sea which is big for a large ship is too big to be noticed by a small one, which bobs over it like a cork.

I knew that the ferry must be coming from the Bluff, so my present course should land me there; however, I wanted to let Bruce know where I was so I headed towards her. At about the same time they saw me and I saw them alter course to close.

In all encounters with other ships during the voyage, my main concern was to be identified. After all, there are plenty of yachts about, so why should anyone think that I was anything but a local yacht on a cruise. But on this occasion I did not have to worry; I saw a crowd collecting on the bridge, and knowing from my own experience that a stray yacht would not cause that sort of gathering, I knew that we must have been recognized. This was confirmed when the ferry, the *Wairua*, turned round and closed to within hailing distance. To check my whereabouts I asked where Bluff was and back came the reply to steer north for nine miles. I thanked them and as they turned back onto their course, told them they looked a nice sight. This, I gathered subsequently, they did not catch, and they thought I said 'See you later', from which everyone assumed I was going to pull in. Still, it was a harmless mistake, and I owe the captain of the *Wairua* thanks for reporting me.

I watched the *Wairua* disappear into the mist and spray astern and then seeing that we were on a good course, I went below for some breakfast.

At about 1030 the Bluff came in sight right ahead and soon afterwards I picked up the lighthouse on Dog Island, which stands across the channel to the harbour. By this time, though, we were out of the limited protection from the wind and sea given by Stewart Island and *Suhaili* began to drift rapidly to leeward before the full force of the storm. I hauled her up as close to the wind as was possible but it made no difference, we were pushed remorselessly clear of the harbour entrance. When Dog Island was abeam we were two miles downwind, but I pressed on in the hope that once we put the Bluff to windward conditions would ease and I might even tack up to Bluff Harbour.

The water was now noticeably lighter in colour and the seas had become much shorter and steeper whilst the swell had almost disappeared. We put Bluff to windward but there was no noticeable change in conditions and soon the water began to take a light brownish tinge, indicating shoals, and I realized we would have to turn for deeper water. Even had the engine been working we would not have made Bluff Harbour in those conditions, and the tidal stream, I learned subsequently, was by then full against us.

I turned *Suhaili* round stern to seas again, streamed my tangle of warps to keep the boat from broaching, and then went to hand the mainsail. The moment I threw off the halyard winch brake I knew something was wrong. Usually the sail sags slightly but on this occasion it remained as taut as before. I took told of the luff and tried to haul the sail down, but after giving for a few inches it jammed completely. I looked up the mast but the halyard was free of all obstructions; then I noticed that it appeared offset at the masthead. I carefully worked my way back to the cockpit to get a clearer view of the masthead sheave, the pulley wheel over which the halyard runs, and sure enough, somehow it had jumped off the sheave and jammed down the side. I could neither hoist nor lower the mainsail.

What a time to choose to do this, I thought bitterly, and then reflected that I had given it cause over the last few hours. Still, this did not help. The sail would have to come in as the boat was threatening to broach despite the warps; the problem was how. The shackle joining the halyard to the mast was eighteen feet above the deck, and I was not going to try climbing the mast to reach it. I would have been thrown off like water off a wet dog. I eventually decided to slacken the reefed sail by unrolling three turns off the boom and then I topped the boom up and frapped the sail to mast and boom. It was not perfect, but it helped. I reefed the mizzen right down again and our motion became comfortable once more. I see from my log book that the wind did not ease from Force 10 until after 1.00 p.m., about the same time that I caught a glimpse of the northernmost island in the chain across the strait. We were well clear at this time and as far as I could judge just about in the middle of the fairway.

I stayed up all afternoon looking out for land and although I thought I saw a cliff face, I am not sure, as by this time I was seeing faint, blurred cliffs everywhere. At dusk I saw a light gleaming away to the north and I recognized it as Nugget Lighthouse, well clear of all dangers. I put the helm over slightly so that we would sail parallel to the coast which was now turning towards the north-east and went below and turned in.

When I awoke the next morning it was light and the wind was down to Force 5. There was no land in sight so I handed the warps and then set the mainsail, what I could of it, and laid off a course that would, I hoped, take us to Otago. During the morning I took a succession of sights and these with the noon latitude told me where I was. By 1320 land was coming into view, and as we drew closer I recognized Otago Peninsula from the description in the Pilot. The wind began to ease in the afternoon, and as I could set no more mainsail our speed fell off rapidly and it was not until 1840 that we sailed slowly round Tairoa Heads.

Before closing the headland I had hoisted *Suhaili*'s identification letters and got out the foghorn. I did not know what I would find round the corner as the largest scale chart I had was of the whole of New Zealand's South Island. I had not expected to want anything better. I decided that I would sail into the harbour, make contact with someone and try and get a message to Bruce. I was not sure whether anchoring would be considered as stopping, but I felt not. It's a perfectly ordinary evolution, and I could have anchored at any of the deserted islands we had passed *en route* and no one would have thought anything of it. The one thing I would have to watch, though, was people trying to get on board or offering assistance. I did not want to emulate poor Jim Peters in the 1954 Empire Games Marathon in Vancouver.

As I came round the headland, sailing about forty yards off

the rocky coast, I made out a signal station by Tairoa Heads lighthouse. I sounded an assortment of blasts on the foghorn but saw nothing to indicate that I was seen or that the station was even manned so I sailed on.

The scene that met my eyes was not quite what I had expected. Apart from a breakwater stretching out from the north shore of the channel the entrance to Otago Harbour was most unharbourlike; instead of the wharves and cranes I had expected to see, there were green hills and sand dunes. I could see no point in hanging around at the entrance as I might wait for some time before anyone came along, so I started to try to sail up the channel. This was not easy as the wind was blowing down the channel and as I got more into the centre, I realized that the tide was ebbing as well. I tacked round and as I came back to Tairoa Heads, realized that I had made about ten yards progress. The current was definitely weaker on the south side though, and I found that the wind came round slightly close in by the cliff face so I headed nearer to the cliff to make what progress I could, and when the wind began to fall away put the helm over to come about. *Suhaili* was not moving very fast and she slowly began to come round, but the wind appeared to have veered and although this should have helped us, it meant, in fact, that we drifted farther into the sheltered bay instead of the sails coming aback and pushing us out into the channel again. The rocks were getting closer. I looked quickly astern to see whether I could gybe her round but the rocks were too close. Lashing the tiller hard over, I ran forward to back the jib manually, but even as I did it I realized that it was too late. We were no longer moving. I need not worry about the rocks as we were aground. I was furious with myself. Thinking so hard about how to gain ground I had never thought that this little bay, bordered by steep rocks, might be quite shallow.

Still, all was not lost. The bottom appeared to be sand so we were not likely to come to any harm. But if we were on the end of the ebb, when the tide rose again we could be slowly pushed onto the rocks so I would have to get an anchor out as quickly as possible. I took down all sails bar the mainsail, which was still jammed, and dived below for the anchor and a polypropylene warp. No time to pump up the dinghy. I lashed the warp to the anchor, stripped off and jumped in. For the first ten yards I walked along the bottom into deeper water carrying the anchor, a 30lb. C.Q.R. ideal for sand like this. Then, when the water rose above my mouth I began bouncing up for air every few paces. Eventually this became too difficult and I towed the anchor the last bit, then when the warp came tight dived down and dug the fluke into the sand.

I turned to swim back and had my first look at *Suhaili* from a distance for five months. To my eye she looked terribly dirty and rust streaks down the side from the Admiral did not help. I looked at the stern; about an inch and a half of anti-fouling was showing so the tide was still ebbing – blast! I swam back and hauled myself on board. It felt cold out of the water but first things first and I hauled the anchor warp as tight as I could and made it fast. Now when the tide rose again we had something to stop us running farther up the beach.

I had just completed this when a voice hailed me from up the cliffs and told me that help was on the way. I shouted back that I did not want help, not yet anyway, and I'd try to get off without assistance. I asked when was low water and got the answer three hours and that the tide would fall a further two feet. That's all I needed to know and I told him I would be afloat again by midnight. My new friend, who incidentally had the broadest Scots accent I've ever heard outside Scotland, now departed to try to contact Bruce for me and I went below to put some clothes on and take another look at the level in the brandy bottle.

It was utterly still. No creaking or movement at all for the first time in 159 days. *Suhaili* was beginning to list, but I knew we were O.K. now that the anchor was out, and I sat back with the bottle in my hand enjoying a cigarette and really appreciating the quietness. Then, for some reason, I remember thinking that if the Board of Trade got to hear of this I'd lose my ticket; I was laughing happily at the thought when I heard an engine outside.

I climbed on deck in time to see a runabout, *Sea Witch*, come speeding round the end of my bay, closely followed by a cray-fishing-boat, the *Anna Dee*. I yelled a warning to watch out for my anchor warp but whether they slowed down in time I don't know. Certainly sometime during the evening a boat's propeller caught it and cut it up badly, which could have been disastrous had I not noticed and attended to it in time.

The runabout swept into the bay and stopped a few feet away. 'I'm Fred Duncan. This is Mr Davis of the Harbour Board, and Mr Wilson – he's a boatbuilder.' Hullo. Did I want assistance? No, I thought I could get off when the tide rose. Did they know where Bruce Maxwell was? Well, he'd been rushing up and down the coast all day looking for me the last they had heard, but someone was trying to contact him. This was wonderful; I had not expected anyone to realize that I was non-stop from England, but they knew that and had already started trying to find Bruce. Nice, friendly efficiency, I thought. How long would I remain here? Until Bruce arrived, I thought, although once I come off I might sail up harbour and anchor.

You can't do that, mate, they've changed the rules; you're not allowed to enter any port. You'd best stay here. At this point the fishermen joined in saying I'd be better shifting to another bay as this was open to the north and the wind was expected to shift to that quarter during the night.

I lit a cigarette and sat on the cabin whilst they decided where I best go. I had forgotten how pleasant company was, and I could have sat listening to them a week. Both boats had radio telephones and after a while the news came through that Bruce had been found and was on his way up.

I'm not used to this sort of service and must admit I found it rather enjoyable; however it was getting dark and it was time I ordered the crew aloft to free that main halyard. I'd never get an opportunity like this again. Whilst I hauled myself aloft and removed the sheave, John Brown of the *Otago Daily Times* and Spencer Jolly, an N.Z.B.C. television reporter, brought me up to date with world news from *Sea Witch* forty feet below. I was not too out of date as I had heard Australian news broadcasts, but I wanted to know how Britain had done in the Olympic Games. Someone thought we'd won sixteen Gold Medals and I suggested this was more likely the Commonwealth. Someone asked What Commonwealth? and I answered rather sharply '*Our* Commonwealth'; he said 'Good on you, mate.'

Sea Witch departed after an hour or so and I was left with Lawrence Waters and John Malcolm and Lawrence's cray-fishing boat, *Anna Dee*. I suppose everyone has memories of phases in their lives, often only a short instant, when they have known complete contentment. I felt this now. The halyard was free and there was nothing I could do for another three hours, when the tide would float us off. In the meantime the *Anna Dee* was anchored about ten feet away and we sat and talked quietly, the only sounds disturbing the peace being the ripple of the wavelets against the hulls of the two boats and the occasional *Squark!* from a rookery in the cliffs. It was so wonderfully peaceful that it was difficult to remember that the day before, *Suhaili* and I had been fighting for our lives; all that now appeared unreal to me.

At about 11 p.m. *Suhaili* began to move. The first sign was the keel bumping on the bottom as the waves rose high enough to lift her. This bumping continued for half an hour or so whilst I watched the anchor warp to make sure the anchor was holding. Slowly it came taut and then each series of bumps brought the bows round in line with the warp until at last I was able to pull her off on the winch. I shortened the cable to pull the boat into deeper water and remove any risk of swinging into the rocks. There was nothing more to be done now. The wind had died and the tide was still flooding strongly in the channel so I decided to wait until the tide turned before trying to move.

I checked the bilges but they were as they had been when I last pumped them that morning; I did not think we had bumped hard enough at any time to do any damage.

A few minutes later Lawrence Waters and John Malcolm went off to 'see if we can find your mate for you' and I knocked up a quick meal. I had just finished when there was a shout outside and going on deck I was greeted with 'What the hell are you doing here?' from Bruce. He had flown until it got dark and then taken a car to travel up from Bluff where he'd been when he received the news that I was at Otago.

I was pretty keen to have news from home and in particular I had looked forward to getting some mail, but I was in for a disappointment. Bruce confirmed that the rules of the 'race' had been altered since I had left Falmouth, and that now no material assistance of any sort was allowed. This had been taken to include mail and so to be safe he had brought none for me. I felt very disappointed at this and pretty bloody angry too, at what I considered then, and still do now, a rather childish and unnecessary restriction.

No seaman would have given the absence of mail a moment's thought. Even today mail to ships abroad is unreliable, and if a seaman gets none, he shrugs his shoulders and says 'There'll be a ton of it waiting at the next port.' Still, I suppose to a person who had never gone without this benefit of civilization, it would appear as vital to my morale. He would be wrong. The only effect then, and now, when I think about it, was to make me angry, angry that if there had to be 'rules' they couldn't have been formulated clearly in the first place, angry at the silliness of some of them.

Still, Bruce told me that my family was all well, which was as good as a letter, and he also brought me up to date with news of my competitors. Moitessier was an estimated 4,000 miles behind, which meant that I had a fighting chance. Loick Fougeron had sailed in his cutter *Captain Browne* and was still behind Moitessier. Commander King had been forced out, having broken his mast and his spare. I was not particularly surprised at this as I had not expected an unstayed mast to last long in the Southern Ocean. But he was safe which was good to know and was expected at Cape Town any time. His withdrawal must have been a blow to the British chances as *Galway Blazer*'s lovely hull could have been expected to make good time and I expected King to leave Moitessier far behind. If only he had had a conventional rig. A junk rig may be the easiest to handle, but junks have huge masts and even then are constantly breaking them. The whip on a mast in a small, pitching boat is terrific, and this has to be restrained by shrouds.

There were three more entries that I had not heard of. Nigel Tetley in a 40-foot trimaran, *Victress*, which according to Bruce was like a palace inside, and an Italian, Alex Carozzo, like myself a member of the Ocean Cruising Club, who had been showing an interest in the Transatlantic race when last I had heard of him, and was sailing his 66-foot ketch, *Gancia Americano*. The third entry was another Victress-class tri,

Teignmouth Electron, sailed by Donald Crowhurst. Bruce wasn't too sure where any of them was, but said that if I kept going at the same rate as I had made to date, a neck and neck finish between Moitessier and myself was being predicted. That was just the sort of news I needed to spur me on.

We chatted for an hour or so before Bruce left in a pilot vessel to phone London and whilst we sat there the wind began to come up from the north-west. I didn't like that at all as the bay was wide open in that direction and Force 4 had been forecast, which could be uncomfortable and dangerous. Left with the *Anna Dee* I began to get worried. The tide still had two hours to go before slack water but the wind was going to be up by then. After weighing the chances, I decided that I couldn't wait for Bruce to come back. It would be best to get clear of the bay now whilst the wind was not too fierce, and risk the tidal stream. The worst it could do was carry me up to Otago, whilst the wind could put me ashore.

I hoisted the mainsail and mizzen, and leaving the sheets slack, went forward and set the jib. *Suhaili* swung onto the port tack and I went aft and tightened the sheets. We picked up speed and headed for the rocks. I threw the tiller over and tacked and rushed forward and hauled in on the anchor as we sailed over it. I did not have time to get the anchor inboard before it was time to tack again. Round we went and this time cleared the rocks. I set the staysail and hauled the anchor inboard.

The *Anna Dee* had stood by all this time, just in case I did not make it, and now seeing I was clear Lawrence came up alongside. I decided that I was not going to stop again, now that I had got going, and I threw across my finished diary, some letters and charts to be given to Bruce.

For some time we kept company and then after wishing me 'Bon voyage' Lawrence and John turned and headed back to port. I was sorry to see them go. In the short time since we had met I felt that I had got to know them well, and I hope that some day my path will lead me back to Otago. I'd like to try crayfishing with them, anyway.

Otago to The Horn

November 21st, 1968 (Day 160)–January 8th, 1969 (Day 209)

For the next nine days I failed to keep my diary. To start with I was tired and when not sailing the boat, I slept to get over the exertions and excitement of passing New Zealand. As I became fresher, I started to sort out the incredible tangle of warp and sea anchor. This job took me three days in all and twice during this time I had to put out the warp again because of gales, which did not make things any easier. Normally with a rope tangle, you look for the key and then it is usually a simple matter to sort things out. But no key was obvious, and to lay the whole thing out was impossible as there just was not room on deck for it. The warp was 720 feet long and the sea anchor warp was 80 feet long with a tripping line of another 100 feet, all of which had enthusiastically joined in the fun.

My experience with sea anchors is limited to this one occasion, but I would never use a tripping line again. It's meant to pull the cone, which acts as a brake, round so that it no longer has a grip on the water and can be pulled in 'streamlined', but in fact, even if you keep it well clear of the sea anchor hawser, the sea anchor twists and the tripping line snarls up with it. I think the answer is to sail up to the sea anchor when you want to get it in, or just heave the boat up to it if you are feeling muscular. All lifeboats on ships are equipped with sea anchors complete with tripping lines; these may have been all right when seamen had sailing and small boat experience, but one does not get it much these days, and I think a long warp is the answer. It's much easier to handle and it 'gives' more, which puts less strain on the boat. Of course you will drift farther but if you are coming down onto a lee shore you should try to sail off it anyway.

We were about 47° South when we took our departure from New Zealand. I had now to decide what course to take for the Horn. Ideally, of course, one would steer straight for it, but there was a complication here in the form of icebergs. The mean northern limit is roughly 45° South, and I did not dare go south of this. In the days of sail, even with a full complement of lookouts, icebergs were still a big risk, but I could not possibly keep watch the whole time and I felt the risk was not worth taking, even if it meant a faster passage. There would be no chance of survival if *Suhaili* hit ice. Even if I took to the life-raft I would perish before we drifted to land, and that was assuming we would find land. Between the Cape of Good Hope and Australia there had been a busy shipping lane a couple of hundred miles away. Since the great sailing ships disappeared very few ships return to Europe via the Horn; they all use the Panama Canal, and the nearest shipping lanes to my intended route were thousands of miles away.

I decided, therefore, to head north of the mean ice limit and try to keep to the 44th parallel, altering towards the Horn at about 100° West longitude, where the ice limit took a southerly dip.

Man proposes, God disposes, for no sooner had I decided on this course than the wind which is predominantly westerly in the Southern Ocean, swung round to the east. During the next twenty-one days I had westerly winds on only one day. This was by far the most frustrating part of the whole voyage:

December 9th, 1968   *Day 179*
Well, well, well. We are north of the 40th parallel and at present steering for Alaska! Same winds, same uncomfortable sea, no change likely by the look of things, except that I doubt if I'll remain sane much longer. Of all the lousy things to happen; easterlies in an area which is renowned for westerlies is one of the most difficult to take because it seems so unlikely. Apart from one day the winds have been easterly for the last fifteen days. We have in that time

managed to creep, crawl, edge and steal, 26° to the east which is a miracle: with westerly winds this would have been almost doubled; in other words a whole week has been wasted and I think that is enough to deprive me of any chance of winning. It's no use my hoping that the others get the same winds, as apart from the fact that I wouldn't wish this feeling of complete frustration on my worst enemy, they will be able to do better in these conditions anyway. A few extra feet in length would make all the difference as we are rocking hopelessly. It's 1745 and the wind is starting to come up as it usually does at this time. I am sitting on the repaired jib on the polythene containers wedging myself between the table and the bunk. Two waves have just broken over us and a torrent of water just missed me as it came in round the hatch, which is closed. We're rolling and pitching abominably and by the noises in the bilges it's time I pumped them again. I managed a meal at lunchtime of bully and baked beans. I did not enjoy it and do not feel like bothering with a meal this evening.

I wish I had an unread novel left that I could escape into, or something that would allow me to relax and forget this feeling of hopelessness which is eating at my insides. I suppose this is reasonable, easterly winds do occur here but 15:1 days of them seems rather unusual and to my present way of thinking diabolically unfair. If the Frogs are meant to win – O.K., but there is no need to torture me as well as allowing me to lose, and the Chinese could hardly have thought up a slower, more destructive method of torturing a person than this. Still, let's look on the 'bright' side, at this rate we'll soon be pushed north into the variables and then, if nothing else, we can move nowhere in calmer conditions!

December 10th, 1968   *Day 180*
No change still. I cannot make it out at all. Three months ago in this latitude I was almost becalmed; now, when the weather should be even better we're bashing into fresh to strong S.E. winds. But the really puzzling thing is the sea. After these days of steady S.E. winds they should be from the same direction, but they're not. As far as I can tell we have waves from the east, south-east, and south, and swell from east and south-east. This rather points to a recent change in wind direction and in that case we may be in the middle or near the front of an easterly air stream that is moving east at

about the same speed as ourselves. One thing that would tend to confirm this is the rather lower swell today, although the wind has not eased. I have been able to set a bit more sail because of this. Still, we are still being pushed N.E. At noon today we were at 38° 49' south, a degree north from yesterday and no change in sight. I am worried as to what happens when this air pattern is past as I am afraid we'll find ourselves without wind in the Variables. I thought of trying the other tack and heading south but then the wind veered slightly to S.S.E. so W.S.W. would be the best course I could make and I'm not doing that. This does, of course, mean that we are steering slightly nearer to east, so I shall continue to threaten to tack. Perhaps if I decided to turn round and head back to New Zealand I'd get westerlies! Oh dear. I wish I were home; at least there'd be dozens of 'experts' to tell me what I should be doing! In the meantime, I'll just have to muddle along as best I can.

1830. It's up again, everything: wind, sea and swell, blowing Force 7 and gusting higher. I took in sail this afternoon and am at present under jib, three reefed main and two reefed mizzen sailing beam onto the swell. There was a lot of nimbus cloud around but when the wind increased the sky cleared. Our motion is not at all comfortable, as apart from pitching into the seas which come from ahead as well as everywhere else, when a large swell wave catches us we are driven bodily sideways. If it gets any worse the warps will have to go out and we'll run. I daren't try to hold her on this course with less sail, as our speed is just keeping us out of trouble at present. The course is good at 060° all considered; the boat is trying at least.

Just now when I was up watching the sea for a bit, a very large wandering albatross, wing span a good 8 feet, swept right in close to the bow and down the windward side. If I had leaned out I could have touched him. This is the closest I have seen one of these giants and they are most impressive. Of course, I did not have the camera with me. I also noticed some green weed growing on deck alongside the cockpit. This part of the deck is constantly wet so I suppose the weed found ideal conditions. Weed is also growing in the littoral zone above the anti-fouling, along with brown algaeic scum. All this is new and I suppose we picked it up whilst aground off Otago. We'll have a scrub round when the weather moderates.

There's a red sky tonight, which, according to the old adage, is a sailor's delight. Well, we will test this and report how true it is tomorrow.

Started the fourth log book of the voyage today. Each lasts sixty days and I'm glad I brought six of them along as we are not going to complete this voyage in under three hundred days. It is now thirty-four days since we passed Melbourne and we are not yet halfway between Melbourne and the Horn. We managed a degree and a half east up to noon today but even if we keep that up whilst these south-easters last, we are almost certain to find ourselves becalmed when they do fade, because of our northerly latitude.

I am afraid that January 9th which I gave as an E.T.A. off the Horn to Bruce has become impossible. Even with solid westerlies all the way it would now be unlikely. We are 80° in longitude from the Horn now and I don't see us averaging 2° 40' a day. Then, I said, it would take approximately ninety days to get home from the Horn, but without the engine this will be greater. When I get home I shall feel like a man who has run 100 yards in 20 secs. in the Olympic Games! Poor old Britain, she has a poor enough champion in this race as it is, but even our best could not do much better in these conditions. Drake and Nelson must be weeping.

I have decided to leave sail set for tonight. I think she'll take it alright.

Finally, on December 12th, when I was in latitude 37° South, over four hundred miles north of where I wanted to be, I decided that if I was going to get myself back into westerlies I would have to head south, and if necessary, west of south, but that I would keep going regardless of the ice limits until I found the westerlies I wanted. In fact, after three days of heading slightly west of south I ran into them again, but I had lost about ten days, and I seriously wondered if this had not deprived me of any chance of winning the race.

When I left New Zealand Bernard Moitessier had been 4,000 miles behind me and we had had even chances as far as being home first was concerned. I allowed Moitessier 130 miles a day and myself 100 and I had to do better than this to win. The best place to gain was in the Southern Ocean, and I had hoped that even without self-steering I would manage 120 miles a day. The waste of ten days, or 1,000 miles, infuriated me,

The Admiral's port vane after the knockdown off the Cape of Good Hope. The vane was pushed inwards far enough to be split on the mizzen cap shroud while the 1½″ stainless steel arms holding the counterbalance have been buckled and twisted completely out of line

After the failure of the first gooseneck, the boom was lashed to the mast for three stormy days until I could effect a repair

Noon, taking the sun's altitude in the Doldrums and
fully dressed for the photograph

Overleaf: Under jib, staysail, reefed main and mizzen, *Suhaili*
could make 5 or 6 knots on a good point of sailing

Shark! The dark outline is *Suhaili*'s rudder

Repairing the spinnaker after it blew out in the Roaring Forties. It was while doing this and trying not to be camera-conscious that I managed to sew my moustache to the sail. Looking forward in *Suhaili*'s cabin, this shot shows the general confusion that weeks of big seas, ever-wet clothing and a bachelor's existence can bring about in a small boat

Overleaf: In the brilliant seas off Melbourne I was caught – literally – with my ▶ pants off while repairing the mainsail

The gooseneck, showing the handle for the roller reefing gear which I made from a rigging screw after the original handle went swimming

Our water-catching system, a rather disreputable bucket under the mizzen. In a good squall I could rely on catching a gallon of rainwater a minute

but on calming down when the winds became favourable again, I realized that I should have headed south earlier and I only had myself to blame.

Not all the time had been completely wasted, and there was one terrific bonus during this period. I got the transmitter working again. For the first week after leaving Otago I had not had time to look at the radio, although I had listened in to Arawua Radio for the weather forecasts and received two messages. But on the first fine day I got out the instruction manual and began to take the transmitter to pieces. I found the fault fairly early on, one of the wires from the handset connection within the set had corroded and earthed. My problem was how to reconnect it effectively as I had no solder. In the end I broke three of my navigation light bulbs and melted down the scraps of solder from the terminals. It was still an awkward job, as I kept losing pieces and I had to go crawling around the deck looking for even pinhead sized drops, but it was eventually completed and I was able to reassemble the set. I switched on and after a bit of juggling managed to get a meter reading. As far as I could tell the set worked, but I needed to get a response from a station to be sure. I waited until after dark and then called Awarua and Wellington. There was no response, but whilst I was listening for a reply I heard Chatham Island talking to fishermen rather faintly on 2 megacycles. I waited until he finished and gave him a call. There was an immediate response and I heard the operator ask for the name again. I transmitted the name and switched off to listen; once more the response was immediate. For some time this went on, but I was about nine hundred miles east of the Islands, which is extreme range on this frequency, and he was unable to hear me distinctly. Chatham Island only has frequencies in the 2 Mc/s band so we were unable to shift to a higher frequency. Eventually I heard him say he was sorry, but my transmissions were not powerful enough for him to make me out and we closed down. It was a pity, but he must have been on his toes to have heard me in the first place and although I would have liked to get a message through at least I knew that the radio was working.

As soon as the weather conditions allowed, I gave the

batteries a good charge and tried calling Wellington again but without response, although I was able to hear them and a variety of stations in the Pacific for some time afterwards.

As we sailed farther into the Pacific I lost the New Zealand commercial stations and had to look elsewhere for time signals for the chronometer. I had kept a careful note of the chronometer error throughout the voyage and knew that on average it lost $8\frac{1}{2}$ seconds a day, but it sometimes jumped a bit, and I liked to check it daily if possible.

Navigation away from land using a sextant depends upon an accurate knowledge of the time. Before Harrison's Chronometer in 1714, mariners had to judge their easting or westing entirely by their experience. It was possible to calculate latitude but not longitude, as latitude may be found from measuring maximum altitude of the sun during the day at noon, but the calculation of longitude depends upon knowing the exact time to the second, when one measures the sun's altitude. Before Harrison and his followers made accurate timekeeping possible, seamen sailed north or south until they reached the latitude of their destination, and then they would turn and sail along the parallel of latitude until they sighted land. This called for sharp lookouts. Harrison, a self-taught Yorkshire carpenter, constructed a chronometer (it can be seen in the Greenwich Maritime Museum) which varied by only 3 seconds a day in varying temperatures and on board a sailing ship of the time at a period when the finest clocks ashore were nowhere near as reliable. The instrument won an award of £20,000 for the inventor from the British Government which at the money values of the time gives an idea of the importance attached to the problem. My chronometer had a rate far outside Harrison's – but it had not been cleaned for some years.

For over four weeks I was without an accurate time check, which caused me considerable worry. The only other method of working out the exact time requires altitudes of the moon, and the annual tables necessary for this are no longer published. In *Spray*, Joshua Slocum was able to calculate his position with accuracy although he had only an old alarm clock with which to keep time because he had the use of the moon tables; I had to trust that the rate of my chronometer was steady and make rough checks by means of timing noon, sunrise and sunset. I reflected that at this stage I was worse off than Captain Cook, as at least he had had a larger boat which would have kept his chronometer more steady. In fact, though, when I did next obtain a B.B.C. time signal as I approached South America, I was only three seconds out, which gave a negligible error as far as my position was concerned.

It may seem strange that I could not receive the powerful American stations at Honolulu, San Francisco and Panama, yet eventually managed to receive one of the B.B.C's overseas commercial broadcasts, but something always seemed to happen just as the time signal came up. At one time I could even pick up American commercial stations, and their D.Js gave me a close approximation of the time, which was better than nothing.

About the time that I turned south to find westerly winds again, I began to have rather disturbing dreams. Most of these revolved about the theme that my voyage was only an eliminating heat, and that there was to be another race after we all arrived back in Britain. On December 16th the theme changed a bit, and the whole voyage was being made by about ten yachtsmen and run in stages. The stage that I went through was from Australia to New Zealand, and as I pulled in for the evening I was whisked off the boat and taken away for a hot bath which was to be followed by a huge meal. For some reason I decided to steal a march on my competitors and I went into the galley to cancel my meal. The cook immediately took a huge steak with fried eggs, mushrooms, peas and chips and threw it overside. This outrage woke me up.

Most of the dreams I had concerned the voyage, but occasionally I would wake up and discover I had brought in some person whose existence I had completely forgotten for years. I used to speculate for hours on this whilst I was sitting in the cockpit. Apart from the people concerned, and my memories of them which gave me something new to think about, I wondered at the capacity of the subconscious mind to store vast quantities of information which we are unable to unlock. So often when one awakes and can vividly recall a dream it appears to be nonsensical, but the experience of recalling forgotten people made me wonder whether these other dreams should not be taken more seriously. We live in a materialist world and I admit that I never used to pay attention to dreams at all, but on my own in *Suhaili*, where life was more basic and not affected by the pressures that face us in our cramped societies, I began to wonder whether we are not missing out on something. Should we so readily dismiss as superstition the faith that men at the dawn of history had in dreams and their interpretation? Their lives were more simple and uncluttered than ours, their days were not spent rushing to an office or factory and concentrating on a job with little time for social intercourse. In a village or town the men met and talked in groups, as they do to this day in the rural parts of Africa and Asia, and from my own experience in India the conversations are often of just this sort of thing, discussed with insight and intelligence that come as a surprise to one who has been brought up in an urban society and is inclined to think that such people are ignorant and without intelligence. None of my more abstract dreams seemed to make sense, but for the rest of the voyage I continued to recall forgotten characters and wonder. Perhaps one day we will be able to open the mind and use more fully our subconsciously-stored information just as we use, say, the multiplication tables.

Even though *Suhaili* was now well south and we had picked up westerly winds, our speed did not really rise to the daily run I had expected. Reducing sail at night to achieve a balance so that I could sleep contributed to the disappointing progress but also the strain on equipment was beginning to show and I had to spend two or three hours each day at least on maintenance. The sails suffered most. Although *Suhaili* seemed to balance quite well with no one at the helm, if a big wave caused her to slew round it took some time for her to recover her course even if she did not gybe and I had to wake up and bring her back. To make sure that I did awaken I was still sleeping without a bunkboard so that when *Suhaili* gybed I was thrown out onto the deck. This was a very effective alarm and although I sustained a few bruises as a result, it was far better than damaging the boat. On one occasion when this happened, I picked myself up to find *Suhaili* heeled right over so that the portholes were underwater, and I looked out at a beautiful nothingness. Unfortunately there was no time for photographs as the booms were straining on their now ragged guys, and if these gave the masts could be pulled out of the boat with the force of the sails crashing across to the other side. As it was, this quite regular occurrence strained the tackles badly and was not good for the already tired sails. More and more frequently I had to take in sails to sew up seams that were splitting, and every time we lost speed.

Sails made of cotton or canvas where the stitching beds into the material generally have less trouble with splitting seams than terylene sails where the stitching stands proud and is very vulnerable to chafe; but terylene sails are stronger and not affected by rot, and I doubt if another fabric could have withstood the strains imposed by this voyage.

I was still a little scared of running into ice, but by this time I felt that I had lost so much ground by being forced north that Moitessier must be close behind and the frustration of being held up led to a desperate reaction. I decided to drop farther south than the 45th parallel and chance the ice in order to keep my lead. The Admiralty Pilot and the chart differed as to where ice might be met. Up until now I had intended playing safe and taking the less risky course north of the limit given in the sailing directions, but now I decided to put my faith in the chart, which put the ice limit farther south. I looked around for some evidence, however slight, to support this decision and give me peace of mind, and discovered that the chart had been published more recently than the Pilot. That was good enough for me and I was able to forget the Pilot's advice completely. As a general rule this is most unwise but I wanted to be the first home and I thought that the risk involved was justified.

My spirits rose as we began to move in the right direction at last. Two days after reaching westerly winds I was feeling energetic and happy:

December 18th, 1968   *Day 188*
I have spent the day so far pottering about. I started by greasing some rigging, then I spliced a length of rope into the port jib

sheet where it's badly chafed. The new length, about half a fathom, is green, whereas the rest is white. It cannot be helped, it's all I have.

I took a scrubbing brush to the weed on the white paint overside but that had no effect so I used the cooking spatula. It's difficult stuff to get off. What interested me is that the weed on the port side is brown, and on the starboard side green. We've had more sun to port which probably explains this. I noticed also that when I managed to remove a piece of weed, it fell into the water and travelled along with us for a couple of fathoms even though about 6 inches from the hull. I experimented, but this only happened near the stern which explains why all the weed has, with a few exceptions, fastened itself there. The only other place where weed is forming is above the waterline round the bow. It has not got a hold yet and I managed to scrub most of it off along with a thin film of algae.

The gooseneck barnacles have not yet reorganized themselves after my last assault, but I thought I detected a large company of them on the self-steering rudder foot plate. I'll attack when the weather gets warmer.

I had a tidy up in the locker at the foot of my bunk and discovered that two of my lighter refills have perished. I have half of one left. This is awkward as all the matches are wet and most crumble when you try to light them. I may finish up having to rig an 'eternal flame'.

The wind backed and freshened quite easily soon after 1700. I had already handed the 'Big Fellow' as I could see the line of cloud marking the front getting close. I wish all fronts passed so quietly! I took in the spinnaker and set the jib and then gybed. The wind is now (1900) fresh to strong and we are bowling along under plain sail with two reefs in the main and one in the mizzen. She has balanced herself on a reach which is marvellous. I was all set to steer but it's not necessary now. This is race-winning form, if it's not too late. We're doing a comfortable 6 knots I should say, but this may go down when the seas have built up. One line of nimbus has passed and I can just see blue sky in a gap in the alto-cumulus. Most waves have white horses on them but the sea is still down, the slight swell still from the N.E. It's really quite impressive as the 'watery' light reflects from the waves against a background of dark grey cloud, and two wandering albatross are wheeling around within a couple of hundred yards of us in their eternal search for food. There were a couple of petrels about during the afternoon but they've disappeared now – just as I wrote that, I glanced out and saw them again!

I feel very happy this evening for some reason. The excellent day's run probably contributed to this feeling. The stillness of the Southern Ocean has been shattered by my bursts of song which included many hymns as I feel grateful. I shall sit up for a while which means a sing-song over a whisky bottle as I cannot see well enough to read by the hurricane lamp. My reason for sitting up is to keep an eye on things. With the barometer steady there will probably be an increase in wind force soon. The alternative is to reduce sail and turn in, but we're moving nicely and I want to get home.

There's another pair of petrels out there now.

Well, to learn another verse of Gray's *Elegy*. I've memorized three verses the last three nights – it's good for the mind.

The sun has just set. It found a gap close to the horizon and then came through washing everything a reddish-gold. The sails changed colour completely. Really beautiful.

Poetry had become more and more important as my supply of unread books dwindled. I found it difficult to read whilst steering as one's eyes stay away from the compass too long and the course becomes erratic, but it was easy to sit and learn poetry. Apart from the enjoyment this gave me, I also thought that the mental discipline involved in sitting, learning and remembering the verses would be good for me. As far as I could tell when I had last met people off New Zealand, I was sane and unchanged, but I did not feel that I could really judge myself in this. If any changes were taking place I could not be sure that I would notice them, as I had nothing to compare myself with. I did use the tape recorder periodically to check my powers of speech, but I was far more concerned in preserving my mind. In order to do this I learned a great deal of poetry, not only the *Elegy*, with some of the finest verses written in the English language, but also Burns, Scott, Shakespeare and Cunningham amongst many others. To give my voice practice, I would usually recite out loud, my *Golden Treasures of English Verse* in hand, to a wondering audience of albatross and petrels. If they were puzzled by the recitations, they were alarmed by my sing-songs. I have no voice and am inclined to shift key suddenly without being aware of the fact. The result is that in order to keep any friends at all I confine my singing to my boat when well clear of land. I was able to give some of the finest performances of my life in the Southern Ocean.

The weather remained unpredictable. It was almost mid-summer in the southern hemisphere, but we were still getting severe squalls. There was usually an advance warning of these given by the clouds. I would watch the clouds to windward for the low dark ones that often meant a squall. As the cloud came closer I would decide whether it warranted a reduction of sail and if so, drop the mainsail and roll it onto the boom. Even under a storm jib and scrap of mizzen, *Suhaili* would scream along down the waves before a good squall. Often these squalls would be accompanied by hail which I could see sweeping across the water towards us. On one occasion we sailed ten yards ahead of a wall of hail for close on a minute. It was a weird experience. *Suhaili* was sailing quietly and yet the air was full of the explosive noise of the hailstones hitting the sea all round. The last time I turned to see how much longer we would be spared, hailstones hit me straight in the face and for a couple of minutes I was blinded by the pain of the impact.

For several mornings I had awoken with itching eyes; I thought that this might be something to do with the battery acid which had splashed into them earlier, but I could not understand why both eyes should be affected. Eventually I discovered the reason. One of my cans of disinfectant had been holed by the constant movement in its locker, and the contents had seeped out into the bilges. The cabin very slowly took on the smell of a well-kept public lavatory, but it happened so gradually that it was some time before I noticed it. I decided that the fumes must be responsible for the irritation and having thrown the tin with the remaining disinfectant overside, I spent some time pouring buckets of water and detergent into the bilges and then pumping them out in order to get rid of the concentrated disinfectant slopping about there. I then opened up both the hatches on the boat to allow a draught of wind through to air the cabin. This was asking for trouble in the conditions prevailing at that time, so in order to try to stop too much water getting below I stood by the forward hatch to close it if a wave threatened to come over the bow. Whilst I was standing there I suddenly saw, to my horror, a large wave building up astern. I flung the forward hatch shut and slipped in its locking pins intending to rush aft next and close the main hatch, but I wasn't quick enough and I had to leap up into the rigging as a wave swept over the stern and along the decks.

This was one of the three occasions when we were pooped and it could not have happened at a more unfavourable moment. With the main hatch wide open to the sea, the water poured down into the main cabin. As soon as the wave had passed I jumped down onto the deck and rushed aft to close the hatch to prevent any more water getting below. I then climbed into the cabin and rigged up the bilge pump. The bilges were full; there was more water in them at this moment than at any other time on the voyage so far, and the noise of the water gurgling and washing about as the boat rolled and pitched brought back frightening memories of the last voyage, when for thirty hours in the Arabian Sea, three of us had baled frantically for our lives with buckets when a seam in the hull had opened up. Things were not so serious this time. With the hatch closed, no more water could enter the boat, but it was twenty minutes before I had the bilges dry again. My bedding, the galley, chart table and radio were soaked by the wave. The galley was easily mopped up, but the chart table and sodden chart took some time to dry out, and I had to sleep wet for three days as I could not put things out to dry and my efforts to dry the sleeping-bag over the heater failed. The radio seemed to have come out of this soaking rather better than on the previous occasion. I wiped it dry, lashed the heater to the radio shelf, and left it running for eight hours to dry out any water that might have got into it. An inspection showed that all was well, and when I switched on, the set reassuringly lit up and worked.

Although most of my clothing had been damp for months,

until this day I had managed to keep my sleeping-bag reasonably dry by protecting it from the leaks round the cabin with a canvas 'counterpane'. When I felt confident that there would be no squalls during the night I used to remove my wet weather clothing and climb into the sleeping-bag wearing my other clothes and allow the heat from my body to dry them out whilst I slept. Clothes that I could not dry out in this way remained damp and mouldered, and I did not look forward to the end of each week when I forced myself to have a change-round, because it meant putting on cold damp clothes whereas those I was wearing were at least warm.

Washing my clothes was no problem. I would fill a bucket with sea water and detergent, soak the clothes, give them a good scrub and then drag them astern on a rope to rinse. If I was lucky it would rain, and I would be able to hang things from the rigging and soak the salt water out of them. If there was no rain I would wring them out as much as possible and then hang them on a line I had strung between the bookshelves in the cabin and dry them out as much as I could with the heater. Salty clothes absorb water vapour, so that if I had been unable to fresh-rinse the clothes before I changed into them, they soon became damp again. What with starting out damp and then inevitably getting soaked during the day when water found its way through my, by now, porous wet weather gear, the clothes absorbed more and more salt as each soaking evaporated, until at the week's end they were encrusted with the stuff and about as comfortable as a suit of armour. When they were in this state a drag overside would improve things as salt was a great deal less concentrated in the sea water.

I thought longingly of the warm Tropics as I stripped off that night and forced myself to climb into the damp sleeping-bag without my warm clothing to protect my skin. But the sleeping-bag had to be dried out and the only effective drier was my body. To give me courage and help me drop off to sleep quickly I took a large mugful of brandy before turning in, but all the same my flesh recoiled from contact with the cold, damp material and for the first fifteen minutes until it warmed up it was all I could do to prevent myself from climbing out and getting dressed.

What amazed me, with my skin taking this constant rough treatment from wet and stiff clothing, was that I did not break out with salt-water sores, small boil-like eruptions on one's skin that itch intolerably. On the previous voyage they had given me a lot of trouble, particularly on my legs. For some reason they never got going this voyage and I have never been able to understand why not. Conditions were far worse and the only difference in the diet was that I had no fresh food at all this time, although I took yeast tablets regularly in compensation.

Two days after being pooped we ran into fog. *Suhaili* was 47° South, about two thousand miles from the Horn, close to the ice limit, and I immediately suspected that we might have run into an area of ice. I checked the sea and air temperatures and found the sea water to be much colder than I had expected. Either we were approaching ice or we had come upon an unexpected upwelling. An upwelling of sea water seemed unlikely as there was no increase in the bird and sea life and the water was still clear blue in colour.

It is surprising how much information is given by signs like this. Clear blue water indicates that there is no plankton in the sea. Plankton feeds upon nutritious plants in the water, and if the water is cleaned-out of these nutrients, will die off and sink slowly to the sea bed. The only source of replenishment is round river mouths, near the land in shallow water, and in deep water by means of an upwelling of rich, chemical-laden water from the bottom. Hence out at sea, thousands of miles from land, the absence of birds points to the absence of fish which in turn points to the absence of smaller fish and plankton. This can be confirmed by looking at the water; bluish water is generally empty of life while green water indicates the presence of minute life forms. A good example of this is the North Atlantic, in the belt covered by the North-East Trade winds. Here the constant winds pushing the surface water slowly before them cause the water to 'heap' towards the coasts of Venezuela and Brazil. This water drops down and spreads out over the ocean floor. Off the African coast, the movement of water away from the surface causes an upwelling which provides rich food for fish, a fact which is being exploited by the new West African fishing industry. Roughly between them there is an oceanic desert, inhabited solely by Sargasso weed, and how this grows in an otherwise lifeless area is still something of a mystery to oceanographers. The water around *Suhaili* now was blue which made me suspect that there was no up-welling, and that the colder sea must be caused by some other reason, to which icebergs seemed a logical answer.

There was no thought of real sleep whilst the fog lasted. The grim thought of *Suhaili* smashing into an iceberg frightened me into staying awake and I began to regret my earlier reckless-ness in heading so far to the south. I kept my lookout going for two days, cat-napping in the cockpit by day when the fog lifted slightly, but staying awake all night staring anxiously into the gloom ahead and imagining all sorts of obstacles looming up. Then after one short spell of sleep I awoke to find the sun breaking through at last; the fog slowly disappeared and I was able to climb wearily below and climb thankfully into my sleeping-bag.

When I awoke, the cabin was flooded with the half-light one associates with dawn and dusk. I looked at the alarm clock and noted that it was 6.15 and decided that as all seemed well I would have an early night and carry on sleeping. Half an hour later I opened my eyes and was puzzled to find that the cabin seemed lighter. In my rather tired and sleep-numbed state it was a minute or two before it occurred to me that day might be breaking. I scrambled out of my bunk and poked my head out through the hatchway to see the sun just beginning to show through the low cloud to the east. Suddenly alarmed that I might have slept very much longer than I thought, I looked at the chronometer which has a dial to show when it was last wound. The needle pointed to 20 hours so I had only slept through about eighteen hours, not a day and eighteen hours as I had feared. The reason for my alarm was that I knew I had eventually turned in on December 23rd and I had been hoping that the Chilean radio stations might spring to life at midnight to welcome Christmas Day. Still, all was well. I had awoken on Christmas Eve and I could now charge the batteries to pre-pare for a radio transmission that evening.

Christmas is very much a family festival at home or on board ship, and indeed my last eleven Christmasses had been spent on B.I. ships. The thought of being by myself at Christmas rather ruffled me. For almost the first time since I left Falmouth I felt that I was missing something, and that perhaps it was rather stupid to spend one whole year of one's life stuck out on one's own away from all the comforts and attractions that home offers. By now, Dad and my brothers would have brought in logs from the old trees in the garden, and the family would be clustered round a roaring fire in the drawing-room, and thinking of getting ready to go to midnight service at the village church in Downe. I recalled winter evenings at home when we played Bridge. The memory of Mother as my partner humming 'Hearts and Flowers' and Diana asking Father if she could go 'Crash' or 'Slosh' had me roaring with laughter. The warmth and fellowship of those scenes seemed to be in such contrast to my present circumstances that I brought out a bottle of whisky, feeling that if I couldn't have the fire I could at least give myself an inner glow.

Two glasses later I clambered out on deck and perched myself on the cabin top to hold a Carol Service. I sang happily away for over an hour, roaring out all my favourite carols, and where I had forgotten the words, singing those I did know over again. By the time I had exhausted my repertoire and had had a few encores I was feeling quite merry. Christmas, I reflected as I turned in, had got off to a good start after all.

The first words in my diary for December 25th are 'Awoke feeling very thick-headed'. Despite this, at 9 a.m. I drank to those at home where the time was 6 p.m. and then began preparing a currant duff. I made an effort over Christmas lunch. I fried a tin of stewed steak and had potatoes and peas, cooked separately for a change, and to go with them I opened the bottle of wine that brother Mike had given me and which I had been saving for this occasion. I rather over-estimated on the quantity though, and this filled me up, so the duff had to wait until the evening before I could tackle it, by which time it had gone soggy.

At 3 p.m. my time I drank a Loyal Toast, wishing that I had been up early enough to hear the Queen's Speech at 6 a.m. my time. Somehow, gathering together to listen to this speech adds to the charm of Christmas. One becomes aware of people all over the world held by the same interest listening as well, and it makes the world seem a lot smaller. I wished that it was!

In the evening I tried without success to call up New Zealand and Chilean radio stations; then I listened in to some American commercial stations that were coming through rather well. There must have been unusual radio conditions as I was able to pick up local stations from Illinois, Texas and California, and it was on the last that I heard a recording from the 1968 manned American moon shot. I had not heard before of *Apollo 8* and her crew, the first men actually to go round the moon, and it gave me food for thought. There they were, three men risking their lives to advance our knowledge, to expand the frontiers that have so far held us to this planet. The contrasts between their magnificent effort and my own trip were appalling. I was doing absolutely nothing to advance scientific knowledge; I would not know how to. Nothing could be learned of human endurance from my experiences that could not be learned more quickly and accurately from tests under controlled conditions. True, once Chichester and Rose had shown that this trip was possible, I could not accept that anyone but a Briton should be the first to do it, and I wanted to be that Briton. But nevertheless to my mind there was still an element of selfishness in it. My Mother, when asked for her opinion of the voyage before I sailed, had replied that she considered it 'totally irresponsible' and on this Christmas Day I began to think she was right. I was sailing round the world simply because I bloody well wanted to – and, I realized, I was thoroughly enjoying myself.

The days between Christmas and the New Year put even this happy rationalization to the test. Once again the weather started to play up and we ran into easterly winds. I was now some 1,700 miles west of the Horn, and the nearness of my competitors was beginning seriously to worry me. As the days of adverse conditions followed each other my frustration increased:

December 28th, 1968　　　　　　　　　　　　　　　　*Day 198*

Awoken at 0410 by the staysail boom banging and found that we were heading south. I climbed on deck in a bemused, sleepy state and was rudely greeted by the sun. That, I thought, has no business being up at this hour, and I'll put it back an hour tonight. The wind had not changed, just *Suhaili* had decided to run! I clambered back into my bunk having sorted things out a bit and next awoke at 0830. My first conscious thought this time was that I was resting against the wrong side of the bunk and then glancing at my cabin compass I discovered that we were heading west. Somehow she had managed to gybe and was now lying hove-to. What interests me about this is the fact that even in a semi-torpor I realized something was wrong from the angle of my body in the bunk and yet we have only been on this tack a few days. Also I was more than half-asleep and unable to think things out for a couple of minutes after this.

I kept climbing up with the 'Big Fellow' intending to set it, but the dark low strato-cumulus building up to windward put me off each time. In fact nothing materialized apart from light squalls before dinner time, when I usually take it in anyway. I console myself for this loss of distance with the thought that it would have pushed us south if I had set it and we are now 47° South which is quite far enough. We are, in fact, still steering south of east; with the present N.N.E. to north-easterly winds nothing else is possible, but I don't want to make matters worse.

The strato-cumulus clouds when they did reach us brought light rain which has reduced visibility but, *so far*, nothing else. The glass is dropping though and this spell of fine weather cannot be expected to last indefinitely.

I tried three times to obtain a time signal today; Las Salinas, San Francisco and Callao, but could not hear anything on any of the advertised frequencies. I don't think I am much out, actually, as last night, when I was listening to the news from El Paso, Texas, the announcer announced that it was 'exactly midnight' within ten seconds of my chronometer with applied error showing the hour. If I knew at what point in this statement the hour struck I would have been in clover. Oh for the B.B.C.!

Breakfast was a tin of baked beans. Lunch – fried cheese on, and dinner a bacon and beans risotto. I have indigestion!

December 29th, 1968   *Day 199*
Awoke late due partly to advanced clocks and partly to the fact that I did not get to sleep until late last night. Some time this

morning the wind has veered to the east. I just give up! Someone is going to have to rewrite the books, or there has been a general and consistent misprint! The best course we could make on a port tack was 160° True so I came round and we are now making 020° True. We were moving a bit better on the port tack as we are heading into the old waves at present, but I think we'd better go north for a degree or so. Poor old *Suhaili*, she just cannot do well in these conditions, she's not built for it. I gave the barometer a bang this morning accidentally, whilst I was polishing its frame, and it jumped 3 millibars. It won't go back down so maybe the pressure has risen. But, in fact, this is not really much of a guide as the wind swings round according to rules known only to itself. I wish it would swing north or south as I can then leave her to steer herself and get the maximum speed.

Later: It's 1245 and I've just tried the other tack upon which we steered a brilliant 180° True so we are back steering 020° True doing a bumpy one knot at a guess with this choppy sea. I got a very rough sun altitude. I could not get an image on account of the cloud so I took the brightest part, and this puts us 48½° South. So, here we sit, imitating a rocking horse moving fractionally northwards; I cannot beat these sorts of conditions. If I believed in an evil spirit, I could well understand that he had decided to make me lose the race, and one would have to give him credit for an efficient job. I just do not understand it at all. Whilst occasional easterlies are encountered down here, days of them must be unusual, and yet the wind has had an easterly component for the last five days. I wonder if my sextant is all right, and yet, come to think of it, it cannot be out much, as the sights I took a few days ago a.m. and p.m., although they did show an error which I attribute to the fact that I don't know my chronometer error exactly, did not differ by more than 15 miles. Still, the wind boxed the compass before, maybe it will do it again.

There is an excellent prayer by John Davis, the Elizabethan seaman who, with his crew reduced to fifteen men from seventy-three was beaten back three times into Magellan's Strait: 'May it please his Divine Majesty that we may rather proceed than otherwise; or, if it be his will, that our mortal being shall now take an end, I rather desire that it may be in proceeding than in returning'. . . . And I think I have troubles! But do appreciate the 'proceeding than in returning' part. What a man, and I cannot help thinking that my complaint about the wind seems absurd when you consider what he had to put up with – without complaining!

I have just taken the time of the sun's p.m. altitude equalling the altitude of my a.m. sight. In both cases the altitude was 54° 37.6′. The a.m. time was 1023; p.m. 1431, a difference of 4 hrs. 8 mins. Dividing this by 2 we get noon at 1227. As I had expected it to be this time exactly for our longitude of 111° 15′ W approximately, unless there are big errors (I am discounting the boat's movement which is small for this time, and the sun's change in declination), there does not appear to be much wrong here.

1700. The wind has veered slightly, and until a short while ago we were making 050° True. I have had to ease her though as we were pounding heavily at times (writing is difficult, my hands are numb with cold), riding over one wave and the bow on falling being buried in the next. The sea has got up quite quickly and is now very choppy. I have noticed that quite often a noticeable increase in wave size has accompanied a squall, but as soon as the squall is past, or within minutes anyway, the waves have fallen again. I am now sitting below fully dressed in foul weather gear, waiting to see what three lines of black, low, strato-cumulus are going to bring.

December 30th, 1968   *Day 200*
Well I had hoped to be at the Horn by now, but at this rate we'll get there in February. I feel very depressed at the moment and thoroughly frustrated. The net result of our day's work is 1° east and nearly 2° to the north. The wind is still slightly south of east. I tacked at noon today and we are now heading south and west. We were making 040° True on the other course but I'm not going any farther north. It is just as well I am on my own at present. I'm not the sort of person that takes adverse conditions calmly and my mood at present is murderous. Tacking north and south and making no progress at all, whilst somewhere to the west and probably not far away now, I'll bet the Frenchman is having beautiful westerlies. Every time I look at the compass I get a feeling of complete helplessness. What the hell is wrong with the bloody weather anyway? From the Cape of Good Hope to Aussie I had two days of easterlies. Since New Zealand I've had over twenty days of them and I've been farther south which should mean even less easterlies. The fact that the

sea was so choppy last night that I could not make the best of these conditions has not helped either. I tried to push her and we were taking wave after wave right over the boat until the thought of the weak floors occurred to me and so unnerved me, or either the thought of what happened in the Arabian Sea so unnerved me that I had to reduce sail. She then refused to hold the course and kept yawing down wind. By soon after midnight I had at last sorted that out and I collapsed asleep and the net result of all that is 1° east which was probably contributed by the current anyway. If the wind would just shift 4 points one way or the other I could make quite good progress but like this I can do absolutely nothing and that makes me furious. Why the hell don't they mark this stretch of ocean as having variable winds instead of westerlies? We're just making south now, hammering into the sea. I've got all sail but for one reef in the main, so as to claw to windward as much as possible, but it looks as if the wind is rising so I'll probably have to pay off a bit shortly.

I am trying to keep at an average of 48° South at present. This will give me 120 miles clearance from the ice-line which a single-handed voyager must keep clear of. Hence tomorrow at noon I'll tack north again and I'll just keep on doing this until the weather gets tired of being easterly or I go insane.

I changed my mind about tacking at 1830 as the wind had veered and we actually made 055° True when I came round. The wind veered round eventually to S.S.E. and we were sailing fast to the east at last. However, the wind increased, building up a south-easterly sea and slowing the collapse of the old easterly sea so I had to reduce sail to ease our passage. We were pounding continually and every wave was coming over the bow.

December 31st, 1968   *Day 201*

I remained up, anxiously watching our progress from the hatchway, until 0200 when I decided to try and get some sleep. I had just divested myself of my foul weather gear and climbed into my sleeping-bag when the boat was thrown into the air and came down with such force that I was knocked breathless, even though lying on a mattress. I hastily reclothed myself and handed the mainsail. The wind was gusting to about Force 9 I should say, every few minutes, but otherwise blowing about Force 6. The sea water and rain were bitterly cold.

Whilst I was up I set the storm jib and reefed the mizzen right down but I left the jib up as we were moving along very nicely. A short while later the wind rose still further and I decided to get the jib in whilst it was still possible. Our motion eased immediately but by this time I was feeling a bit tired and decided to go to sleep and as the glass was still falling and the sea rising, I streamed the warp and handed the mizzen. This left us running on a course of N.N.W. but could not be helped. I have to sleep and it would be insane to leave the boat hard pressed in these conditions without anyone to tend her.

I turned in shortly after 0500 as all seemed safe, after a hot whisky and water to put some warmth into my bones. Whilst I was handing the mainsail my watch strap broke. Fortunately I was able to grab the watch before it slipped overside and I've put it in the cutlery drawer. When I awoke I stared stupidly at my bare wrist for some time before I could remember what had happened to the watch. Eventually I remembered and reached behind my 'pillow' – three sweaters rolled up – for my faithful and now battered and rusty alarm clock. It was 1230 so I had managed about $7\frac{1}{2}$ hours sleep. We were still heading N.N.W. comfortably but the easterly sea had disappeared and we only had a nasty S.S.E. sea and swell to contend with. Best of all the glass had risen and is still doing so. I decided we could take the sea on the beam if under reduced sail and accordingly set a bit of mizzen to push her round. We rolled too easily like this so I handed about 20 fathoms of warp – my Charles Atlas course! – and set the staysail. We are at present heading 050° True heeling about 15° to port on average but rolling with the beam sea. The occasional wave is breaking over the boat but otherwise she is quite comfortable. One always receives warning of the waves that are going to come over us because they break before arriving and you can hear them breaking. It's still raining and I can just detect the patter of the rain on the deck and cabin through the howling of the wind in the rigging. I'm 'cowering' below in my bunk because it's warm and there is nothing I can do at present except wait for the wind to ease. The rain has changed to hail. I can see the crystals on the skylight. One must be philosophical about all this, I suppose, and at least the wind is round; once it eases we'll belt off to the east again.

1900. The wind is easing and the glass still rising. I have just returned from handing 50 fathoms of warp. I would have set the fully reefed mainsail but the sea is still very high and I think it safer to wait for it to go down a bit first. The odd wave is still breaking over us and there are sharp squalls every ten minutes or so. So I am back in my bunk, about to continue reading Bertrand Russell's *History of Western Philosophy*.

The New Year brought a change at last. In fact, I did not really notice the passing of 1968, I was too busy trying to force the boat eastwards. The one thing about adverse conditions is that a reaction to them sets in and I always found myself pressing the boat much more as soon as the weather allowed:

January 1st, 1969   *Day 202*
I managed to set some main last night but had to take it right down to the identification letters early this morning. The wind was quite bearable but the sea so choppy we were hardly making any progress at all. Once again I was unable to get to sleep until well after midnight and so overslept. I have managed to hoist all plain sail today as the wind has veered round to the S.S.W. and eased, but we are not going very fast on account of a S.S.E. sea and swell that has yet to die. I wish the wind would stop boxing the compass; it has now completed two revolutions in the last fortnight, which means there is always a cross sea of sorts, and a short one at that. Poor old *Suhaili* is too short to make much in these circumstances. I would like to set the 'Big Fellow'; the wind is suitable but the sea must go down first.

1550. 'Big Fellow' up despite dark clouds to windward – I wanna go home! I had left the storm jib, which uses the same halyard tack and sheet as the 'Big Fellow', set because it was not coming to any harm and it saves work to hand it and set the larger sail at the same time. As I have been busy sewing up some seams on the mizzen, I have not, in fact, had much spare time today. The procedure for changing the sails was as follows: Let fly the tack. This allowed the storm jib to come inboard and I unshackled it. Next, slack away the halyard until the sail is on deck and unshackle it, and lastly unshackle the sheet. I then shackle up the peak tack and clew of the 'Big Fellow' and hoist it up halfway on the halyard. This is to keep it clear of the water once I haul it forward on its tack. With the tack made fast I haul the sail up taut and then trot aft to adjust the sheet. Lastly I take in the jib, first letting go the halyard, then its stay on the Highfield lever. I lash it down with two ties and leave its sheet, this way I can set it again in about $1\frac{1}{2}$ minutes. I have to leave a sail set right forward as *Suhaili* will luff up without it, hence I always set a sail before taking another one in. When I have to hand the 'Big Fellow' again, I set the jib first as, in addition to keeping the bow off wind, it provides a lee which makes hauling in the 'Big Fellow' much easier. Some time ago I spliced a length of rope onto the Big Fellow's tack and this serves as an inhaul when handling the sail. It has made the job very much easier.

With Cabos de Hornos, Cape Horn, about 1,500 miles away I began to think increasingly of the possible problems that could be encountered in what is by repute one of the roughest parts of the world. I had already read Richard Dana's account of rounding it from west to east in *Alert* in the southern winter in his classic *Two Years Before the Mast*, and also everything that appeared in the Pilots. We were going to round the Horn the easy way, running before the prevailing winds, and should not have to face the difficulties that in the sixteenth century forced John Davis to turn back, or more recently, gave Joshua Slocum and in 1965 David Lewis such harrowing experiences. They were heading from east to west, and in order to avoid the prevailing westerly winds to the south of the Horn, had chosen to take the far more hazardous route through Magellan's Strait where the very fierce gusts of wind known as 'williwaws' can come at you from any direction. On average one will get more favourable winds for an east-west passage in the Magellan's Strait, but the sudden shifts in direction make it very hard and difficult.

Nowadays there is not the wealth of experience available to the sailing man that existed sixty years ago when a good part of the Merchant Marine was made up of sailing vessels. The Press and broadcasting companies have built up a mystique about the Horn to the extent that most people believe that the wind there blows at near hurricane strength the whole time. But the Horn is like any other part of the Southern Ocean in that it is affected by a constant stream of eastward-moving depressions, and this means that the weather varies like the rest of it in these latitudes, between calms and gales. It is true that when it really blows the effect is on the whole worse at the Horn because of the constriction of the sea between South America and Antarctica. The high mountain ranges down the west coast of South America effectively block the eastward-moving airstream and force it to funnel through the gap known as Drake's Passage, between Cape Horn and Graham Land five hundred miles to the south. Even so, the weather is not unmanageable for a well-found boat, and it appeared to me that provided one went sufficiently south to avoid the williwaws, I should not meet anything that really threatened *Suhaili*. If the wind ever reached hurricane strength we might be in trouble, but this force is rare even at the Horn and is unheard of anywhere else on the traditional round-the-world sailing routes.

Danger to any ship comes not from wind as much as from the seas that the wind builds up. It would take a fantastic wind force to dismast a well-found yacht on a flat sea, but when there are large waves to roll a boat heavily, an extra strain is imposed upon the masts and rigging. The other danger is that a boat might yaw and broach before a breaking wave, which could roll her onto her beam-ends and almost certainly snap the masts; but this would take a really huge sea if the boat had a sufficient length of warp out to hold the stern into the wind. The greatest danger seemed to me to be that a really low depression, like that we had experienced in the Foveaux Strait, might arrive and we would be faced with the wind blowing from one direction and the waves coming from another, the 'wind against tide' conditions that all seamen hate, but on a massive scale. Still, *Suhaili* had ridden out these conditions before, and at least we should have no lee shore to contend with this time.

Dana's account of rounding the Horn in winter tells of nothing that would cause *Suhaili* trouble, except ice, and even this was unlikely in January. Nevertheless it does not do to take chances with the sea and I began to check the boat over with an eye to emergencies.

The most obvious threat to the boat's safety was the Admiral. I had kept the main tubular structure after the self-steering packed up as the guard rails along each side of the boat, which were there to stop me falling overside, were fastened to it.

However, two of the four legs had sheared and if another went – which might happen at any time – the whole structure would tear loose and could easily rip up the deck and remove the mizzen mast. As soon as the boat's movement allowed, I took a hacksaw to the feet and then threw the whole structure overside. For the record, it is at 48°23′S 97°35′E. I re-rigged the lifelines through the rigging screws to give me some sort of security. The overall effect of this was that I reduced my world by a few feet each side of the boat. Suddenly *Suhaili* was smaller, but she seemed more comfortable in herself, rather like an old lady who has taken off a too tight corset. Her evident relief communicated itself to me. *Suhaili* was both safer and lighter while I had something less to worry about, something less to go wrong. It was as if we had cleared the decks before an action.

January 8th, 1969   *Day 209*
It looks as if we'll be off the Horn on the 17th.

Cape Horn

January 9th, 1969 (Day 210)–January 17th, 1969 (Day 218)

January 9th, 1969   *Day 210*

Just heard on the Voice of America that the Chilean Navy has been asked to look out for a 'damaged ketch' battling towards Cape Horn. The lone yachtsman, 'Me', has a lead of 3,000 miles on his nearest competitor. That's splendid news even if the lead must be down to 2,000 miles by now – still it's not lost yet and we have a fighting chance.

I don't know what the damage referred to is.

I put out a call on 2182 Kc/s but although I could hear people I was obviously unheard. Perhaps we'll have better luck tomorrow.

Gave the batteries four hours of charge today having fixed the fuel pipe in the morning.

It's become quite chilly this evening and I have the heater on. As usual there is quite a thick mist and it seems very damp. Condensation is dripping off all the rigging.

January 10th, 1969   *Day 211*

Awoken at 0430 by the boat's violent motion. We had luffed up. I discovered the cause the moment I poked my head out of the hatch, the mainsail was in two pieces, and had split right down a seam. I handed it and turned in again as I had only just dropped off. The result of this, of course, was that I overslept and awoke too late for a morning sight at 1015. This means no longitude today as the mist always falls about noon. Whilst making breakfast the boat lurched and my hand was covered with 'Red Hot' porridge. I have two blisters the size of half-crowns on my wrist as a result; they'll last until I want my foul weather gear jacket, when they'll be ripped off. I unbent the mainsail from the boom as the sewing it requires will take a lot of time. Apart from the seam, the material has frayed at the leach and I shall have to recut it. In the meantime I have set the old mainsail which appears to be in rather better condition than I thought. I may leave it up as it's better material, lighter and slightly larger. . . .

This evening as I was having coffee in the hatchway, I saw a flock of small birds about a cable's length away. Their motion was rather jerky and they may only have been petrels but I have not seen petrels in as tight a flock as that before nor at that height. I doubt if we are close enough to land for them to be land-based, though.

Still, as I am not too sure of my longitude I have decided to play it safe and have altered course to the S.S.E. for the night.

No answer on the radio but I picked up the B.B.C. News on 6 Mc/s which was rather pleasant.

January 11th, 1969   *Day 212*
Steered from 0800 till 2000, tiring but exhilarating as the wind has risen steadily and we have been surfing along. I've just reduced sail for the night and put her to head about 120° True, a safe course to miss the land. I missed noon on account of mist and cloud but I managed two sights and these put us 240 miles west of the entrance to Magellan's Strait at 2000 tonight. The glass has dropped rather heavily and everything points to a blow so I'll sleep clothed in foul weather gear tonight. I am going to press as much as I can for the next week to get round and clear. I look forward to writing this log a week today!

I managed to damage my blisters today but they seem to have repaired themselves. Now is not the time for open wounds on one's wrists.

Tried on 2182 again but although I can hear people clearly there was no response. Too much static for the B.B.C. on 6 Mc/s.

January 12th, 1969   *Day 213*
Slept badly. Awoke to find blue in the sky for a change and despite

occasional squalls there was about an average three-eighths blue all day so I managed to get good sights. We were 480 miles from the Horn at noon.

Nasty weather all morning. There was a strong wind increasing in squalls, a high sea and swell and I had to reduce sail in order to control her – my arm ran out of strength after an hour or so. Broke one of my blisters: damned painful.

The lighter ran out of gas today and all the matches are wet, so I have lit my 'eternal flame' – the hurricane lantern. I have six containers of Lifeboat matches but that is only sufficient for about 100 days so I'll keep them in reserve.

January 13th, 1969   *Day 214*
Awoke – no that's not the right word as I only dozed all night – got up at 0500 when the wind suddenly rose from the N.N.W. I took in the main and stayed up watching her as the sea rose very quickly. Handing the main I broke my other blister so I drained it and put a bandage over the wrist.

We ran well all morning but at midday I discovered that the jib-stay was stranding; in fact three strands had parted at the lowest piston hank so I had to hand the sail and set the storm jib and stay-sail. I am not going to climb the mast at present and I'll have to go up to bring the old stay down so that I can get its measurements, so for the meantime I have spliced a short strop which will connect the Highfield lever to the jib tack and the jib will have to support itself from there up. In order to remove the old stay and put it out of the way I had to crawl along the bowsprit and then, hanging on with my eyelashes, use both hands on spanners. It was a far from pleasant job, as apart from the fact that one moment I was under water and the next about 15 ft. above, we were rolling and yawing; in fact, this is the first time I've worn my safety harness for about three and a half months I think. I wanted to get on with sewing up the mainsail today but as I could not keep myself steady using both hands that was out of the question.

The wind has been up to expectations for Cape Horn, Force 8 and gusting above. I keep putting off lying to the warps as we appear to be getting along nicely and the sooner we get past the Horn the better. The glass has begun to rise too but it did that yesterday evening.

I am sitting up at present to obtain a time signal and to put out a call on 2182 Kc/s. The cabin is festooned with wet clothing hanging and dripping everywhere. My choice of trousers now lies with the least wet pair! I cannot afford the heater any longer as the 'Eternal Flame' (which blew out today) is using Kerosene rather heavily. Once into the Trades I'll allow myself a match a day and put it out between breakfast and dinner.

I have 110 cigarettes left. I refuse to ration myself at present so in a week we'll just have to start a cure – or I'll smoke tea leaves! I have six bottles of whisky and four of brandy left which is pretty good, indicating that I have consumed fourteen bottles of spirits so far and one of these I only had one tot from before it spilt. This is an average of one bottle every sixteen days – heavier than my usual consumption but good for the present time.

Tried a call on 8110 and 2182 Kc/s but there was no response. I even prefixed my calls with 'Pan' × 3 ['Pan, Pan, Pan' is an emergency prefix] but it made no difference although I could hear a ship quite close, by the strength of his signal. Listened to the News on B.B.C. after the time signal.

January 14th, 1969   *Day 215*

Another disturbed night; I'm getting rather tired now. I awoke at 0400 intentionally to take a lookout and the sun and my red eyes glared balefully at each other. Poor sun, he was just getting up and it was not much of a good morning. Having gybed I set the staysail and went back to bed. I awoke again at 0800 and made pork and beans for breakfast. I've been playing with the radio all morning trying to find someone to talk to but all the frequencies I hear voices on I do not have crystals for and no one answers on 2182. I'll try again this evening.

Oh dear, the main gooseneck has broken again; this time the brass casting has sheared, I think because the nut holding the jaw in place worked tight and the jaw jammed. The whole weight of the boom then went onto the casting which sheared. It happened when I decided to set the mainsail this evening. This is all very depressing. Earlier on when I gybed, after discovering that we had moved about due east yesterday and were beginning to get a bit cramped to leeward, the jibsheet caught up forward and between clearing it and getting back to the cockpit to harden it, the foot of the sail flogged itself loose. I put some tacks in it, sacrificing a needle to stop myself falling overside in the process.

So, now, there is no jibstay, the jib is damaged, the main goose-neck has gone and the new mainsail which has rope at its reefing points, is split. Not to fuss, I've put the kettle on, and I shall settle down and try and work out a way of fixing up a jury gooseneck. I could set a sail, the old mizzen for instance, using one of the running poles as a boom and I might do this tomorrow. I don't want to lie unable to sail properly just here. Without the main she won't sail close-hauled.

Later: I think I've come up with an idea for the gooseneck (writing by candlelight again). It means I'll need a new boom when I get home but that's a small price to pay. My concern was to find some way of fastening the boom to the gooseneck jaw. Ideally two flat pieces of metal fastened each side of the boom and extending so that they could bolt into the jaw would do the trick, but, as I don't have two such pieces of metal that's out. I have one though, the self-steering rudder tiller, so I am going to remove the broken fitting and cut a slot lengthwise down the centre of the boom and bolt this piece of metal into the boom. The tiller already has holes in it, three to be precise, and before it became too dark I cut metal away from round one of these end holes so that it will fit into the jaw and I drilled one bolt hole. The wind has died this evening and if it is calmer tomorrow I might get the job done in a day. The main problem is finding sharp drill bits. I shall not have roller reefing on the repaired job of course, but fortunately I ordered all my sails to have reefing points sewn into them.

I could almost set the old mizzen tonight. I've brought it out of storage and refastened a couple of slides to the luff. I had removed them as the new mizzen mast has a different sort of track from the main. I think I'll wait till tomorrow though; I have not had a good night's sleep for four nights and I feel a little fatigued.

I thought I heard a seagull this evening.

January 15th, 1969   *Day 216*

Had trouble getting to sleep last night and then I slept very lightly. The alarm woke me at 0500 and I discovered that the wind was veering so I gybed and set the spare mizzen loose footed as a mainsail. I breakfasted on pork and beans and then got to work on the main boom. It cost six drill bits but I had the metal plate bolted onto the boom by midday. I applied fibre glass to the job to help check splitting and I then put two turk's heads round the join. Thank goodness that when I was an apprentice such 'old fashioned' stuff was still taught. A good turk's head is the strongest rope whipping I know of and by the time I came to start the third round I had to use a spike to get the rope through. I want to put two more on when I get the opportunity. I left the boom until 1800 before reshipping it as I wanted to give the fibre glass a chance to harden. Unfortunately the wind and sea got up during the morning so that by the time I had started the ropework we were shipping the sea over the bow. 'I thought of Dana, gritted my teeth, and carried on!'

The day's run of 90 miles was remarkably good and I can only conclude from the course made good, 137°, that we were helped by the current.

Whilst I was engrossed doing my turk's heads, I was suddenly startled by an albatross flapping away from the right under the bow. It must have been asleep and did not wake until the bow wave hit it because it nearly got caught in the bobstay.

The glass is depressed. It's dropped over a millibar an hour since 0500 and I am worried. It's never dropped quite like this before and we are in an area famous for its rough seas. The wind has risen this afternoon and I have reefed the mizzen that I have set as a mainsail. I have also hauled down the tack so that the foot just clears the cabin. I could set the main with its three reefs but apart from the fact that I want to leave the fibre glass as long as possible, with three reefs it's larger than the mizzen as now set. We are just about hove-to now. I don't want to leave too much sail on her in case it blows up during the night and the course we were making would put us in the ice zone by Friday if we don't slow down. I am hoping that the current I think is there will carry us eastwards. We want 200 miles to the Horn as from noon. Of course, the falling barometer and N.E. winds may herald a depression in which case the wind should back which would suit us admirably. I just hope it won't be too fierce if it does back.

I don't mind admitting I feel a bit scared tonight. I would probably be more so if I weren't so tired. Well, the Lord's Will be done, but I'm sleeping clothed.

DATE..17ʰ..January........19.69.   LOG OF YACHT......Suhaili...............

1	2	3	4	5	6a	6b	6c	7a	7b	8	9	10
HOURS	COURSE by COMPASS		Deviation.	Distance by Log	WIND			TIDAL STREAM		Barom'r		
					Direction	Force	Leeway	Direction and Rate Knots	Allowance	Therm'r		
0 (Midnight)	070°	18°E			WNW	5				1000		
1 (a.m.)	080°	18°E			WNW	5				1000		
2	080°	16°E			W y N	5				1000		
3	070°	18°E			W y N	5				1000		
4	070°	18°E			W y N	6				1000		
5	060°	18°E			W y N	6				1000		
6	070°	18°E			W y N	5				1000		
7	060°	18°E			W y N	5				1001		
8	070°	18°E			W y N	5				1001		
9	060°	17°E			W	5				1002		
10	070°	17°E			W	5-6				1003		
11	070°	17°E			W	5				1004		
12 (Noon)	090°	17°E			W	4				1004		
13 (1 p.m.)	090°	17°E			W	4				1004		
14 (2 p.m.)	100°	17°E			W	4				1004		
15 (3 p.m.)	100°	17°E			W	3				1005		
16 (4 p.m.)	080°	17°E			W	3				1005		
17 (5 p.m.)	060°	17°E			W	3				1005		
18 (6 p.m.)	060°	16°E			W	1-2				1005		
19 (7 p.m.)	070°	16°E			W	1-2				1005		
20 (8 a.m.)	090°	16°E			W	1-2				1005		
21 (9 p.m.)												
22 (10 p.m.)	090°	16°E			Var	light airs				1004		
23 (11 p.m.)	160°	16°E			NE	1				1003		
24 (12 p.m.) (Midnight)												

Day's run.......104......Nautical Miles   Engine started....................
Time under way..24...h...........m.   Engine stopped ....
Average speed....4:33...knots   Engine running ......h.......·.m.

FROM. FALMOUTH .TO................ H.W. DOVER   H.W. at...... TIDAL STREAM turns........at..........
              AT   ........A.M.   ........A.M. SPEED......kts. turns........at..........
                             ........P.M.   ........P.M.   turns........at..........
                             B.S.T.   LW. at......   turns........at..........
                                             11

DAILY REMARKS AND NOTES, SKETCHES, ETC.

Jib staysail & Mizzen Mizzem (2 refs)

1500 LAND Ho!!! 2 small mts brg 150(?) Diego Ramirez Isl.

0910 P/L running 145°/325° through Lat 56° 22'S Long 68° 35'w

1005 Land 2 pts on Port bow

1135 Gybed

NOON LATITUDE 56° 12'S LONGITUDE 68° 22'W

4/8 Cloud cu & c.str. Mod wly Sea & Swell

1600 Gybed. Set Main 3 refs set spare jib goosewinged 1649 P/L 177°/357° Lat 56°21'S Long 67°33'w

1855 Handed goose-winged Jib.

1900 Short run squall   1915 Cape Horn Brg Nᵉ YIPPEE !!!

CLOCKS ADVANCE 1 HOUR TO GMT — 4 HOURS.

2315 Handed all sheet let out all Mizzem.

	FUEL and OIL—GALLONS					FRESH	SIGNATURE
	OIL FUEL	PETROL	PARAFFIN	LUB. OIL		WATER	
On Hand							
Received							
Total							
Consumed							
Remaining							

An incident today worthy of note. First, whilst having a cup of coffee this afternoon I decided to check the level of the whisky. I reached out for the bottle and poured in a tot and then realized that I had my ready-use bottle of paraffin in my hand!

January 16th, 1969   *Day 217*

It was a depression. The cold front arrived during the night and I awoke when the storm jib sheet slide came out of its track at 0500. It was blowing Force 10 at the time so I took in sail, streamed the warp and seeing she was comfortable, went back to bed. I took off my foul-weather gear as it's pretty wet and doesn't allow the heat of my body to dry my clothing properly. I slept through the alarm set for 0800 and awoke at 1000. The glass was rising by this time and as the wind and sea have subsided I have set more sail.

My right hand is giving me trouble. The last of the blister came off at 0500 and a width of flesh an inch wide from the fork between thumb and forefinger to the wrist is now raw and weeping copiously. I tried drying it but being a burn I cannot place it too close to the heat. It's painful at present and whenever I expose it outside (where it's hailing at present!) it hurts like blazes.

I shall not turn in tonight as Diego Ramirez Island is to leeward and I want to keep a lookout.

Just heard the B.B.C. News. Apparently a wrangle over the shape of the conference table has held up the start of the full-scale Vietnam peace talks! I ask you, no wonder the young people of today show little respect for their elders.

It's bitterly cold outside. We are under jib, staysail and reefed mizzen and that is quite sufficient in the squalls that are arriving every half hour or so. Unless we get some help from the current we won't pass the Horn till about midnight tomorrow night. The glass has stopped rising and has, in fact, fallen 1 millibar in the last three hours. I am hoping that it's just diurnal variation but without much confidence. The wind appears to be backing a bit too, so we have quite likely another depression on the way.

January 17th, 1969   *Day 218*

It's not quite 0100 and I have just tried to steer through a squall and got soaked for my pains. Up until this one I have nipped up and taken a roll in the mizzen and she has remained steering about due east, but this time I decided to steer whereupon we rolled heavily, a wave came over the windward side soaking me from head to waist and as *Suhaili* rolled the rest of the wave came over the other side completing the job.

When there are no squalls it's clear and quite light outside and if it weren't for the biting wind it would be enjoyable on deck. I have the bandage over my burn but it's throbbing painfully. I've just finished the dried peaches and I've consumed a quarter of a bottle of whisky since yesterday morning. In fact, I prefer coffee or cocoa to whisky which explains my low consumption; I find that they warm me up more.

I picked up Diego Ramirez just after 0500. It was bearing about S.E. and S. at 15 miles which was excellent. Land appeared to the north a couple of hours later.

It's now 1845. We are not quite south of the Horn which is clearly visible about 8 miles away. The wind died this afternoon and I have a lot of sail up at the moment. However, dark cloud is forming to windward and I can see rain falling on the land so I'll probably have to reduce sail shortly.

It was a short rain squall and when it lifted I could plainly see the two tower rocks that mark the S.W. of Isla Cabo de Hornos. We've passed it!!! Spliced the mainbrace and broke out Aunt Aileen's fruit cake. I carefully removed the foil wrapping and the aroma hit me. The flavour and taste are even better than the smell. I've cut a reasonable slice as I'll make it last a bit if I can. It has withstood over seven months in its tin magnificently. To add to my pleasure there is a piece of *The Times* in the tin so I have something new to read as well.'

In my log book I wrote YIPPEE!!!

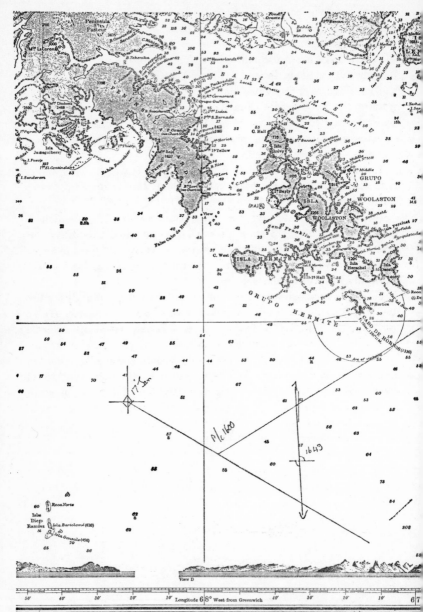

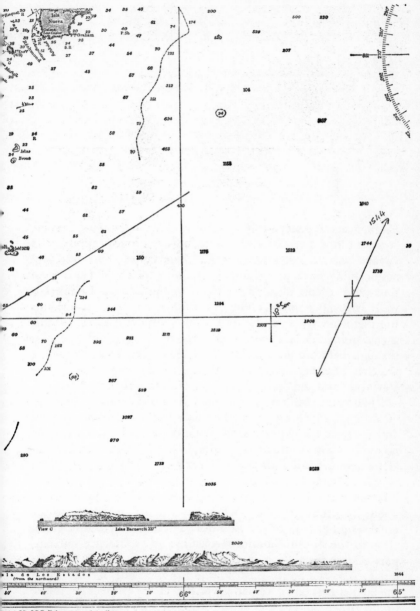

Islas
Nueva
Caica
Los Casas
P.ª Graham

40
F.Sb

Islas
Evouth

View C   Islas Barnevelt 227°

Isla de Los Estados
(from the northward)

50'   40'   30'   20'   10'   66° 66°   50'   40'   30'   20'   10'   65° 65°

...rving C.B., O.B.E., Hydrographer of the Navy.

Dog Watch

CAPE HORN was inevitably something of a climax in the voyage. It would have been very easy to assume that once round it, the voyage was as good as over and one could relax and sail comfortably back to Falmouth. A quick look at a chart soon puts paid to this idea. Cape Horn to the English Channel is well over 9,000 miles along the sailing ship route, and this represents nearly a third of the whole journey. And not all this is easy going. To start with there are about 1,300 miles to pass through before one even clears the Southern Ocean and the weather becomes more predictable as one passes through the Variables and the South-East Trades to the Equator.

I planned to sail up leaving the Falkland Islands to the west, as although this takes one rather close to the ice limit the wind and currents are slightly more favourable. If I had still made no radio report, I intended heading in towards Port Stanley and attracting attention there by means of a rocket, just to let people at home know I was safe. From there I would head out into the South Atlantic until roughly level with Cape Town at about longitude 30° West, when we would alter course to the north and head up to the Equator. There is no point in going close to the South American coastline as an adverse current, part of the circulation in the South Atlantic, would slow us down. Also the South-East Trades are met with farther south the farther east one goes. However, the closer one can get to the South American coast near the Equator, the narrower will be the belt of calms, the Doldrums, so I planned to go within a couple of hundred miles of the Brazilian coast, as close as I dared without running into the south-moving current.

Once clear of the Doldrums one meets the steady and reliable North-East Trade winds and you sail close-hauled heading west of north until the next weather division between the North-East Trades and the westerlies, is met with. This area, the Variables, is known also as the Horse Latitudes because of the number of horses that had to be thrown overboard from sailing transports when a becalmed ship began to run short of water. The last part of the voyage, the 1,200 miles from the Azores to Falmouth in the westerlies, would not be dissimilar to the Southern Ocean except that the seas would not be so large – and I would be nearly home, which would make all the difference.

When I made my original plans I had intended keeping farther east at the Equator and using the engine to motor through the Doldrums. I had calculated that from Cape Horn to Falmouth would take about 90 days in those circumstances. Without the engine I had to replan rather more carefully, as with Moitessier close behind me I did not dare risk wasting a single hour if I wanted to beat him home. A couple of hundred miles farther west could make as much as a week's difference in the time it would take to sail through the Doldrums and although this added to the total distance to be covered, it would probably reduce the time the voyage would take. On the last voyage, *Suhaili* had crossed the Equator in longitude 24° West, and had been becalmed for four days. This time I intended crossing at about longitude 28° West, about 240 miles to the west.

This route gave me the quickest way home and I just had to hope that the weather would perform as expected. It's all very well to talk about an ocean 'race', but in circumstances like those of this voyage, one pushes one's boat as hard as one can, bearing in mind the continual strain being imposed on the boat itself. I had never really taken my sailing as racing in the generally accepted way. To me it had always appeared more of a contest simply to get round and I was inclined to keep to a speed that seemed comfortable to *Suhaili* and myself, one that did not impose unnecessary strains on either of us, and hope that this would get us round safely – and first.

My latest information on the other people trying to get round was scanty, based upon what Bruce had told me off Otago and the radio programme I had picked up before the Horn, in which the estimate was that I was 3,000 miles ahead of Moitessier. I thought that Moitessier must now be overhauling me fast as I had lost a lot of time, but in fact he was not sighted off the Falkland Islands until eighteen days after I had passed them, at which point the distance between us on the chart was approximately 1,500 miles. It is, of course, impossible to say who would have been first home had Moitessier kept on. My position on February 10th, the day *Joshua* was sighted, was in the Variables, and my speed had fallen as a result. Moitessier would have been slowed in the Variables and Doldrums just as I was, but even if one ignores this and allows him his full average speed of 117 miles a day all the way home from the Falklands, he would in theory still have had fifty miles to go to Plymouth on the day that I arrived in Falmouth. This may satisfy a mathematician, but no seaman would be so foolish as to say who 'would have been' first. There are too many imponderables at sea.

Moitessier's sighting caused considerable confusion amongst my friends at home as the first information to come through was that the sail had a '2' or an 'S' on it. *Joshua* has a 2 on her sails and my new mainsail had had an S on it, and it was not until the colour of the hull was reported as being red that everyone knew for sure that it was Moitessier.

At this stage in the voyage, barring accidents, I had no one else to worry about. Ridgway, Blyth, King and Fougeron had withdrawn. Tetley, Crowhurst and Carozzo were too far behind to hope to catch up. In fact, although I did not know it at the time, Carozzo had already withdrawn, and Donald Crowhurst was still in the Atlantic. What had interested me was that Tetley and Crowhurst were both sailing multihulled boats. Although there are plenty of catamarans and trimarans about these days, no one as far as I knew had ever sailed one in the Southern Ocean for any length of time before. A multihull is subject to far greater hull and rigging strains than a monohull like *Joshua* or *Suhaili*. When the wind hits a boat, a monohull will heel over and reduce the force; a multihull will not heel to the same extent and there can come a point when the strain becomes too great and either the rigging breaks or the windward hull is lifted so far out of the water that the wind can get underneath and turn the boat right over. The danger of this is slight when the helm is permanently manned as the helmsman can run off before the wind in time to save the situation, but when singlehanded, a sudden increase in the wind could capsize the boat before a sleeping man could reach the sheets. Personally, I would not like to take a multihull in the present state of their development singlehanded through the Southern Ocean, although Nigel Tetley and *Victress* have proved that with good seamanship it is possible.

With 9,000 miles to go *Suhaili* was in reasonable shape and there was no reason why we should not make Falmouth. Superficially she looked a mess. The hull was covered in weed above the waterline, and gooseneck barnacles had begun to grow on the anti-fouling again. Paint was peeling off the hull and cabin and there were large rust streaks which had run down the paintwork from the rigging and the Admiral's feet, which I had not removed as the decks would have to be plugged and I needed fine weather for the job.

The copper strip on the leaking seam seemed to be holding out despite the pounding the boat had taken during the last five months; I was only having to pump the bilges once a day in normal conditions, and although this increased if the weather got really bad, it was still a great improvement on the early days.

My main worry was the rudder. The pintles which hold the rudder to the sternpost were badly worn and there was a good ¼-inch play on them. Before I put rope lashings on the rudder head to hold it tight and reduce the strain on the pintles I had been able to hear them jumping every time a wave hit the rudder, and with the cabin acting as a sounding box each slight bump magnified itself into a fearful wrenching thud. If the pintles wore through I hoped the lashings would hold the rudder until I could get to it and haul it inboard. Then I would have to think of a way of refastening it in place or rigging up some other form of jury steering. It might go at any time, but the boat would still be manageable somehow, and there was no point in worrying about the problem until I was faced with it.

Despite my protective mixture of tallow and white lead, the rigging had developed a layer of surface rust. I had lost my wire brush overside so had taken to rubbing down the bad patches with wire wool. The wires themselves were otherwise in good shape and would have lost very little of their strength. None of the standing rigging broke on the voyage.

The running rigging – halyards, runners, the jib forestay and so on – took much greater wear and needed constant attention. The jib forestay was broken but I had plenty of suitable wire on board to make a replacement and it was only a question of awaiting the right weather conditions that would allow me to climb the mast before I rigged up a new one.

The goosenecks were loose and looked as if they would go at any time, particularly the mizzen. The main had gone completely, but my jury arrangement looked firm and worked well and I just had to hope it would last me home. If the mizzen broke I thought I had enough bits and pieces of metal left to knock up something that would do the job. Roller reefing is a great advantage and there is no excuse for making life difficult for oneself by not having it, but men sailed for centuries without it, and there was no reason why I should not do the same.

The sails were getting a bit tired. Once white, they were now weathered and brown, with angry reddish lines on them where they made contact with the standing rigging. I had commenced the voyage with one new suit and had taken along my old suit for emergencies. This had proved wise as my new mainsail had just split and I had been able to set the old one in its place and not lose time. Most of the sails had my stitching on them; in fact, after steering, sewing had become my major occupation. I planned to repair the split mainsail even though its shape would be altered slightly by this, but I could not afford to lose 300 square feet of sail, and I did not know how long my old mainsail would last. Apart from the mainsails I had two of every other sail I needed and all were in serviceable condition.

As far as my food supplies went I had no problems. At a rough estimate I still had sufficient for six months, even allowing for the increasing number of tins that were going off. The worst affected were the tinned vegetables and scarcely a day passed without my hearing the hiss of a tin collapsing, which meant up to half an hour's ferreting through the lockers to find the victim before he could contaminate the air and possibly the bilges. However, I had plenty of dehydrated peas and instant potato left, and about twenty-eight pounds of soup powder which was an excellent flavoured thickener. The tinned meats were beginning to taste a bit funny but so far they appeared safe to eat and I put the taste down to my boredom with the flavour. Unless an unexpected number of tins went off when we reached the warmer climate there should be no worries about food.

Drinking water was down to about four and a half gallons, mainly because on the run to the Horn I had been unable to collect rainwater from the spray-covered sails without it tasting brackish. I hoped to start collecting again once round Cape Horn and I was confident of being able to gather all I wanted once we got into the Variables to the north of the Falklands. If we received insufficient rain there to refill all my polythene containers I had about 130 tins of fruit juices and seventy of beer left which would certainly carry me through to the Doldrums where rain squalls are frequent and heavy.

The engine I had come to consider a write-off, but I decided that if I got a spell of fine weather I would try to strip it and find out why it had seized up. I did not think that with the tools at my disposal I could do much about it, but it was worth trying and could cut a few days off the voyage if I managed to get it going once more.

The battery charger was still functioning although I had to remove the cylinder head each time I wanted to use it in order to free the valves which had taken to sticking since the exhaust pipe had been sheared off south of Cape Town. With the charger working and the batteries delivering power, I should have had few worries about the radio, but my inability to contact anyone was a cause of growing concern. As far as I could tell the transmitter was working, but I was never able to get a response when I called up a station that I could hear using one of the frequencies fitted to my set.

If further repairs became necessary to the boat or equipment I still had a comprehensive tool kit. The only thing I was running short of were drill bits, mainly because when drilling in a moving boat one is constantly being thrown about and unless one withdraws the drill fast it gets snapped off. Paraffin for the galley and lamps was holding out well, and although the consumption had been high in the Southern Ocean, mainly because I had used the cabin heater frequently, there was half my original stock of 35 gallons left. Meths for heating the primus was in plentiful supply, with over $1\frac{1}{2}$ gallons remaining; more than sufficient, particularly now that I was down to a single burner, which imposed a natural rationing system.

My sextant had given me some anxiety earlier in the voyage when the two mirrors had begun to tarnish. Since then I had taken to holding the instrument out in the rain to wash it clean of salt, and although the tarnish continued to spread, the mirrors were still largely clear and I was experiencing no difficulty in taking sights. The chronometer still worked well, and as my latest landfall on Diego Ramirez had been accurate I had no fears as to my ability to find Falmouth.

The most worn of all my equipment were my clothes. Of my original three pairs of jeans, two were badly worn and I had had to put canvas patches on them. Shirts and sweaters were holding out well, but none of my protective clothing was in good shape. The rubber sea boots were cracking and they leaked. I continued to wear them only because they kept some of the spray and all of the wind out, and if I had to have wet feet I might as well keep them warm; one advantage of their present condition that I noted in my diary was that when they filled with water, it ran out at the foot and I did not have to take them off to empty them. The waterproof jacket and trousers were slightly porous by this time, and to try to keep the worst of the damp out I had taken to wearing an old pair of waterpoof trousers over the new ones. Clothing was not so important now though because the temperature would start to rise as we worked our way north and by the time we reached the

Tropics I would probably be doing without clothes altogether.

The other part of the team, myself, was in good physical shape apart from the inevitable cuts, blisters, and bruises which, though inconvenient, were nowhere near serious enough to cause me to give up. If anything, I was probably fitter than when I set out, although I could have used a few long nights' sleep.

My medical and surgical stores were virtually untouched apart from some eyedrops, aspirins, and Elastoplast for small cuts and abrasions.

There were no signs of salt-water sores, boils or any of the other symptoms that normally indicate one is run down, and the ancient scourge of seamen, scurvy, had made no appearance after more than two hundred days at sea. I had plenty of Board of Trade anti-scorbutic lime powder left, which I had been mixing with water and taking regularly since my fresh lemons had run out off New Zealand. This, and the tinned vegetables I carried, gave me a great advantage over the seamen 150 years ago who had had to make do with salt meat, and after a few months at sea, rotting vegetables. In Dana's *Two Years Before the Mast* there is a chilling account of the effect of scurvy on two members of the crew, and of how, after a passing ship had been hailed and some fresh potatoes and onions obtained, the two men quickly recovered. Dana, of course, was an American sailing aboard an American ship. What is appalling is the realization that a preventative against the disease had been known for sixty years prior to Dana's experience, and that British seamen were already at that time becoming known as Limeys from the habit aboard British ships of issuing lime juice to prevent scurvy. The term 'Limey' is often used these days to describe us rather contemptuously. Personally, I have always felt rather proud of the description.

It was much more difficult to assess my mental state as I had no yardstick. I felt quite sane and seemed able to reason things out accurately. If anything, I felt that my reasoning had become sharper, and the long hours at the helm with nothing to do but learn poetry and daydream, or think about any subject that occurred to me, had slowly made me more aware of the world of which I am a part. Thinking about the origins of the human species and its erratic development to its present position as the dominant animal, led me often to considering the social set-up that man has built for himself. I was fortunate that I had some excellent books with me, H. G. Wells's *Outline of History* and Bertrand Russell's *History of Western Philosophy*, to name but two which gave me other people's opinions to consider and measure against my own. Few people today query the origin of our species. We started out as a lowly cell and have developed slowly into our present highly complex form. Regardless of our colour or nationality, all babies are similar, whether red, yellow, white or black, and it is solely the circumstances of upbringing that decide the child's future. In every country I have seen, a caste system of some sort exists, however much it is denied. Even amongst the most civilized and democratic countries, true equality of opportunity is something that has still to be attained.

The sea and ships are great levellers. There is certainly no room on a small boat for a person who is incompetent or won't pull his weight, whatever his 'caste'. All share the same risks in a storm, and no earthly influence will select you above the rest to be saved if the ship founders. Seamen have a reputation as blaspheming, heavy drinkers ashore, which is not surprising when one thinks of the rough masculine life they lead at sea. I am always amazed when looking over the *Victory* in Portsmouth that a thousand men could be jammed into that small space for years at a time. A harsh discipline (to our modern eyes), teamwork, self-reliance, trust in their officers and in each other, formed the pattern of their lives, but they were also brought face to face with the colossal natural forces that one meets at sea. Their whole existence depended upon their ability to come to terms with the wind and sea, and to use these forces to drive their ship.

It is not surprising that most of them thought more than their counterparts ashore about the cause of these forces, and not in the least surprising to me that so many were strongly superstitious or developed unshakeable religious beliefs, and sometimes both. I have found myself thinking deeply on the matter when out in rough weather in a small boat. It is all very well for someone sitting in an office to explain logically how the waves can build up before the wind, for we have discovered the natural laws that control this, but to a seaman, the explanation of these laws does not always seem to be sufficient. However practical you like to think you are, the feeling comes that there is more to it all than just natural laws, and if you have been brought up in a society that bases its philosophy upon the existence of a Superior Being, you come to consider that this Being is responsible, and to accept that he exists.

The rules are there, the physical laws that we have slowly learned. If we obey them we have a chance of survival. It is no use knowing that your boat is heading towards the eye of a storm and praying to God to see you through it safely. That's not his job. It's your task to steer the boat away from the eye, and you are asking too much if you expect the boat to survive when you deliberately ignore the rules. My own philosophy is developed about the phrase 'The Lord helps those who help themselves'. It is no good lying in your bunk, listening to the rising wind and feeling the boat beginning to strain and praying for God to take in a reef. No one but a fool would expect anything to happen. One has to get up and reef the sails oneself before the boat's movement will ease. If the wind continues to increase one takes in more sail until eventually one has to heave-to. When everything has been done that you know you can do, you put your trust in your Superior Being, and just hope that what you have done is right. This will probably seem obvious to everyone, believer or otherwise, but there is a great deal of comfort to be gained by thinking that there is something out there that can protect you. Because of this belief, throughout the voyage I never really felt I was completely alone, and I think a man would have to be in- humanly confident and self-reliant if he were to make this sort of voyage without faith in God.

From a more practical point of view, if you are trying to do a particularly difficult job, and failing time and again, the knowledge that the Lord will assist if you help yourself keeps you going at it, and in my experience the job usually gets done. A simple example of this occurred when we were making for Cape Horn and I was bending on the old mainsail. The halyard slipped from my grasp and pulled through its sheave about fifteen feet, well beyond reach. I could not afford to lose it and if I did not catch it quickly it was likely to run right through which meant I would have to climb to the top of the mast to retrieve it, next to impossible in the sea conditions prevailing then. Three times I tried to reach the halyard and failed. It was obvious that if I was going to get it back I was going to have to climb some way up the mast. I told my God the problem and explained how I intended setting about it, and asked him to give me a hand. A minute later I was back on deck with the halyard shackled on to the sail. Now it could be said that telling him what I intended doing helped me to think the problem out calmly, and the feeling that he would give me a hand encouraged me, and that this Superior Being is just a figment of my imagination. The fact remains that the job was done, and because I thought there was someone there I was encouraged to keep trying – and surely that is what God is all about.

On my own in *Suhaili*, dealing with the elements in a straight-forward manner and with only the basic rules of the sea to go by, things appeared in a far less complicated light than they do when surrounded by the diversions of civilization. The answers I came up with then seemed both simple and honest. I stored them for future reference in the private corners of my mind; right or wrong they will always be there.

Cape Horn to the Equator

January 18th, 1969 (Day 219)–March 6th, 1969 (Day 266)

My first impulse on rounding the Horn was to keep on going east. The feeling of having got past the worst was terrific and I suppose this impulse was a way of cocking a snook at the Southern Ocean itself, almost as if to say 'I've beaten you and now I'll go round again to prove it.' Fortunately this phase passed very quickly. A spell of cold uncomfortable weather quickly put things back into their proper perspective; I thought of hot baths, pints of beer, the other sex and steaks and turned up into the Atlantic for home.

From Cape Horn to Port Stanley in the Falkland Islands is about 470 miles. It took us six days. During this time I made repeated efforts to establish radio contact with Port Stanley and Punta Arenas, the nearest Chilean port in Magellan's Strait. One evening, when I was turning in, I heard English voices loud and clear and almost hit the deckhead with excitement. The frequency being used was almost on top of one of mine and I wasted no time putting out a call. I listened hopefully for a reply but the voices continued conversing with each other and had obviously not heard me. I tried the three other frequencies I had close to them but was still unheard. It was so pleasant to have the cabin filled with English voices again that I left the receiver on and just sat back to listen.

What I had found was the British Antarctic Survey radio stations which operate in this area. This was their 'chatter hour' when they discuss the day's work and swap news. It was fascinating; I learned that one vehicle had proved no use on a certain surface and was out of use until the *Shackleton* arrived with new tracks. It became like the B.B.C's 'Archers' serial to me. Each evening for over ten days I listened in without fail and my new friends brought me up to date with the latest news. Sometimes I heard only two voices, but more often a third station came in as well. This was apparently manned by a new boy down south who, when being grilled by the other two, gave his reason for volunteering as 'he found it a bit warm at home'. It was a very one-sided friendship; I felt I knew them well but was never able to introduce myself as they always used a different frequency from mine. A month later when I had lost contact with them, I heard on the B.B.C. News that one of the islands where we had a survey station had had an eruption and that the Chilean Navy had been asked to evacuate the team; I was on tenterhooks until I heard they were safe.

Still without any radio contact, I decided to head close to Port Stanley and attract attention. I did not like to go too far away from the islands anyway as this would have meant entering the pecked lines on the chart which some Admiralty cartographer has encouragingly marked 'Icebergs and loose ice may be fallen in with to the southward of this line'. But the wind came up from the north-east and I had little choice but to sail east or north-west. I decided to go east, thinking that this wind must be a temporary affair. I should have known better by this time. The wind strengthened into a gale and before long we were hove-to and drifting steadily over the Admiralty's pecked lines. It was not a happy day at all.

January 20th, 1969   *Day 221*

The wind continued to rise until by mid-afternoon it was Force 10. I handed the mainsail finally just before it really got nasty and I think this was about the most painful job in the voyage so far. Spray and rain were hitting me like bullets and my wretched burn did not stand a chance. The scab went within seconds, leaving raw meat exposed to the bullets. On top of this it is very cold and by the time I had the sail lashed I could not feel a thing. They started to thaw as soon as I got below and I was almost in tears with the pain as the blood began to circulate again. I have put a bandage over my hand again. It soon gets wet but at least it keeps the wind out. I knocked back a gill of whisky after furling the mainsail and for all the good it did it might as well have been water. I did not even feel it going down. A second 'slug' a few minutes later had a wonderful effect. The glass had dropped 16 mbs. in eight hours. The N.E. wind has now died and I am expecting the wind to back and come on furiously any minute.

The wind backed at 1800 and for a couple of hours we were nearly stationary as I waited for the gale. However, despite the lines of dark cloud that swept over us, each accompanied by a short squall, the wind did not really get up so I reset the mainsail. It did not take more than four minutes to get it down and furled and I wanted to get on.

It's bitterly cold out. I am keeping an ice watch from the hatchway and frequently popping down to check the level in the whisky bottle. My sinus always gives trouble when my face is exposed to the cold like this and it's started to ache now. I don't know, I'm beginning to fall to pieces physically – must be getting old!!!

After twice falling asleep standing in the hatchway, I decided to turn in as I had seen no signs of ice at all and we were not going very fast. I climbed into my sleeping-bag still wearing my blue waterproof overalls as with all the clothes I had on it was difficult to remove them, conscious of my cold feet as the cold air infiltrated through the bottom of the sleeping-bag. Both the pairs of stockings I was wearing were wet, and the seaboots didn't even have a psychological value now.

At 1000 we were virtually becalmed, the sun was shining, and we were steering west. I took a sight, tacked, set more sail and had some breakfast:

January 21st, 1969   *Day 222*

I have a headache, probably a hangover from checking the whisky too often. I did not sleep well though, yet again. I half remembered dreams when I awoke; the worst, which recurs, is that this is just an elimination for a race round the world. I suppose someday I'll read that and laugh at it, but just now, with a headache and having just been sick (so it's not the whisky!) plus the fact that my joints are aching and I'm dog tired, it's a nightmare.

I tried to turn in early this evening and I took a couple of Codeine, my first of the voyage, but as soon as I got into my sleeping-bag and was beginning to doze, the wind changed direction. I altered the sheets to suit but then the wind died. Since then it's come up now and again in light puffs and as each time it does this I have to change the position of the tiller, I cannot turn in. If this goes on much longer I'll have to heave-to. I cannot exist endlessly without a decent rest. If only we could have, for once, the winds that are meant to prevail here.

January 22nd, 1969   *Day 223*

It's 0100 and the Codeine seem to have eased my headache which is as well because sitting up with one's head feeling like an anvil is not fun. I don't really know what the wind is up to. Briefly it came from the N.W., the direction that is supposed to prevail here, however it's now north-easterly and I expect it will soon be N.N.E. again. This is a bit rough as this will be the third time it's been north-easterly since passing the Horn and that is exactly what we do not want. I feel close to despair. Nothing I do seems right; if I take in sail the wind drops, if I increase sail, it rises. The moment I think I've got her steering nicely it changes direction, so I'm up and down the whole time; and for what? We've averaged 75 miles a day since passing the Horn. I wanted to pass Port Stanley to report so now we get N.E. winds which make that impossible, unless I want to lose time. I was making up for it, but I cannot go on a starboard tack or we'll hit the south coast of the Falklands and a port tack puts us into the ice area. At present I dare not close the land because as sure as eggs are bloody eggs, the wind will turn S.E. if I do and then I'll be pushed onto a lee shore. Perhaps if I weren't so tired I'd view it differently.

Once I managed to get a semblance of balance, I turned in for six beautiful hours. I spent the day on repairs. Put another splice in the starboard flying jib sheet; it's lost about 4 ft. now and if it goes again it will have to be renewed, which presents a problem as apart from my warps which are not really suitable, I'm almost out of rope. Sewed up a hole in the 'Big Fellow' and got on with the main.

Winds up from N.N.E. It's about time we had some steady westerlies in my humble opinion. I don't wish to appear a complainer but we've had more easterly than westerly winds since the Horn and I don't reckon we're getting a fair go.

At 0430 on the 23rd the wind backed sharply to the west at last. By 0830 it had become strong and I had to start reefing during which I lost quite a bit of skin, though as my hands had skin as thick as an elephant's now I did not feel the loss.

It became obvious that a call to Port Stanley was out. At noon we were over a hundred miles east of it and I came to the conclusion that the two days I would lose by heading in and back out to my present position were not worth sacrificing with the Frenchman so close behind. It would mean that my family would not know that I was safely round the Horn, but I would be home sooner, and I hoped to meet a ship on the way and get us reported.

Soon afterwards I discovered the reason for my sickness. With my fresh water down to $3\frac{1}{2}$ gallons in the polythene containers, I had decided to try and hang onto this, using for my coffee and cocoa some of the rainwater I had put into the forward fresh water tank after I had pumped out the original contaminated supply. Not until I made up some lime juice did I really taste the water by itself and it was vile. I stopped using it, went back to the polythene container, and soon recovered. A few days later I ran into my first really good rain squall, and before it passed had gathered over five gallons of drinking water. This gave me a month's supply without rationing.

As we ran farther north it suddenly struck me that we had a straight unbroken horizon, instead of the constantly undulating line which had become so familiar during the four and a half months we had been in the Southern Ocean. It took me a moment to realize the reason for this, that South America had at last come between us and the endless progress of the Southern Ocean to the west.

One night, just before sunset, we began to run through patches of royal blue sea. The ocean as a whole was slate-grey in colour and I was alarmed at first in case these patches marked the ice which I had never seen at sea. I made up close to one patch to investigate it and as we came alongside it suddenly came to life. Hundreds of silver tongues began to flick out of the surface. I was unable to make the creatures out clearly, but they were rather like tadpoles with very long tails, their total length being about six inches. They seemed capable of quite rapid movement and I stood no chance of catching them with my bucket.

I hunted through my copy of Professor J. L. B. Smith's *Fishes of South African Waters*, but could find nothing there, and except that they appeared to be the fairly advanced larval stage of something, I still don't know what they were.

Daily maintenance around the deck and as far up as the lower spreaders presented few problems, and had become routine. The one thing any singlehander fears is something breaking at the top of the mast, and at last this happened to me:

January 26th, 1969   *Day 227*
I set the Big Fellow just before noon to get a bit of extra speed as the wind was dying. About two hours later as I was sitting below stitching away on the mainsail, I heard a slight bang on deck. I looked up and then down; the Big Fellow was beautifully set in the water alongside. Fortunately the sail itself is not damaged but the halyard has broken which means I shall have to go aloft. I tried this evening but was unable to steady myself sufficiently and having swung out and come in again landing with my eyebrow (which is now the size of an egg) before I had even reached the first spreader, I gave up for the day.

In the event I never did reach the top of the mast, but my diary describes the attempts I made which resulted in my nearly killing myself:

January 27th, 1969   *Day 228*
As with her steering N.E. the seesawing lessened, I decided to go aloft and re-reeve the Big Fellow halyard. I should have known better. I got halfway when she luffed and that was that. I hung on for half an hour hoping she would come back but no one answered my prayers and eventually my strength ran out and I had to come down. We are scarcely moving and she wants more sail so, as soon as my arms and shoulders have stopped aching I'll set the 'Big Fellow'

using the main topping lift as a halyard. In the meantime I'm having a cup of coffee and pondering the point that 'If one thanks God when things go right, surely it is reasonable enough to blame him when things go wrong.' From this it will appear how depressed I feel at present through the lack of prevailing winds and frustration of every attempt I make to help myself.

After lunch, as it seemed calmer I had another attempt at reaching the masthead. I made the upper spreaders quickly enough but whilst I was gathering my breath she started to pitch again. I waited ten minutes or so for a change, during which time the Big Fellow was washed off the deck into the water, and as I could see more and more of it going overside, I decided to make a quick dash for the top and hope my legs would hold onto the mast. I had gone about four feet when she swung. Both hands were on the tackle which I did not dare let go of or I would have fallen 32 feet. My legs couldn't hold on round the mast as the mainsail was in the way and I swung forward. I managed to cushion the return swing and fend myself off the mast with my feet, and I swung straight out towards the mizzen. Somehow I got caught the wrong side of the mainsail which stopped me being swung forward again and I was able to grab one of the back stays with a leg and then get a hand free for the same purpose . . . and there I hung, lurching wildly, until she eased up. The moment she eased I swung back to the spreader and then made my way back to the deck as fast as I could. It's quite obvious that I will need really calm conditions to reach the top and after this last attempt I am in no hurry to make another! We'll just have to make do without a main topping lift until I can get up, each time I want to hoist the Big Fellow.

Almost as bad was dropping my last cigarette – except for twenty which I was pretending I did not know about as I intended keeping them for an emergency. My fingers were so thick-skinned and insensitive that I did not notice the poor half-finished thing slipping from them and rolling overside. This was probably a unique opportunity to give up smoking and I was half prepared to do so. For a whole day I managed without and then that evening, as I was having a cup of coffee and thinking how nice a puff would be, I remembered hiding a squirrel store of cigarettes soon after leaving Falmouth. No mole ever dug as furiously as I did into my large clothing bag. Arms, head and shoulders disappeared as I scrabbled to the bottom, and emerged clutching a precious 400 fags. In my diary I promised 'I'll keep to 4 a day', and then added more realistically 'or thereabouts'.

With the Falkland Islands behind me – or rather bypassed – and *Suhaili* well within the ice zone, my main desire was to make as much northing as I could. My policy of pushing *Suhaili* at a pace we could both take had proved right so far. Here we were, still a going concern with the worst behind us. Just the same, I wanted to beat Bernard Moitessier and *Joshua* home, and I felt that we could afford to go a little harder from here on:

January 28th, 1969   *Day 229*
I awoke to find a dull overcast sky and dying wind so I set more sail and by noon had both the spinnaker and Big Fellow up. The sky cleared then but soon a line of dark cloud began forming to the S.W. and I decided to shorten sail. That's when the fun began. I had the spinnaker half down when the wind arrived. *Suhaili* gybed herself immediately and heeled right over. I dropped the spinnaker and rushed after to release the mizzen boom guy and pull the helm over. After an age she gybed back again and I was able to get the spinnaker in. I next hoisted the jib. It was half up when she gybed again, again without warning which she usually gives by rustling the sails. I hoisted the jib, rushed aft and brought her back again. The wind was rising very quickly and was blowing Force 6–7 by this time. However, I managed to get the Big Fellow in without incident. Then I took a reef in the main, but as she still had too much sail I took two more reefs at the same time and at last I began to win control of the situation. I was soaked. I had been very hot in the sun so I was in shirt and jeans only when I started to take in sail and what with her gybing and luffing a lot of water came over the decks and I caught my share. Still, no complaints, as this wind is south and west and good and strong, so we're moving north rapidly, and that suits us fine. The glass is rising and the weather is much warmer – all to the good except I would not mind this wind for a week. The sky is completely clear of cloud; one wonders why, as usually there is cloud about when it's windy.

On February 3rd we officially left the Southern Ocean when we crossed the 40th parallel in longitude 41° West, and a few hours later a school of dolphins gave us a playful welcome as they leapt round the boat, the pilot sitting with flattened tail on the pressure wave from *Suhaili*'s stem, his lithe grey body swaying slightly as he led us through the green water. There was no sudden change in the weather, but day by day the temperature rose, allowing me to venture on deck without first pulling on my faded and scuffed wet weather gear, and soon it was warm enough to spend the day without a shirt. The water was still a bit cold for swimming as we were only just clear of the ice limit, so I continued washing by means of a bucket of heated sea water in the cabin. This was rather a messy business as it meant the whole of the after end of the cabin got liberally sprayed with salt water detergent suds. However, it did mean that the cabin got a scrub out afterwards.

The wind started to become erratic a few days later, sometimes coming on in nice strong gusts but soon easing off, leaving us rolling slowly but not moving. These occasions could not be wasted and as soon as I had *Suhaili* headed in the right direction I got out my tool kit and began to strip the engine. Starter, dynamo, fuel pump, injectors and exhaust manifold soon came off and I started removing the cylinder head nuts. A special spanner is usually used for this job; I did not have it and my tools, a cold chisel and hammer, would have made an engineer's hair curl. Too bad, the cylinder head had to come off and I used what I had. When I eventually had the cylinder head off, the pistons could not be seen for congealed oil and flaked carbon, but a piece of wire wool and the back of a knife used as a scraper soon cleared that. I now tried forcing the pistons to move but they were stuck solid. I took a hammer and using the wooden handle tapped round the edge of each piston and tried again – nothing happened. I filed down a knife so that it would fit between the piston and the cylinder liner and tried scraping, but although on two of the cylinders I was able to force the blade down as far as the piston rings, on the other two I got nowhere. This appeared to be the cause of the trouble and for two days, when the opportunity arose, I scraped patiently away at the slag. It was a tedious and not very rewarding job as in that time I only got down a tenth of an inch. Further progress was barred when the knife broke, cunningly slicing my finger at the same time.

By this time I had had enough of the engine and I replaced the cylinder head to keep the wet air from the innards, and gave it a rest. A couple of days later, my enthusiasm restored, or rather my determination not to be defeated by an inanimate and unco-operative lump of metal refreshed, I returned to the assault. This time I cut some discs of lead from the self-steering vane counterbalances and put sufficient of them into the cylinders to stick out one inch above, and replaced the cylinder head. I tightened the bolts on the cylinder head slowly, hoping that the pressure would shift the pistons, but all I succeeded in doing was jamming the lead in the cylinders.

I extracted the lead by drilling it out, bit by bit, put Diesel oil in all the cylinders and left them. Next time I attempted to free the engine I used a nut and bolt jammed between the teeth of the flywheel and its case and slowly opened the nut and bolt out. The thread stripped and I had the devil of a job getting the jammed bit out. So I put the cylinder head back in place, covered the whole thing in grease and left it. If I had not got an engine I was no worse off than the old clippers and I would have to manage without. After I reached home the engine was examined and it was found that two cylinders were cracked, due undoubtedly to my inexpert attempts to free them. Out of my experiences there is a lesson for people who take an engine cruising: remember to turn it frequently.

One thing that I had almost come to accept as a part of my existence, constantly damp clothing and jammed locker doors, disappeared as we ran into the warmer latitudes. I revelled in my new and luxurious state. Everything went on deck to be aired. The settee cushions were scrubbed and left to dry in the sun and I washed down the whole interior of the boat. Widow Twankey's laundry never had anything to match my washing line and I reckon I got an extra knot from *Suhaili*'s increased windage. Whilst the cabin was clear I went through all the lockers checking the tins, and had to throw nearly a hundred away. These must have had quite a smell because shortly afterwards I felt a slight nudge against the hull, and going on deck I discovered a 7-foot nurse shark doing its best to scrape the anti-fouling off the hull. I tore below, grabbed the rifle and put a bullet in its brain as it came close to the surface. It must have been killed instantly as it did not even twitch but just rolled up and slowly sank from view. I could clearly see the ragged hole in the top of its head made by the bullet, and a dark brown cloud slowly spread from the opening. Half an hour later another appeared and I gave him the same treatment. I would have tried to spear them using the harpoon without the gun, but the decks were cluttered with gear and I like to get one thing done at a time.

The next day I took my first, somewhat nervous swim since re-entering the Atlantic. The water was still nippy but very refreshing and I had a good work out, swimming as fast as I could and trying to keep pace with *Suhaili*. It was whilst I was climbing out of the water I noticed three small pilot fish darting about round the rudder, and I grabbed the underwater camera to take some shots of them. These fish were unusually curious; whereas one usually had a difficult job trying to find the subject in the viewfinder, in this instance I could not make them go far enough away to get the focus right. I found myself kicking at them with one foot while holding the camera in one hand and hanging onto the boat with the other. Most of these photographs, not unsurprisingly, are expert portraits of a foot.

For nearly a week the pilot fish remained with us, their lives occasionally hanging in the balance as I debated whether to catch them and have fried fish. They were saved by the thought of their usual food, shark excreta. I often saw them whilst I was swimming and although their initial curiosity was replaced by nervousness, they gradually grew to accept the fact that this large red guardian of theirs had a strange white parasite that needed to splash about in the water each day. I did not just swim on these occasions, I used to take photographs and check over the hull and particularly the rudder pintles. It was also a good opportunity to clean the hull.

February 15th, 1969   *Day 247*
Went swimming with the camera and photographed my gooseneck barnacles before I gave them independence! Many were 6 ins. long

and bloated. The main spots were on the stern and abaft the stern post with a good few on the keel. The anti-fouling has obviously lost its power now as there are a large number of small ones growing on the hull. With one or two exceptions though they came off very easily. The exceptions had all secreted a white foundation substance onto the hull and . . . would easily hold me when the boat made a surge.

We passed Buenos Aires about 1,800 miles to the west on February 9th and for a week sailed rather slowly north, the average speed being about 70 miles a day on account of the light variable winds, broken only by vicious squalls which were fortunately advertised by the low cumulus cloud that accompanied them. Instant action was essential when these squalls arrived and I used to drop the mainsail the moment they hit, and sail through them under jib, staysail and mizzen, usually with a bucket quickly lashed under the mizzen gooseneck to catch water. Between the squalls the sun was hot, hotter than I realized, and the cabin heated up like an oven. The humidity would rise every time a squall approached, forcing me to evacuate the cabin and seek whatever shade existed on deck from the sails until the clouds gave me some protection. The transition in four weeks from the cold round the Horn to the near Tropic conditions here was too quick for me. My body had become acclimatized to the Southern Ocean and wanted longer to adjust.

Still, routine work had to be done and at this stage I was still trying to get the engine to turn:

February 19th, 1969   *Day 251*
I awoke after a fitful night at 0720; the sun burning my face as I lay on deck was responsible. There was no wind to speak of but we occasionally got puffs from the N.N.W. to N.N.E. For a while I tacked to get the best northing I could but I had to give up as I was covered in sweat even that early and panting for air.

I spent the morning renewing servings and greasing wires. I would have liked to go up the mast but if I take in the Big Fellow we'll stop and in any case I doubt if in this heat I'd reach the top.

A shark appeared at 1210, smaller than the other two. I decided to leave it alone in case my previous action in killing two has offended someone. It took my hook lure and line by way of thanks. . . .

I suppose some clever all-knowing bastard will read this and say that I've done everything but the obvious, work on the engine. Well, I tried it but in fifteen minutes I had built the temperature in the engine-room up to 98°F and that's when I gave up. I also tried to get the charger to work but without success.

This took me to lunch, after which I decided to rest as I'm feeling exhausted. The wind, within ten minutes, veered round to the N.E. so I roused myself and tacked. Three minutes later it was north and west. I tacked again and left it. I'm not Superman or immortal; I'm an average human and I know when I've had enough. The work in the sun this morning has given me a headache. I don't wish I'd never started this, I just wish there was something tangible I could get my hands on to let off steam (instead of doing it by writing here!) I'll win, if my water holds out. I have 7 gallons left.

Later: I have definitely got mild sunstroke. I feel awfully tired, my head aches and feels very hot – blast! I'll have to spend tomorrow below just as I was getting enthusiastic about smartening up the rigging and once I get started I usually keep going for other jobs as well. I'll have to make a hat.

The only cure I had for sunstroke was to keep myself in the cabin, rushing out periodically for a quick dip to cool off; rest, which I probably needed, was not allowed me.

February 20th, 1969   *Day 252*
I awoke at 0310 when I rolled out of my bunk. On staggering onto the deck I found us aback in a squall. I tacked thinking we could manage better on a starboard tack, then decided to try the port tack; got a glimpse of the stars so knew we were heading S.E. and tacked again. I cannot read the compass at night as its light packed up on the way out and my last torch gave up three weeks ago, hence I now watch the stars at night to get my course. A squall came up next so I took in the Big Fellow and set the jib. To do this without tearing the sail, I tacked and let the Big Fellow lie tacked until I got it down. Worked beautifully.

Turned in for two more hours when another squall awakened me from a blissful dream concerning a female acquaintance. I was a bit annoyed at being woken just then! It rained briefly about half a cup's worth and then eased and I went back to bed but couldn't recapture my dream.

I feel a bit better this morning but still have a slight headache and it hurts my head to stand in the sun. I feel stiff, though, and very tired.

Spent the day making a hat. The result will serve its purpose but I am unlikely to pose a threat to Dunn's. The only person who could possibly take offence is Clampett of the Beverly Hill Billies. I'll soak it overnight and stiffen it with some paint tomorrow.

Very little progress up to noon despite all my tacks yesterday. It's been quite hot today but not so bad as the last four days. I have kept out of the sun as much as possible. We're still not moving much and the course is just north of east or west on either tack; the wind has been light from the north all day.

It is flat calm this evening; the sea is like a badly rolled sheet of glass in which the Celestial Sphere is only slightly distorted. I was lying on deck trying to keep cool and for up to half a minute at a time the only sound was that slight buzzing in my ears which you seldom hear. Then for some reason an unseen hand would give the boat a gentle push and the stillness would be disturbed by the crack of the mainsail as it swung from side to side, and the rippling of the water round the hull. Rather pleasant, but I would trade it for a southerly gale. Perhaps this time the wind will change direction.

The hat was eventually finished. Made from an old piece of canvas, it looked like no other hat I have ever seen; however, after I had put some paint on the wide brim to stiffen it up a bit, it ceased to flop round my ears and over my eyes and I took to wearing it whenever I was on deck.

With light, fitful winds most of the time, punctuated by short explosive squalls, poor *Suhaili* was not sailing at her best. She is too heavy to ghost through calms, even with every sail I could put on her.

February 21st, 1969   *Day 253*
We are now becalmed and we made a day's run of 18 miles. Yesterday we managed 36, the day before 40. Our week's run between Fridays 14th to 21st February, is 345 miles. Does anyone wonder

that I am in despair! Still, I collected nine pints of water this morning. It would have been a great deal more but my hands were full. In the first squall the water was pouring off the booms like a waterfall.

Having boxed the compass the wind steadied from E.N.E. for the best part of the afternoon. It was light but we did at least move.

I have just had the news and I also picked up Lourenço Marques for about ten minutes. It was quite strong but there was a lot of interference.

February 22nd, 1969   *Day 254*

I could not sleep last night and eventually at 0330 I got up to get cool on deck. It was as well I did as I saw a squall coming up and this gave me time to get ready for it. The wind arrived at 0350 and it really blew for about 45 minutes. I don't know what course we made as I could not see the stars but I think about west. I managed to collect 4 gallons of water from the mizzen; it was pouring off so fast that I held the container under the gooseneck and did not bother with the bucket. It became flat calm for about ten minutes after the squall had passed and then the wind came up from the east. At 0630 I could see another squall coming so I took one reef in the mainsail to take the bite out of it. I got two gallons of water out of that. At 0825 we had a three gallon squall but I only collected one as I was busy trying to photo the water pouring off the sails. The main problem was keeping the water off the lens. At 1005 we had a two gallon squall which was the last. However, I now have sixteen gallons of fresh water which will keep me going for two months if I ration myself. I was beginning to feel rather sleepy by this time. However, I wanted to know how far we had come and after noon I decided to slap some High Vis. Orange on the cabin top as it had been nicely freshed off. It does not look attractive, of course, but as I cannot keep a lookout twenty-four hours a day I can at least make the other fellow's job easier. I have just sufficient paint left for another coat nearer home.

At 1620 I decided to have a sleep. No squalls were in sight and we were doing quite well sailing north. We did 87 miles to noon, which was a great improvement.

Awoke at 2210, had a tin of grapefruit juice and went to bed again. Lovely and cool.

Then at last the winds began to come at us from the east. The South-East Trades are bent round slightly in the west of the South Atlantic and I prayed that we had reached them at last. We wanted to go north so we could go on a reach to the Equator, *Suhaili*'s, and any ketch's, best point of sailing. My relief both physical and mental was terrific. We had not seemed to be getting anywhere before and the excitement that had arisen soon after passing the Horn at the thought of getting home again had soon been replaced by my usual attitude:

Memories of home seem like a dream now, the only reality is my small cabin and the endless empty sea around it. I no longer get excited thinking of home; I mentally shrug the thought of it all off just as I would the memory of the plot in a book. It's nice to think about, but it does not really exist.

Now that we were moving again my spirits shot up. Like most sailors I immediately began calculating when I would reach my destination using the best day's run achieved so far; a totally unrealistic calculation, of course, but tremendously exciting.

I began to think about arriving home again, and decided that it was time the crew put up with a bit of 'hard usage' to get things smartened up.

February 23rd, 1969   *Day 255*
I started work on some netting beneath the bowsprit, but only managed to get a few preparatory servings on the shrouds as the wind and sea got up and started soaking everything. This is not an essential job by any means but is one I want to do, hence I am indulging myself.

It was pleasant on the bowsprit. I had my hat on to protect my head and I wore shorts for a change (I don't usually bother with clothes when it's warm) because otherwise it's uncomfortable sitting on wires! I got nice and wet which in this weather is a treat.

We seem to be taking rather a lot of water again. I can only conclude that this is due to removing the gooseneck barnacles as the sea has not been particularly rough and that is all I have done to the hull for some time. It's annoying but as it only requires one session on the pump a day, it's not really troublesome – just worrying.

I was beginning to pay more attention to the outside world now as well. I listened faithfully to the B.B.C. News every evening. It was coming through loud and clear, and the report of the difference between the British Ambassador in Paris, Mr Christopher Soames, and General de Gaulle over their respective accounts of a discussion on Britain's position in relation to the Common Market aroused me to greater efforts:

February 24th, 1969   *Day 256*
General de Gaulle's insult to our Ambassador cost my French competitors about five miles today. I awoke full of indignation and seeing a squall coming decided not to change the Big Fellow for the jib but to steer her through it, which I did, and despite light winds overnight we managed another 111 miles.

I don't think the five miles will affect the issue of the race somehow, and I cannot see de Gaulle being tumbled from office by it, but it made me feel better. . . .

The wind is getting up a bit this evening (it's 1700) and I shall probably have to take the Big Fellow in soon, but I'll hang on a bit. I'll teach that old so-and-so to insult our Ambassador!!

On February 24th we passed Ilha de Trinidade, leaving it 140 miles to the west. This group of islands now belongs to Brazil but at one time they belonged to Britain. I don't think the land crabs and birds which were the sole occupants of the islands at the time were particularly affected by their change in nationality. There is also a story that Captain Kidd hid his treasure on the island and a serious attempt was made to find it sixty years ago by a Welsh miner; but if it is there, he didn't find it.

The Trade Wind belts are always a pleasure to sail through. The wind seldom, if ever, reaches gale force; at the same time it rarely dies away completely, and its direction is constant. The average strength of about Force 4 is ideal for sailing. Add to this the fact that the North-East and South-East Trades cover the Tropics and I think you have the picture. The sun shines down brightly but the wind reduces its heat to a comfortable and bearable temperature. I had gone brown by this time and usually pottered round the boat without clothing just for the comfortable free feeling it gave me. The sea, which for the past weeks had been flat and shining, now sparkled as the waves caught the sun, and I spent hours just watching it and enjoying the speed we were making.

I can never understand the people who say that they get bored in a sailing ship. In a power driven vessel, yes, whether a large liner or small cabin cruiser, because somehow using an engine instead of the natural forces seems to take the poetry out of the movement. Watching the ever-changing waves alone can keep me perfectly happy for hours on end; there is so much variety. And when the sea is flat calm suddenly it comes to life with small marine animals that you never notice as a rule. On one occasion in the Variables when I was cleaning weed off the hull, I became aware of two small beetle-like insects skipping across the surface of the water. It was fascinating to watch the way they stalked their food, minute plankton, and consumed it. How these fragile beings can survive when the surface of the sea is broken by the waves is something I don't know. Presumably they submerge and seek safety in the depths, but if so they must be able to live without breathing, have gills, or be able to carry a very large air bubble down with them.

Even in the middle of the oceans, where the sea is so clear that you can drop a silvery object into the water and watch it disappear into the blue over a hundred feet below, occasional fish appear, usually in small groups of four to ten. These are mainly pelagic species, the strong swimmers, such as dorado, bonita, and so on, and they would always appear fascinated by *Suhaili* and her white-skinned parasite. I frequently had reason to curse myself for forgetting the pump for my speargun. All these fish are good eating and the fresh meat would have done me no harm and made a pleasant change of diet. I tried catching them with the harpoon on the end of a length of line, but although I managed to hit one and and scare many I never landed any. A trolling line is seldom very effective deep sea; the ideal conditions are when the boat is sailing at about 5 knots and the surface of the sea is broken. For cruising over long distances, if you like fish, a powerful speargun is essential. On the Cape Town to London voyage we caught two fish on a trolling line and a dozen more with spearguns, when far away from land, but on this trip I only caught a bonito. Close to land, of course, on a good coastline, you can live on the fish you catch, provided that you have a plentiful supply of water. Fish are rich in protein and at least two pints of fresh water are needed daily to wash the system. Even so, an exclusive diet of fish will ultimately lead to loss of body weight and anaemia.

The Equator to Falmouth

March 7th, 1969 (Day 267)–April 22nd, 1969 (Day 313)

WE ran into the South-East Trades in latitude 24° South and twelve days later shot across the Equator, having averaged nearly 120 miles each day. It did not take me long nowadays to get *Suhaili* balanced and I found some spare time on my hands with which to prepare her, and me, for our confrontation with civilization. I gave myself a haircut and trimmed my beard, and then trimmed the weed off *Suhaili*'s hull. I also gave the upperworks a scrub down. All the ropework was checked and where necessary new servings of marline put over splices and given a good coating of Stockholm Tar. I had time, as well, to check the sails and stitch up the split mainsail, usually working below but sometimes dragging the sail into the cockpit and working there despite the spray that frequently came over.

We were getting close to the shipping lanes again and I started to worry about seeing a ship to report us. I had seen only one ship, a Japanese bulk carrier, since leaving New Zealand. She was heading towards Rio from the Cape of Good Hope but had been too far away for me to be able to attract attention. Keeping a lookout for shipping was all very well when I was awake or in daylight, but after I had turned in at night I had to rely upon a rather weak oil lantern to avoid being run down.

This lantern disappeared one night from its accustomed position hanging from the pushpit aft, and I was left with the choice of rigging up an electric light or leaving the paraffin pressure-lamp going all night. I just did not have the petrol left to keep the batteries charged sufficiently for an electric light, whereas with 15 gallons of paraffin remaining, the pressure lamp using 1 pint a night could easily be left going without straining my resources. I started off by leaving it wedged in the lifebuoy on the top of the main hatch and pointing up towards the mainsail which, when illuminated like this, seems to show up fairly well. But one night of this was enough to show me that if I wanted to keep the lamp I would have to put it in a less exposed position. The cockpit wouldn't do as spray was constantly coming over, so I finished up with the lamp fastened in the vice on the saloon table and shining up through the skylight. This reduced the actual light showing from the boat by three-quarters, but it was the best I could do. It also made the cabin very hot, which made dropping off to sleep difficult, but unless we wanted to be run down, we had to show some sort of light.

As we approached the Equator the steady Trade Winds began to be broken:

March 5th, 1969   *Day 265*
The wind is beginning to fluctuate and we are getting some quite severe squalls. At one point this afternoon the weather looked so threatening that I handed the mainsail. It was as well that I did as when the squall hit we heeled right over and made about 5 knots under the other three sails alone. This evening we have run into a northerly choppy sea so we must be on the edge of the Doldrums, although we cross the mean limit of the S.E. Trades at the Equator at this time of the year and this, with luck, will be to-morrow.

Burning on deck by day and stuffy below for the first half of the night, but as we are moving, who cares?

I spent the day reading when not steering or trying to race the boat swimming. I was never exhausted before the stern came level with me, not because I am fit – I have little stamina now – but because we were moving well. Day's run to noon 118 miles . . .

The next day we crossed the Equator and the stomach pains that gave me my greatest scare of the whole voyage began:

March 6th, 1969   *Day 266*

I have had to work today with the wind south of east. She won't
balance to steer north, so I steered. Quite nice but too hot for comfort.
I don't know if it's the sun or unaccustomed labour, but I do not
feel at all well this evening. I feel a bit sick and tired and I have a
headache. I also have agonizing indigestion.

Tried the radio this evening but no one seems to be listening.
Not much on the news.

Can't get to sleep.

Finished all the cigarettes at lunch today – it's a horrible habit
anyway!

Having at last to give up smoking was more of a relief than
anything. For some time I had been convinced that cigarettes
were not doing me any good, but whilst I had them on board I
did not have the willpower to give them up. Now I had no
choice and surprisingly enough I did not miss them at all.
But as soon as I got home and they became available, I started
smoking again.

From a health point of view I would have to have stopped
anyway. The indigestion developed until I had a permanent
pain in the middle of my stomach. I got out my *Ship Captains'
Medical Guide* and by the time I had finished looking up my
symptoms and the possible causes, I was really alarmed. It
appeared that I could have anything from appendicitis to
stomach ulcers. I put myself on a diet of spaghetti cheese and
rice puddings, which was most unsatisfying, but it did ease
things a bit. I also started taking indigestion tablets, but the
pain remained despite all this. Then its source appeared to
shift and I got really scared. I took out the charts and measured
off to the nearest decent-sized port, Belem, at the mouth of the
Amazon, which was about a thousand miles away. That was at
least ten days sailing, and in ten days if I did have appendicitis
without any antibiotics on board to keep the thing in check, I
would be dead. I cursed myself for leaving antibiotics off my
medical list, and for not having my appendix out before I set
sail, but it was too late for recriminations now. I decided to
hold onto my course for home and just hope there was nothing
seriously wrong. With any luck I might sight a ship and if that

happened I could ask them to arrange a daily radio schedule in case the worst came to the worst.

I still feel guilty about this. If I had had appendicitis and had made a contact it would have meant great inconvenience to any shipping which diverted to pick me up. It would have been even worse if I had managed to make a radio contact and a search was necessary in order to find out where I was. The authorities go to a great deal of trouble for ships and yachts in distress. Apart from the expense, which is relatively unimportant, men's lives are put at risk in aircraft and boats to look for the man in trouble. Everyone who sets off in a small boat has this responsibility to the search and rescue organizations, that he should be ready for any emergency himself, and he should not set off unless he is capable and his boat fit for the job, as his negligence may be paid for by other men's lives. I have always felt strongly about this, and yet here I was, possibly in trouble which I could have coped with myself if my medical stores had been properly thought out. I did not feel very proud of myself.

On March 9th, after a couple of days of light breezes, the wind suddenly came up strongly from the north. This was the second time *Suhaili* and I had crossed the Equator from south to north and each time the Doldrums have proved untroublesome, largely, I think, because I went as far west as I could. The next evening I sighted a ship coming south. I let the lights get close and then started calling it with the Aldis. After five minutes without response, I lit a hand flare and then continued calling. Still no answer. I was beginning to think I had run into the *Flying Dutchman* and was about to give up when I realized that if I did have appendicitis this might be the last opportunity I would have to save my life, so I brought out a distress rocket and set it off.

The result was most spectacular; the whole sky was lit up by the blue flare which drifted slowly down on its parachute, burning brightly for about three minutes. I waited half a minute and then called the ship on the Aldis again. This time, after a minute or so, I got a flicker in acknowledgement and my hopes rose. I was all right, I could reassure my family with the news that I was still alive. Even more important for the present, I could ask for someone to keep in contact with me. I started calling the ship in the usual way used by Merchant Navies the world over but before I had even started sending *Suhaili*'s name he had lost interest. I lit another flare but received no response, although I continued to signal until his sternlight disappeared over the horizon. 'The lousy bastard', I wrote in my diary.

It really was quite unforgivable. There is a sacred tradition supported by law as regards distress at sea, that unless you endanger your own ship you will go to the assistance of a ship in distress. There was next to no sea running, the wind was between Force 2 and 3, but this ship had completely ignored my flares and my signals, not even bothering to investigate what in any circumstances were unusual happenings. I only hope that if that ship is ever in trouble her signals are not treated as mine were – although I was not feeling so charitable at the time.

I saw a number of other ships in the ensuing days, two of which came really close, within half a mile, and not one of them answered my signals. This was a shattering revelation to me. I was trained as a merchant seaman to understand that keeping a lookout was the primary duty of the Officer of the Watch when at sea, and that if the Captain ever came on the bridge and saw a ship that you had not observed you were for the high jump. I remember once in the Arabian Sea being occupied working out a sight, during which time I watched ahead but not past the beam. The Captain came out onto the bridge just as a Pakistani destroyer, unseen by me, roared up from astern. I got the rocket of my life, and rightly so. It did not matter that in the circumstances the destroyer was bound to give way to us; something could have gone wrong, and I was on the bridge to keep a lookout for just that. It was a lesson I have never forgotten, and a few years later when I was Master of a coaster in South Africa I gave the second mate a bawling out for sitting in the wheelhouse chair whilst on watch because he could not keep a proper lookout from there. Now I was seeing the other side of the coin, and learning what it was like to be largely dependent on ships' lookouts. I came to the conclusion that you could not depend upon them at all, and that's not a comforting feeling for a singlehander.

After a few more days, the intense stomach pain began to ease off. I kept to my milky diet for a while longer and then cautiously went back to solids.

March 13th, 1969   *Day 273*

There has been no complaint from my stomach for a day or so now, so I think I can, in retrospect, diagnose my trouble as a combination of chronic indigestion and acute imagination, and it shows the dangers of giving a layman a medical book! I still have the indigestion and I'll be glad to get onto fresh food again, although apart from that there is nothing wrong with me. Five to six weeks to go with any luck.

I think now that the real trouble was the bully beef, which had started going off. The tins were sound but the considerable changes in temperature that they had experienced must have affected the contents. Anyway, I left bully beef out of my menus for three weeks and had little further trouble.

It took thirteen days to get through the North-East Trades. Once again there was little steering for me to do as *Suhaili* balanced herself well. Coming up from Cape Town before, we had been able to leave the tiller lashed and untended for sixteen days, only keeping a lookout from the hatchway, and we had spent most of our time playing Canasta. It seemed harder work this time as I had to do all the sail tending on my own, but I had learned from my previous experience, and although I was pushed farther west than I would have wished, we made a quicker passage as I allowed the sheets to be slightly looser. The sea itself really posed a greater problem as there was a limit as to the amount of sail I could leave up without having *Suhaili* banged too heavily by the waves.

March 11th, 1969   *Day 271*

I awoke after an excellent night's sleep, full of good intentions. These mainly concerned the charger. However, the wind rising and a disgraceful sea getting up, I had to drop the idea. I really have not done too much today. I made what I consider to be an excellent fish pie – from flying fish I found lying on the deck this morning (I've mastered cheese sauces at last) – despite the boat's crazy motion, and I've done some scribbling, but that's about all.

It has not been an easy day though, on account of a confused sea on top of a heavy N.E. swell. It made me giddy watching it and this a very unusual. We've been ploughing under a great deal and the lower fathom of the jib is permanently wet. Despite this I have kept sail pressed on her, apart from a couple of turns on the mizzen for a short time, and the reward was 125 miles run to noon, which I am jubilant over. This is close-hauled and on a nasty sea. We covered 1½ degrees of latitude which is how I am measuring progress at present, and this is half a degree more than expected. I have changed charts and at last can see Britain. She is taking water a bit, but it is only to be expected when pushed like this. I'm not bothered as long as she doesn't strain herself. The worst bangs are, in fact, from beam seas breaking against the side, although on one or two occasions our motion has been like an elevator falling in its shaft without a brake to check the bang at the bottom.

The urge to smoke has not really bothered me. Quite often during the day I say I could do with a cigarette but it has not become an overpowering obsession. It's like steak; I can't have it at present and that's that.

On March 17th I celebrated my thirtieth birthday. The temptation to philosophize in my diary upon passing this milestone was irresistible:

March 17th, 1969   *Day 277*
Firstly all those sevens are obviously propitious, but I still doubt if we can get home by April 17th as I had hoped. I'm feeling very lethargic. Quite frankly I think I have been on my own long enough and am getting stale. I need something to break the monotony, and getting home is the best cure I can think of. After finding our noon position, the big time of the day is 2100 when I listen to the B.B.C. News. I occasionally scribble a bit, thinking ahead to the book I shall have to buckle down to when I get home, and over the last few days I have described the business in the Foveaux Strait and off Otago. It won't do for the book as it stands, but it's still fresh in my mind now.

It does not depress me that this decade is past. I have enjoyed it and managed to do more than most people. Certainly I do not regret a day of it, although perhaps I would like to mark time at this stage for a few years. There seems to be so much left to do in life and I'm itching to get on with something new. This voyage is about played out as far as I'm concerned. Barring accidents we'll be home in a month and that will be an anti-climax for me, however the race has turned out.

It's rather depressing to think that in another ten years I shall be forty, which seems middle-aged from my present position; however, I can remember feeling the same about thirty, ten years ago. I think this is an ideal age actually, young and fit enough for sports, and yet with ten years of adult experience behind one. (I hope in ten years time I am as content.) Perhaps the most interesting thing that has occurred in the past ten years is the change of outlook of people. When I was twenty I had difficulty in identifying with people of thirty, and yet before I sailed I found I could identify more easily with people of twenty than those of forty. These are generalizations, but I wonder why this is. I suppose better education is the answer.

Now that I have got over my indigestion, apart from a recurrence today as a result of cooking a mixed grill for a celebration lunch, I feel well, but I have noticed that my fingers are becoming less sensitive. The other day when the deck bolt on the starboard runner sheared, I had to rig a tackle on the runner. I transferred a shackle pin from my left to right hand, and despite directions to the contrary, the pin slipped from the hand and fell overside. I was angry about this at the time as I am running short of shackles now and cannot afford to lose any more.

I called Dick [my brother in the Royal Signals in Germany]; we had arranged this schedule before I sailed; on 16 Mc/s at 1300 and 1400 G.M.T. as arranged, but could hear nothing except Latin American stations in reply.

Tried to set the Big Fellow today. Each time it twisted up into a ball, and on the last occasion managed to wrap itself round the forestay which took some sorting out. As usual it was torn when I took it in so that is that until I get some repairs done.

Usually on the run north in the North-East Trades, one finds the winds veering round towards the east the farther north one gets. For some reason the winds decided not to co-operate with me, or so it seemed at the time, and continued to blow from north of north-east. Then when they at last began to veer, they dropped strength; we had reached the Horse Latitudes. To put it mildly, this was frustrating. The Horse Latitudes usually commence about twenty to twenty-three degrees north of the Equator; we ran into them at 18° North, about level with the Cape Verde Islands. By this time I had come to consider any light winds from an awkward direction a personal insult, deliberately designed to hold me up, and the only way I could let off steam was by swimming until I exhausted myself and then trying to find an absorbing job to keep me occupied. It may seem incredible that I got out paint and grease and began to overhaul all the rigging screws, deliberately putting new servings on the threads and the splices, but I did it to stop the feeling of helplessness that would have built up otherwise.

March 23rd, 1969   *Day 283*
Oh God, this is hopeless. 67 miles to noon and we are still heading N.W., the best I can manage with a N.N.E. wind, a heavy northerly swell, and northerly, N.E. and easterly seas. I feel bloody dispirited. I can do no more than we are doing in these conditions. Despite the good conditions yesterday we in fact made less northing than when we were all but becalmed. What the hell can I do? This is what gets me, the answer is absolutely nothing, but sit and hope for more average conditions.

Yet, as usual in the Variables, the weather could change suddenly:

March 25th, 1969   *Day 285*
Well, today beats everything. It got up to a full gale by lunchtime and I've spent most of my time reducing sail. I raced as long as I dared, feeling that if it's going to blow a gale from the S.S.E. I might as well take full advantage of it, but the seas were confused and I had to ease her to stop the pounding. By 2000 it was Force 9.
I don't mind gales in this weather; at least it's warm.

Our position at this time was approximately 24° North, 41° West and we were beginning to meet small clumps of Sargasso weed floating on the surface. When at school, collecting cigarette cards, I remember seeing on one of them a picture of a Spanish Galleon covered with long, trailing tentacles of weed in the Sargasso Sea. Columbus was the first to sight the Sea, and the seamen of the day were convinced that they were on the border of a vast malignant ocean of weed, that would trap their ships and keep them there until they starved or were killed by the primeval sea-monsters that lurked there. The thought of this picture fascinated me for years, and I visualized a vast number of nautical antiques just waiting to be collected by an enterprising adventurer.

The reality was disappointing. If you take a tea tray and drop five grains of rice onto it you will have an idea of the proportion of weed to water in the Sargasso Sea. The weed is broken off the coasts of the Caribbean by storms and is carried into the Sargasso Sea by the Gulf Stream. It propagates by fragmentation. It grows on the surface of the sea and only in a few tangled clumps does it go deeper than nine inches. The fascinating thing about the weed is the life it supports, most of which is normally found only along the sea coasts. I used to drag clumps of the weed aboard and shake out the small yellow crabs and shrimps that hide in the leaves, always hoping that I might find a Sargasso fish, a small, cleverly disguised fish found only amongst this weed. I have yet to find one, but on one occasion as I was picking over a lump of weed, an eel or snake about five inches long sprang clear and shot off very quickly with a jerky, sinuous movement. It had the same dull yellow colour as the weed, but moved too quickly for me to get a close look. I tried to find some reference to this creature in the books I carried with me, but there was no mention of it. As all sea snakes are venomous I was rather careful how I picked weed out of the water after that; I did not want to take any unnecessary risks even with what appeared to be a small edition of something. But I collected about sixteen crabs and rather more shrimps and periwinkles and put them with some of the weed in a perspex box aquarium that I made. The crabs' favourite food appeared to be tinned sardines, so from then on these figured prominently on my menus. I also tried bully beef but their opinion of it seemed to coincide with my own. The fatality rate was high amongst my passengers, and every day

I had to pick out and bury a few corpses. The most robust crab hung on until four days from Falmouth, by which time I think the water had become a bit too cold – or he had become allergic to sardines.

The Variable winds in the Horse Latitudes nearly drove me round the bend. It was hopeless trying to leave the tiller un-tended as *Suhaili* would yaw and gybe so I had to steer the whole time, discontentedly watching pieces of weed drifting slowly past. When I grew tired in the evenings I would leave the tiller lashed, but I generally had to get up three or four times during the night to gybe back onto course, or as on this occasion:

March 29th, 1969   *Day 289*

Awoke for the news at 0200 G.M.T. Ike is dead. Well, he has been ill for a long time now and has been fading recently, but I still have a slight feeling of personal loss. I can still remember the excitement when we went back into France in 1944 and although, of course, Monty was 'our man', he had to share the honours with Ike. It is never pleasant for a proud nation to have to admit it is no longer the biggest power and to place its armies under a foreign leader; few men could have handled the situation with such tact and under-standing.

The only break in the monotony of the days was when we crossed a shipping lane, as apart from the hope of sighting a ship and getting a report through, the lane was usually well marked with rubbish such as bottles, dunnage, and even hatch-boards, that littered the sea. Some of this rubbish is a real threat to a small boat. A hatchboard may weigh as much as a person and they are bound at either end with heavy metal bonds. If a boat hits one of these when travelling at speed the hull could easily be stove in. Even more menacing farther north are the pitprops that litter the sea lanes. *Suhaili* might have survived a collision with one of these but she is much more strongly built than the ordinary boat. A fibreglass or plywood hull would not stand a chance.

On April 2nd, at 2 p.m., when about six hundred miles south-west of the Azores, we sighted a Norwegian cargo vessel ahead and immediately hoisted *Suhaili's* signal letters and *MIK*, the International Code for 'Please report me by radio to Lloyd's, London.' As the ship came closer I got out the rifle and fired three shots into the air. When it was a mile away and through binoculars I could see no one on the bridge, I fired two more rounds. We passed about 150 yards apart, close enough for me to read the name and home port, Tonsberg, but it was not until we were abreast the bridge that the O.O.W. appeared to take a lookout. By the time he had found his binoculars he had moved past and he did not bother to turn and answer my signal lamp. You can take as many precautions as you like, have the brightest lights and the biggest radar reflector ever made, but if the O.O.W. is not doing his job, you've had it.

Four days later, after drifting with still only occasional bursts of wind from the south-west, we crossed another shipping lane; a busy one as there were ships in sight all afternoon. I spent the whole time trying to signal them but all ignored me until the B.P. tanker *Mobil Acme* appeared. I quote the conversation from my signal logbook:

Sent: British *Suhaili*. Round the world non-stop.
Received: Please repeat name.
Sent: *Suhaili*. Please report me to Lloyd's.
Received: Will do. Good luck.
Sent: E.T.A. Falmouth two weeks.
Received: R[oger].

I was jubilant. At last after four months I had managed to get a report through. I started to imagine the effect at home and at the *Sunday Mirror* when the news got through. I knew that my family would not have given up hope for me; I had pictured my father shifting a pin on the chart in the hall and telling everyone quite categorically where I was within a couple of days. I did not know then that Bruce had already been out in the Azores helping to organize a close lookout for me by the American, Canadian and Portuguese Air Force units there, and by the local fishing fleets; although on occasions I heard aircraft, I did not see any until I was nearly in British waters.

Later that night I switched on the radio for the B.B.C. News, thinking that there might be a mention which would confirm that I had been reported, but there was no comment. I began to think that perhaps the *Mobil Acme* had not reported me after all, although of course it was quite on the cards that Moitessier had already arrived and there was little interest in those who followed him.

In fact, the *Mobil Acme* must have cabled London immediately, as within two-and-a-half hours of the sighting, Lloyd's had phoned my family and told them that I had been sighted off the Azores. This was highly efficient work on everyone's part and brought an end to the anxious waiting at home. What pleased me was that I later heard that the *Mobil Acme* had added to their message to Lloyd's, 'Standard of signalling excellent.' This helped reassure people that I had not gone barmy and was also, from a professional point of view, a pretty compliment. I can say the same for the officer on the bridge of the *Mobil Acme* at the time, but then of course we probably went to the same signal school down London's Commercial Road.

We were due west of the Azores with 1,200 miles to go to Falmouth when we met the *Mobil Acme*. If the prevailing westerly winds held we should have had no trouble reaching Falmouth in two weeks. But that very night the wind swung round to the north and there it stayed for the next forty-eight hours, keeping us down to 89 and then 79 miles in the day's runs. The excitement of meeting the *Mobil Acme* and the thought that I was so close to home had led me into the yachtsman's trap of calculating an E.T.A. based on the last good run, but the unfavourable winds and apparent silence of the B.B.C. combined to bring about a feeling of anti-climax.

April 7th, 1969   *Day 298*
Up at 0400 when the wind arose from the S.W. I took a reef to ease her and help her reach, and went back to bed for a couple of hours. Steered all day.

I saw land to the S.E. during the early part of the morning. It faded as soon as the sun got high. This will be Corvo and Flores – 'where Sir Richard Grenville lay!' My sights put us 30 or so miles off at noon and I steered a course to pass well to the north. I'll visit the scene of the battle some other time.

The glass is dropping and as the wind is now S.W., we can expect a cold front and northerly winds shortly. I am heading *Suhaili* well north at present in order to gain sea room, as if we get a bad blow I'll have to run like last time we passed here, and I want as much room between me and the islands for this as possible. We're reefed down at present and running with a bias to port. Going comfortably at about 4 knots. I would steer her but I cannot see any stars and I have a shocking headache; anyway she is doing very well by herself at present.

This headache developed and I was sick the next day, probably due to food poisoning; anyway I did not eat anything for a day and felt better for my fast.

This good burst of south-westerly winds gave us a nice push homeward, but on April 11th, after three days and 359 miles, they eased.

Great, it's 2200. We are completely becalmed and there are ships all around so I dare not sleep – not that I could with the booms banging as they are. I feel completely licked. I don't think, even in the Variables, I have felt so low the whole voyage. Just sitting here, unable to do anything. There is some malignant being watching over me which takes a delight in playing with my hopes and frustrating my wishes.

This was heartbreaking; so close to home, as far as I knew unreported and unable to make radio contact to report myself, and now the winds had deserted me. But the next day, Saturday, April 12th, another sighting broke my solitude at last. From then on I found myself thinking of myself as a sailor rather than a sea creature. The spell which when I had rounded the Horn had made me want to sail on was finally broken. The sea was not now my environment but an obstacle between me and home. I suddenly wanted to see my own people and my own country – and the sooner the better.

I was sitting quietly in the cockpit repairing some flags when a ship came up over the horizon astern. I rushed to hoist my signal letters and got out the Aldis, but although she came close enough for me to read her name, *Mungo* of Le Havre, she motored by before I could finish signalling a message.

April 12th, 1969   *Day 303*

I took down the flags and began to do a few repairs when about five minutes later I looked up and saw the ship returning. This was very unusual and rather encouraging and when he started signalling my hopes rose. I received: 'What do you want?', and sent that 'I am non-stop round the world reported missing.' They asked what name and when I told them they began to wave so I knew I was recognized. I was by this time signalling with the fog horn and I sent R.T. 2182. This was acknowledged and I switched on the radio. For an agonizing minute the transmitter refused to work, but then we were through.

Now the news. Moitessier is apparently going round for a second time. I am thought to be 'Le Premier' and was reported missing some time ago. I asked him to send a message to Cliff Pearson [of the *Sunday Mirror*] for me and he agreed and when I told him to send the account to Marconi's he laughed and told me there would be no charge for this sort of message. I think at one point he doubted if I really was not a hoaxer and he asked my name and when I told him I heard him say 'Yes, that's right'. We spoke in a mixture of English and French. I was pretty excited at the thought of getting a message home at last and my English was scarcely coherent, so I don't know how he understood my French.

He asked me if I wanted a position and I told him I was in approximately 44°30′N, 22°00′W. He said I was exactly 44°25′N, 21°58′W. Any seaman will agree that as I had not yet got my Meridian Altitude I was pretty close. It's reassuring.

We chatted for a bit. I said I would be glad to get home and he said he could understand that!

At 1630 another French ship appeared, a tanker, *Marriotte*. She came over and gave three blasts which I acknowledged, so it looks as if the news is out. I'm sitting up for the B.B.C. news at present.'

That night, with the bit now well between my teeth, I kept the Big Fellow set, and although the wind died away to a whisper I stayed up with him, steering, and we made 98 miles to noon on Sunday, April 13th.

Suhaili in the Variables. A swim for the singlehander can be defined as the time when he is most likely to discover how well his self-steering arrangements are working

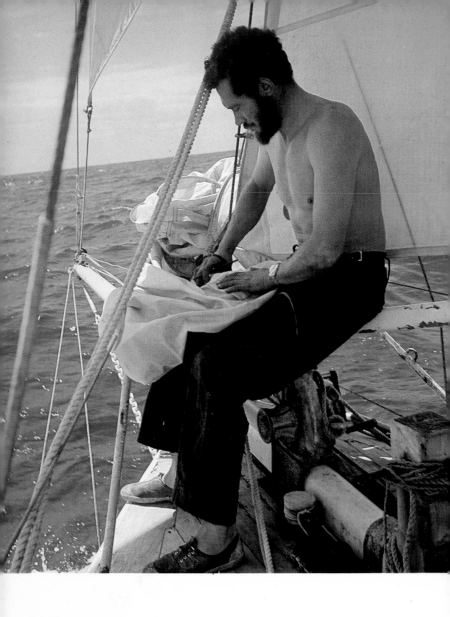

Repairing the jib

Sargasso weed

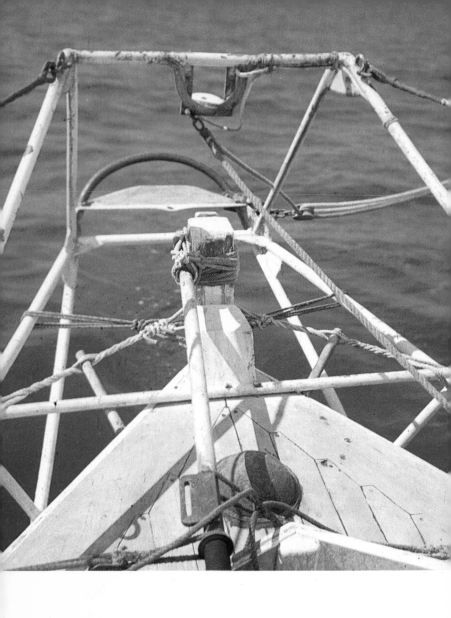

The tiller lashed to the rudder head, an arrangement which served us from Australia to Falmouth. The lashings between the rudder head and the 'pushpit' were to reduce wear on the pintles

Fathomer, our 'Good Shepherd' came roaring down the sloping seas towards us, with the Supporters Club waving wildly from her foredeck

Overleaf: We would have an early morning chorus from *Pirates* ▶
or *Pinafore* . . .

'Where from ?' asked the Falmouth Customs.
'Falmouth', I replied

That evening, I switched on the radio for the B.B.C's 6 p.m. News and when it was over spun the dial through the frequencies as usual. I picked up the G.P.O. High Frequency station at Baldock and decided to give him a shout. This had been a pretty fruitless exercise for three months, but my luck had changed at last and to my delight my call was immediately acknowledged. This was wonderful and after we had chatted for a bit the operator asked if I wanted to speak to anyone by phone. I asked for my home number. Mike answered and I'm told that he nearly went through the roof. Father was out, so I then spoke to Mother and Diana. The Chief Engineer in charge at Baldock, Mr Johnston, has since very kindly presented me with a tape of the conversation. It sounds a pretty exciting moment, as indeed it was, but the best news was that all the family were well. It is often forgotten that the worrying is not only confined to those left at home. I had had no news of my family for five months and I had had plenty of time to think of them.

Mike confirmed that Moitessier in *Joshua* had sailed on round the Cape of Good Hope and into the Indian Ocean, and I was able to discard the unworthy thought that the *Mungo* might have been misleading me and that Moitessier was right on my heels. Certainly I had expected him to be close and the Indian Ocean was the last place where I imagined he would be; as we now know, Moitessier eventually sailed on into the Pacific, where after 307 days at sea, he dropped anchor in Tahiti. So of the nine who had set out, only three of us were left, all British, which I thought to be a Good Thing.

Nigel Tetley in his trimaran *Victress* was off the coast of Brazil and Donald Crowhurst in *Teignmouth Electron*, the other trimaran, was thought to have just rounded the Horn. Mike also told me that Mother and Father and Diana would be coming out from the Scilly Isles in *The Queen of the Isles*, and that Ken, Bruce and Bill would be coming out in Guy Crossley-Meates's ex-air-sea-rescue launch, *Fathomer*, from Falmouth, where they had already installed themselves in the Marine Hotel. I only hoped that Bob and Di had remembered the specific details of my postcard booking from Australia and were keeping the best room for me! The rest of the family was already moving in on Falmouth, so it looked as if we were going to have quite a party.

Just the same, when I had finished writing up my diary, I got out the whisky bottle. Barring last minute accidents, *Suhaili* was going to be the first boat ever to sail round the world non-stop and I went on deck and poured a dram over her stern. As an afterthought I sacrificed another dram as a libation to Shony, one of the old British Gods of the Sea, before I took a good long swig myself. In the circumstances I thought he would have approved, but for the next two days my diary contains only 'Steered all day' and 'Steered all day, but it's getting very calm.'

On the following day, Wednesday, April 16th, I got through to Cliff Pearson at the *Sunday Mirror* and told him that I just might arrive in Falmouth on Sunday, April 20th, but as I was almost becalmed even while I spoke to him, it was very difficult to be more definite. Cliff told me that the Supporters Club in *Fathomer* intended to make contact on the Friday or at dawn on Saturday. He asked me to give any future positions in the code Bruce and I had worked out before I sailed and which had been approved by the G.P.O. The *Sunday Mirror*, as one of the sponsors for my voyage, naturally wanted as much exclusive copy on my return as they could get and they thoroughly deserved it. But already, Cliff told me, other newspaper boats were in the Scillies watching *Fathomer*'s every move. From my vantage point it all sounded good fun, and I wished I was a hound rather than the hare. I arranged to make a contact with Bruce on the Saturday morning and signed off.

With all these carefully laid plans on the boil, the wind dropped completely, and at the same time my long suffering battery charger gave up the ghost, which put me in a spot as my batteries were no longer taking a full charge and would not last for long. Once again I started to take the charger to pieces, but with the Big Fellow, staysail, main and mizzen set in the light airs, *Suhaili* needed my constant attention, and in the event I never was able to fix it. On Friday the batteries were further drained when I received a message via Land's End Radio from B.I. and spoke to George Martin of the *Sunday Mirror* in London.

April 18th, 1969   *Day 309*

George told me to watch out for a Beechcraft G–ASDO, which
might be out looking for me. He also said *Fathomer* was being
'tagged' – real cloak and dagger stuff this – most enjoyable!

I am a little worried about my position as I did not get good
sights today and I met a whole crowd of trawlers just before noon.
These would, I think, be on the 100 fathoms line which, according
to my sights, we were 30 miles short of at noon. There are some
humps so maybe that's where they are, but I'd like to get stars
tonight if the sky clears. 280 miles to Falmouth at noon. . . .

It's 1830 and a most remarkable thing has happened. I was
sitting on the containers reading *Timon of Athens* when I heard a
scuffling in the starboard bunk and there, in the medical box, was
a small grey bird with a slender pointed beak. It was the size of a
wren. I have let it out.

That evening we were getting up amongst shipping and I
could see navigation lights all round so I did not like to sleep; I
kept watch from the cockpit, fortifying myself with coffee laced
with whisky. Shortly after midnight a well-lit ship that had
been overtaking, slowed down astern of us and appeared to be
taking up station half a mile away. At the same time I noticed a
smaller boat which I had assumed to be a fisherman coming in
fast and taking up station. After watching both rather anxiously
for some time, I decided to challenge the larger with the
Aldis lamp. Back came the reply: '*Queen of the Isles*'. They
closed in with flash bulbs popping and I was able to speak
directly to Mother and Father for the first time for 309 days.
It was a wonderful moment, but conversation was difficult
in the rising wind and sea, and all too soon I had to give up
trying to make myself heard and concentrate on reducing sail.
The smaller boat closed soon afterwards and identified herself
as *Fathomer*. They then stood off for the night, and with two
watchdogs on guard I felt it safe to turn in.

When I awoke the next morning there was nothing in sight.
My watchdogs had lost me. Visibility was down to two miles
and the wind was up to Force 7. At 0815 I switched on the
radio and made immediate contact with Bruce; he asked me
'Where the hell' I was and I had to reply that I did not really

know. I could almost hear him groan at this but there was nothing we could do about it. The sun was hidden and I could not get a sight. By 1000 the wind had risen to Force 8 from the south-east and rather than strain *Suhaili* this close to home, I handed all sail, streamed the warp and hove-to. I spent the next two hours standing in the hatchway keeping a lookout for boats and hoping for a glimpse of the sun, which eventually rewarded me just before noon. I took a sight and worked out our latitude and radioed it out to Bruce. By this time all the newspapers were working together trying to locate us and it did not matter if anyone else knew my position.

I was tired and depressed. There was nothing I could do until the wind changed or eased and I turned in. This was the limit; to come this far and then get a contrary gale just when I could almost smell home, was too much. I did not sleep for long though. At 2.30 p.m. I drifted awake to the sound of a siren. I leapt out of my bunk, imagining some vessel bearing down on us, but the sound came from the *Queen of the Isles*. I waved to my parents and then looked around at the sea. Whether it was because I had had a rest or because there was a ship close up I don't know, but the wind and sea seemed to have eased, and rather shamefacedly I went about setting some sail and getting in the warp. *Fathomer* appeared just as I got under way again, riding the sloping seas incredibly comfortably for such a small boat. As she closed I picked out Ken, Bruce and Bill waving wildly on her foredeck, Bill, as usual, covered in cameras.

Apparently the three of them had been discussing the best way to handle this meeting. From my radio messages they assumed that I was still perfectly sane but they were a little concerned that after all these months of solitude I might be under some tension at the prospect of getting amongst people again, for they had a better idea than I did of the plans that were being made to greet me in Falmouth. They agreed not to say anything to me until I had spoken and they had had a chance to gauge my reactions. For my part I was waiting for them to speak first. The boats closed to within fifteen yards as we grinned owlishly at each other, and Ken later swore that I then ruined a Moment in History when I at last shouted to him, 'I see you're still wearing that same bloody silly hat!' He promptly took it off and flung it into the Atlantic.

Fathomer and *Queen of the Isles* kept station with me all Saturday night. Following the gale the wind stayed stubbornly in the south-east, and as we would be pushed north towards the Bristol Channel if we stayed on the starboard tack, I went about and stood south. It seemed that the wind and weather were determined to give the lie to any E.T.A. I gave Cliff Pearson in Falmouth, but as before I sailed I had given April 14th as the date round about which I expected to be home and I was only six days out in my reckoning now, I did not think he would complain if a couple more went astray.

At 7.15 on Sunday morning I tacked round and headed north-east towards Land's End, 150 miles away. After a large plate of porridge I took a sight and shouted my position to Captain Evans of the *Queen of the Isles*, who had done the same thing: although in shouting distance we agreed that in practice we were two miles apart. In the afternoon *Fathomer* shot off for the Scillies to refuel and bring out fresh bread, newspapers and cigarettes for the *Queen*. I had not had a cigarette for over six weeks, and although I certainly felt the better for it and had not really missed them, to talk of them in such casual terms had a far more disturbing effect upon me than I could have imagined. As I drank my after-lunch coffee, I felt an addict's craving coming over me.

With the *Queen of the Isles* acting as my temporary Nanny, I was looking forward to a last good night's sleep before I closed the land. *Suhaili*, with reefs in the main and mizzen to reduce the pounding, was sailing comfortably to the Force 5 south-easterly winds, and with the prospect of some light rain during the night I turned in. I was too excited to sleep, which was just as well, because when I went on deck at 10.30 p.m. with a cup of cocoa, the horizon ahead was dotted with the lights of a French fishing-fleet. From seeing too few ships I was now seeing far too many. Navigating through a fishing fleet at any time is a tricky business, but to do it at night can be positively nerveracking, particularly for a small boat under sail. By the very nature of their work, fishing boats are constantly changing course, and as fast as you work out the course to steer to avoid one vessel, the last one you observed has completely changed its mind and is bearing down on you with every intention of maintaining its legal right of way. Multiply this process by thirty or forty boats and the sea suddenly becomes a very small and dangerous place.

I went about and headed south to try to sail round the fleet, but when a couple of hours later I made up towards Land's End again, they were still square-dancing in my path. At this rate I could have gone on dodging about all night without making any progress at all, so I said 'To hell with it', held my course, and four exhausting hours later found myself in clear water at last. The *Queen of the Isles* had uncomplainingly sat on my tail throughout all these manoeuvres, and although she received greater respect from the fishermen because of her size, she was as relieved as I to be clear of them.

At 5 a.m. on Monday, April 21st, the wind went round to the south-west, and leaving *Suhaili* running under reefed main, heading at last for the Lizard, I turned in.

I was up again in three hours. *Suhaili* had followed the wind as it backed slightly, so I had to gybe again to be sure of clearing Bishop's Rock off the Scillies, and Land's End. I also wanted to keep well clear of the strong tidal stream that runs between the two. At 1135 I picked up Bishop's Rock lighthouse, bearing 100° True, my first sight of home for 312 days. I suppose that seeing the slim silhouette of the Bishop on the horizon should have been an emotional moment. Over the centuries it has been the last and first sight of Britain for generations of seamen, but my recollection is that I noted the sighting in the log simply as a navigational mark. My emotions, more prosaically, were concerned with a pint of beer, a steak, a hot bath and clean white sheets.

Fathomer rejoined at 2 p.m. and took over from the *Queen of the Isles*. As if this were a signal the party started. A couple of helicopters clattered overhead with cameramen hanging crazily out of the open doors, and craft of all shapes and sizes joined us, one of them a tiny red skiboat from St Mary's. He probably had an easier time looking for me than I would have done looking for him, because most of the time he was completely hidden from me by the waves. A Coastal Command Shackleton appeared on the scene and made half a dozen low-level runs over the little convoy, scattering the helicopters out of its path like startled chickens.

Ahead of me I could see the grey shape of a minesweeper closing rapidly over the horizon. This was something I had been waiting for. H.M.S. *Warsash*, an R.N.R. ship, commanded by Lieutenant-Commander T. A. Bell, had been deputed by Rear Admiral B. C. G. Place, V.C., D.S.C., R.N., Admiral Commanding Reserves, to escort me in. This was a wonderful choice of ship in view of my R.N.R. connections, and when I saw her I would not have changed her for a dozen aircraft-carriers. She swept round to my stern keeping properly to leeward, flying *QKF*, the International code for 'Welcome'.

Tom Bell came right in, handling his ship beautifully. There was a cheer from the deck and as I acknowledged it I saw standing amongst the crew my three brothers. We exchanged the usual family ruderies and then *Warsash*, who like her sisters is not designed for slow speed work, pulled off to one side and thereafter kept station ahead of me until I began the run into Falmouth.

That night I advanced the ship's clock for the last time to bring us into British Standard Time. I was pretty well exhausted. I had had little sleep for the past few days, and I knew that the next day, if it was to be my last at sea, would be very tiring. Already my voice was hoarse from three days of shouting messages to other ships, and if one discounts my singing it had probably had as much work in that time as in the previous 308 days.

I turned in at 1000 with Wolf Rock and Tater Du lights in sight, getting up at 3 a.m. on Tuesday morning to gybe round towards the Lizard, which was well in view. By dawn I had passed through the overfalls off the Lizard (to the annoyance of my watchdogs) and with a good westerly was heading up under full sail towards the Manacles buoy. Falmouth was then eight miles away and I could clearly identify Pendennis Point and St Anthony Head, which mark the entrance to the harbour.

The convoy was growing hourly. Off the Manacles we were met by the Falmouth lifeboat and the tug *St Mawes*, both dressed overall and looking as smart as paint. The lifeboatmen were in their full rig of seaboots, oilskins and distinctive red 'cap comforters'. I took an immediate fancy to their headgear and after I got into Falmouth, John Mitchell, the mate of *Fathomer*, presented me with his: it has now become one of my prized pieces of sailing gear.

The *St Mawes* was originally the *Arusha*, a B.I. tug stationed on the East African coast, and for this day the Company had chartered her and put her into her old livery, her black funnel with its distinguishing two white bands gleaming in the early morning sunshine. She bustled in flying an enormous Company house flag and I hoisted my own, together with the burgees of the Ocean Cruising Club and Benfleet Yacht Club, and for good measure I hoisted *Suhaili*'s signal letters *MHYU* on the port yardarm.

On board the *Arusha* I could see Captain Lattin and Captain Ben Rogers, who had been my first captain at sea on the *Chindwara*, and many other familiar faces. The Company had been my home since I left school, I had learned my seamanship in it, and they had given me every possible encouragement in preparing for my voyage. To be greeted like this was wonderful.

I was six miles – less than two hours – off Pendennis Point when at 9 a.m. the wind swung suddenly to the north-north-west and rose sharply. I was forced away to the east, reducing sail progressively as I went and the wind rose to Force 7 and 8. This was when I got really angry. *Suhaili*'s inability to sail close to the wind isn't an unduly worrying factor at sea, but for close work like this it was infuriating.

As I drove to the north-east away from Falmouth and towards Dodman Point, the helicopters and light aircraft which had been fluttering around disappeared. I imagine that with the prospect of a full day's tacking before them, they wisely decided to refuel and leave me with my seaborne escort of yachts and small craft, which stuck gamely and wetly to me for the rest of the day.

At least the wind was offshore and by creeping in towards the land I was able to keep to smoother water and a higher speed. I threw in another tack towards Porthmellon Head and out again to Dodman. It was cold and wet, but nothing was going to stop us now. *Suhaili* and I had been away for 313 days and covered over 30,000 miles together; heaving-to at this stage was unthinkable. Off Dodman we wore round and began the tack towards St Anthony Head. We raced across the harbour entrance until I was clear for the run in. I wore round for what I thought would be the last time, easing the sheets to give us a fast and comfortable finish. As we neared Black Rock, which lies between Pendennis Point and St Anthony Head, there seemed little for me to do except wave to the bustling fleet of small boats that was closing in round us. On Pendennis Point I could see the sunlight reflecting on the lines of parked cars, and on the front, people were waving to us. We were nearly there, and that pint of beer was almost in my hand when the Harbour Master's launch came bursting through the mêlée and I was told that the *Sunday Times* had established the 'finishing line' between Pendennis Point and Black Rock. At that moment another competitor nearly dropped out. I had left Falmouth between Black Rock and St Anthony Head and saw no reason why I should not take the same route coming in, and I said so in terms that were unfortunately picked up by the B.B.C. TV microphones at the time. Nevertheless, showing more forbearance than I usually do, I wore round to make another tack to the west. Half an hour later, at 3.25 p.m. I crossed the finishing line and a cannon fired.

The first people to board were Her Majesty's Customs and Excise officers from Falmouth. As they jumped across, the senior officer, trying to keep a straight face, asked the time-honoured question:

'Where from?'

'Falmouth,' I replied.

Pilot's Notes

This epilogue is not intended as a guide to a sailor wishing to make a similar voyage to my own in the future. It is merely my own and thus subjective analysis of the voyage in retrospect as I made it, under various headings. I hope, of course, that the text of the book will in itself be of value to yachtsmen and others in making an assessment of my voyage and drawing conclusions from it.

The Boat

Suhaili was not my first choice. I wanted a longer and faster boat, and I found that *Suhaili* was just too short to cope with some of the seas we met, as she fitted exactly between the waves and could not gather way. A few extra feet in length would have made all the difference.

Apart from this, *Suhaili* was an ideal boat for the voyage. Being pointed at both ends I had a choice as to how I could heave to, either bow or stern on. The fact that we were pooped only three times, none really seriously, points to the advantages of a pointed stern when running. The waves could get no purchase to push the boat, which is what frequently leads to broaching, but broke harmlessly down each side.

Suhaili is very similar to the Colin Archer design of boats, using the waveform principle in her lines, in that the waveform created by the boat's passage through the water coincides with the waveform of the sea. With her 3 to 1 length to breadth ratio,

Suhaili could not be expected to move as fast as the modern ocean cruising craft of the same length, but she is far more sea-kindly than these, and although it would have been nice to have had a faster boat, for a voyage in the Southern Ocean it is safety and not out-and-out speed that counts.

The rather high cabin gave trouble; it was too exposed and it is not surprising that it was shifted by the waves off the Cape of Good Hope. Stronger fastenings are probably the simple short-term answer here.

I was worried that the two rudders hanging exposed over the stern would receive damage from the waves, but although the tiller bar leapt in my hand on one or two occasions, especially in a cross sea, the main rudder stood up to the waves very well. My only real fear was that the pintles would wear through before I finished the voyage.

The hull was basically very strong indeed, the only point of weakness being the floors which, built to Indian standards, were not as strong as those we are accustomed to putting in boats for use in the rougher conditions around Europe. The only strain to the hull was caused by the floors beginning to give, which showed when *Suhaili* came out of the water at the end of the voyage.

The cockpit was a bit exposed at times. I did have canvas dodgers but I never rigged them as they got in my way. However, it was never the cold and wet that drove me from the tiller, but tiredness.

Suhaili was very cramped below, and it was difficult for me to leave everything I might want in a hurry where I could lay my hands on it immediately. There is no way out of this in a small boat.

Rough weather. I nearly lost *Suhaili* in the Southern Ocean because I was handling her badly. I had always left her beam-on to the seas before, in gales, but the size of the seas in the Southern Ocean were such that *Suhaili* was being battered to breaking-up point. I found that by streaming a warp as a bight, with both ends made fast to the kingpost forward and leading down on either side of the boat and out astern, and then setting the 40 sq. ft. storm jib with both sheets tight so that it was held hard amidships, *Suhaili* would lie very comfortably stern to wind. To start with I streamed a full 100 fathom coil of 2-inch polypropylene rope, but later I used to reduce this slightly, depending on the state of the sea, when I wanted to move the boat to leeward. She drifted to leeward slowly with this system but was never subjected to jerking even when riding over the steepest waves. The stretch in the rope provided sufficient give to prevent the waves smashing into the boat. I found the foredeck dry in a Force 10 on one occasion when hove-to like this, and the waves never pooped her.

I came to the conclusion that a sea anchor was of little value in these conditions; a warp was far more effective and less trouble.

Navigation. The basic navigation problem on this voyage was different from the usual in that I had plenty of sea room and it did not matter too much if I was pushed off course. I was usually aiming roughly for a point thousands of miles away, and a day's run of 100 miles at right angles to my track made a degree difference in my compass course. The errors I made were in misjudging the weather belts. For instance I think I lost one to two weeks in the South Atlantic on the outward leg by heading towards the Cape of Good Hope too early. I should have stood south until I met the westerly winds in the Roaring Forties and then turned eastwards.

Again it would have been a lot quicker if I had headed to the south of Tasmania instead of going up into the Australian Bight where I was becalmed. Admittedly I deliberately went north in order to sight a ship and get word through that I was all right after my wireless blackout, but it would have been better if Bruce and I had planned Hobart in Tasmania as a rendezvous. Finally, and my most serious error, I should not have allowed the south-east winds which we met after leaving New Zealand to push us so far north. I think I got caught in an easterly air stream, and if I had headed south early on I would have met westerlies and made a much quicker passage to Cape Horn. In all, these errors cost me between three weeks and a month.

The only action I can think of on the credit side was heading farther east then the usual sailing ship routes just before crossing the Equator on the way out. I probably gained four days through this; but it was a gamble and I could easily have been becalmed and lost a lot of time.

The charts I took were sufficient as I did not plan to put in anywhere, but the Admiralty ice chart would have been a useful addition. A larger-scale chart of Foveaux Strait would have been useful as things turned out and since I planned to go through there from the start I should have taken one. I had more charts than I needed for Cape Horn, but better safe than sorry. In retrospect, a large-scale chart of Otago Harbour might also have saved me from some embarrassment!

For fixing my position at sea out of sight of land I used my ageing Plath sextant, and an old but reliable chronometer. I gave up using my patent log with its 100 foot log line as it proved inaccurate, and once the log line became covered with gooseneck barnacles it was nothing but a drag to our progress. I had no electronic navigational aids because I could not afford them before I set out, but a Direction Finder and Echo Sounder would have been useful. As a general rule I took one sight only at a time instead of the more usual three from which you can get an average position, but I took some care over this one. My reasoning was that as it took me well over a minute to get below, take the chronometer time, write down the readings and scramble back on deck, an average of sights taken over a period of 2 to 3 minutes would be of little greater use than one sight taken with care. As a rule I took one sight early in the morning to obtain the longitude, and the Meridian Altitude at noon for the latitude. If approaching land I would take another sight in the afternoon, and although I was always prepared to take star sights I never found it necessary. On the occasions I managed to check my navigation I was usually within a mile or so of where I expected.

As far as Pilots, Tide Tables and Light lists are concerned, I had all I wanted.

Sails, Ropes and Rigging. All my sails were terylene apart from the nylon spinnaker. The advantage of using synthetic sailcloth is that it does not rot and weight for weight it is much stronger and not so easy to tear. Against this must be weighed the stitching of terylene. In the older materials such as cotton or canvas the stitching will bed into the material, whereas in terylene the stitching remains proud and chafes easily. I spent more time repairing sails on the homeward run than on any other form of maintenance. For all this, I doubt if natural fibre sails would have lasted the voyage, and apart from the mainsail which split and the jib that broke loose, the sails I took lasted well. I had my mainsails and mizzens fitted with reefing points in case the mechanical roller reefing packed up – which it did.

All the running rigging, where I could not use wire, was nylon, terylene or polypropylene. Size for size these materials are stronger and more durable than natural fibres and they are also rot-proof. All the ropes that had to be replaced were 'left-overs' from the previous voyage.

The standing rigging of plough wire, 1 inch circumference 6×7 construction for all except the four lower shrouds on each mast, which were $1\frac{1}{2}$ inches circumference, were protected by a mixture of tallow and white lead. None of these wires broke.

Halyard winches. Both halyard winches on the mainmast were unreliable because the band brakes slipped. As a result both mainsail and 'Big Fellow' collapsed on me more than once, and when winching up there were occasions when the handle whipped back and gave me some bad knocks. In my opinion the brakes were not made strongly enough and although I stripped them frequently to tighten the band, it soon loosened again. Before long I took to leaving the handle on the winch and lashing it rather than risking brake slip.

Engine. This seized up entirely through my own negligence. Since returning from the voyage I have fitted a new engine of the same make. Any engine needs to be turned regularly just to lubricate the parts. This I failed to do with the result that the inevitable condensation within the engine caused rust.

Radio. The Marconi Kestrel range are quite expensive, but you get what you pay for, and once I had located the fault after the Cape Town affair, the radio worked perfectly. I very much doubt that other radios would have withstood the punishment mine took and still functioned.

The *Kestrel II* usually covers transmitting frequencies in the 2, 4, 8 and 12 megacycle bands, and has a power output of 50 watts. The set I took was given an additional frequency in the 6 megacycle band for use round Australia, and was specially adapted to transmit on the 16 megacycle band with a power output on 75 watts. Generally, the higher the frequency used the greater the transmitting range, and I had good circuits with Cape Town at ranges exceeding 3,000 miles. The power for the set came from four 6-volt car batteries.

The receiver, which would pick up all transmissions up to 4 megacycles, and then chosen frequencies up to the 17 megacycle band, worked excellently throughout the voyage.

I found that the permanent backstays, suitably fitted with compression insulators, made an effective and convenient aerial.

The problem of using a low-powered set at great ranges is that you are competing with the much more powerful sets fitted in merchant vessels. In addition, if a merchant ship is unable to make radio telephone contact, it can always book a call using wireless telegraphy (Morse). The only effective way of making a contact with a low-powered set is to book the schedules before starting the voyage. My schedules were made with the G.P.O. station at Baldock before I set out, and after I had moved beyond their range, they handed me over to Cape Town. Had the transmitter continued to function, Cape Town would in turn have handed me on to Perth in Western Australia and so on round the world. On the homeward run, my set was just not powerful enough to break in unscheduled to the shore stations.

A radio receiver of some sort is of course essential on ocean voyaging in order to obtain time signals for navigational purposes, but this can be done quite adequately with a small transistor radio. *The Admiralty Volume of Radio Signals Volume V* contains the frequencies and times of all the world stations that transmit time signals.

Charger. Until someone solves the problem of charging batteries from a propeller dragged through the water alongside or behind the boat, there is no alternative to a small internal combustion engine connected to alternators or dynamos (alternators for preference as they will charge at lower revolutions). My arrangement, a 3 h.p. Norton-Villiers petrol engine connected to two dynamos worked very well. The petrol engine gave trouble but it was not designed for use at sea and periodic duckings. It was basically a motor mower engine bought off the shelf.

Lights. For all purposes I relied upon paraffin lanterns or the pressure lamp. The only fault I could find was in the riding lights I hoisted when I turned in at night, which usually blew out if the wind rose above Force 2. Electric lighting would have been excellent but I could never have found room for sufficient petrol to keep the batteries charged to meet the extra load.

Heating. My pressure lamp could be adapted so that it worked as a heater and throughout the passage in the Southern Ocean this was its only use. Apart from the physical comfort the heater gave me, its real value was as a morale booster, and on many occasions I lit it just for its cheerful red glow. I tried to dry clothing with it but it could not compete with the moist atmosphere inside the boat, and the only solution to this would have been a coal fire. But the heater did as much as a paraffin burner could do.

The Admiral. The principle was fine, the real difficulty came in overcoming the inherent friction. Once I had taken a rasp to the nylon bearings for the vane stanchions the Admiral was very reliable.

I do not know of an alternative arrangement for a boat with a mizzen boom jutting out astern. The vanes were often immersed when *Suhaili* heeled but provided there was nothing restraining them they came to no damage. The port vane was bent inwards and split because I had the vane lashed in a fore-and-aft line at the time.

The ropes connecting the various parts of the system used to stretch after a time but it was a simple matter to resplice them slightly shorter.

Had the self-steering rudders been stronger, there was no

reason why the Admiral should not have lasted the voyage. The rudder bars used were 1 inch diameter water pipe and they fractured with the strain. A slightly larger tube or a solid rod, say $1\frac{1}{4}$ inches diameter, might have been the answer.

Tool kit. Adequate, but an extra set of metal drills would have been useful.

Stores

Food. If I were to do another voyage like this I would take a much greater variety of food. I relied far too much upon basics like bully beef and tinned vegetables, thinking that as long as I kept myself well fed I would not be too worried about variety. This was a mistake. I got fed up with the run of stews and bully and baked bean salads, and for several months ate less than I ought to have done through sheer lack of interest; I arrived home with sufficient food left on board for about three months because my consumption was less than I expected. There was no excuse for this, because there are plenty of different kinds of foods available in tins, but I just did not have the time to rush about finding what was available. I would make time if I were undertaking such a voyage again.

I soon cut my meals to two a day, breakfast and dinner. Lunch became a cup of coffee and a biscuit. I found that if I ate more I got that rather full feeling. I did not require the extra food for the work I was doing and I derived sufficient energy from just the two meals.

The breakdown of my Primus enforced a natural rationing system upon me. It is worth noting that the standard sets of spares prepared by the manufacturers are for limited replacements and repairs only. I should have worked out my own list of requirements and bought them accordingly.

The tins lasted quite well, but towards the end of the voyage the contents of one in every three opened were bad and had to be discarded. I think this was mainly due to the tins rubbing against each other and removing the varnish coating, but in some cases the tins seemed quite sound but the contents had gone off.

The fresh onions and potatoes I took along went bad within

a couple of months. I took old potatoes and hard, dry Spanish onions, which normally keep well. The problem was to keep these dry and well ventilated; in *Suhaili* I found this impossible.

I took two gross of eggs, individually coated in grease. This worked very well before on the Cape Town–London voyage when none had gone bad, but this time for some reason the eggs started going off within a month. It may be I had a bad batch, but next time I shall try beeswax as a covering instead of grease.

I think one of the ovens that can be placed over a primus would be a good investment. I did not take one because I could not see myself doing any baking, but this again was a mistake, and I could have made bread which would have been an invaluable addition to my diet.

I had Vitamin C tablets, calcium tablets and yeast tablets, which I took regularly. I think that the general good health I maintained throughout the voyage could be due to them. It was particularly noticeable that on this voyage I never came out in the salt-water sores which had plagued us on the previous voyage.

Water. I never used the contents of my fresh water tanks. I started with 15 gallons in polythene containers and kept the supply up by catching rain in a bucket hung from the mizzen gooseneck. But one cannot, of course, rely on rain for fresh water in the Trade Wind belts.

Clothing. Because I was short of space I restricted my outfit to three sets of everything, including wet-weather gear, except that I took six sweaters. There is an old rule for sailing which states that if you think you have enough sweaters, take another. This outfit was quite sufficient, and it would not have mattered how many changes I had in the Southern Ocean as I could not dry things out properly and I would have been reduced to damp clothes in the end. My biggest mistake was not taking along an extra pair of seaboots. The pair I had perished before I reached Australia and from then on I had to put up with wet feet.

Life-saving appliances. I took along a one-man inflatable liferaft equipped with two solar stills and the usual repair and emergency kit. For working on deck I had a safety harness and a 6-foot line which could be clipped on to the rigging, but I seldom used this as I found it a hindrance. However, it should be remembered that I knew the layout of my boat and always work on the principle 'One hand for yourself, one for the ship'; I always make 'new hands' wear a harness.

There was a small 'diver's' lifejacket on board, but again I did not use it. It got in the way for one thing, and if I had fallen overside, although I would have swum in the direction of the nearest land, one has to be realistic, and it would probably have been best to get it over quickly.

Medical. I do not feel qualified to give a list of the items one should take. My medical box had all I needed although perhaps an antibiotic would have been a good idea. *The Ship Captain's Medical Guide* was my Bible as far as illness was concerned, and like all Merchant Navy Officers I hold a St John's Ambulance Brigade First Aid Certificate.

Alcohol. I am by nature a social drinker rather than a drinker, and my supply of alcohol lasted well. I found that for long periods I took no alcohol at all, usually breaking out a bottle or a can only to celebrate a good day's run or a particular milestone. When cold, wet and tired, I have always found that a good hot cup of coffee or cocoa is far more stimulating. Alcohol is, of course, a dehydrant and should be used with great caution. My heaviest consumption was during the passage through the Southern Ocean when I laced my coffee with it.

Tobacco. I could well have done without cigarettes. My consumption before I sailed was between 10 and 15 a day, and dropped to about 11 a day on the voyage. When I at last ran out I did not really miss them and felt a lot better for going without; it is obviously the availability of cigarettes that makes it difficult for the smoker to give up. I started smoking again the moment I returned.

Self

I started the voyage fairly fit but tired from the month and a half slog preparing the boat. Within a couple of days of sailing

I was back into a seagoing routine and quickly losing my shore-side flabbiness. I lost weight on the first part of the voyage as far as I could tell and certainly my legs became a lot thinner, but over the whole voyage I actually put on half a stone in weight. This was mainly in muscle in the shoulders, arms and chest, which all grew during the voyage. My legs became quite weak through lack of proper exercise and I found when I got home that walking a couple of hundred yards was tiring.

If I had had the time before leaving I would have sought advice on a properly planned programme of exercises. Such exercises as I did, like press-ups and knee bends, were hap-hazard and of unknown value, except for my morale.

Apart from the accident with the battery acid, my eyesight gave no problems and appears to be as good now as before I sailed. I never had any problem differentiating between colours. My senses of smell, hearing, taste and touch appear to be similarly unchanged, with the obvious reservation that my hands became less sensitive as the skin thickened.

The speed of my reactions did not change appreciably throughout the voyage, but my mental approach to problems appears to have undergone a fairly marked change. I now like to consider things a bit longer and I think more deeply before coming to a decision. Obviously this comes about as one grows older, but I think the voyage has accelerated the process.

Being able to keep in contact with the outside world was a mixed blessing. I used to get quite excited on the days I was to make a report, but a depressing feeling of anti-climax used to follow when I had signed off. Apart from two months in the Southern Ocean when I was unable to receive any radio stations, I was able to keep up with world news quite well, and I never felt that I was out of touch with events.

No great extremes of heat and cold were met with. The temperature dropped to near freezing point off the Cape of Good Hope and rose to well over 40° Centigrade in the Tropics. Generally, there were no sudden rises and falls in temperature, but I did find it took me some time to adjust to the heat in the Variables in the South Atlantic after five months in the Roaring Forties. I had a mild attack of sunstroke there because I underestimated the sun's heat.

Appendix I

Stores lists

A. FOODSTUFFS ETC.

216 × 12 oz. tins Corned Beef
144 × 1 lb. tins Stewing Steak
48 × 14 oz. tins Stafford Pork
   Sausages
16 × 1 lb. tins Bacon (rashered)

24 × 15 oz. tins Pilchards
24 × ¼'s tins Sardines in Oil

350 lb. Potatoes
250 lb. Onions
12 pkts. Mustard and Cress seed
36 Lemons
24 Oranges

72 tins Green Peas
72 tins Runner Beans
72 × 10 oz. tins Carrots
72 tins Mixed Vegetables
144 × 1 lb. tins Heinz Baked
   Beans
36 pkts. Surprise Peas
36 pkts. Smash Instant Potato

2 × 56 lb. bags Granulated
   Sugar

1 × 25 lb. tins Flour
4 × 7 lb. tins Pinhead Oatmeal
2 × 7 lb. tins Lentils
1 × 56 lb. bag Long Grain Rice
1 × 8 lb. tin Semolina
14 lb. Pearl Barley
7 lb. Dried Yeast

48 × 15¾ oz. tins Heinz
   Spaghetti in Tomato Sauce
12 pkts. Vesta Risotto

6 tins Marvel Instant Milk
216 × 14 oz. tins Condensed
   Milk
48 × 15 oz. tins Butter
12 × 3 lb. tins White Cap
   Cooking Fat
1 × 1 gal. can Saladaise
40 × 12 oz. tins Processed
   Cheese
288 Greased Eggs

24 tins Peaches
24 tins Apricots

2 × 7 lb. tins Dried Currants
3 × 6 lb. tins Dried Sultanas
24 × 8 oz. pkts. Cooking Dates
1 × 7 lb. tin Dried Prunes
1 × 7 lb. tin Dried Apricots
1 × 7 lb. tin Dried Peaches
72 × 19 oz. tins Orange Juice
72 × 19 oz. tins Grapefruit Juice
72 × 19 oz. tins Tomato Juice
1 × 10 lb. tin Lemonade
   Powder
1 × 10 lb. tin Orangeade
   Powder

14 × 1 lb. jars Honey
1 × 2 lb. tin Blackcurrant Jam
1 × 2 lb. tin Plum Jam

1 × 2 lb. tin Strawberry Jam
1 × 2 lb. tin Raspberry Jam
1 × 2 lb. tin Damson Jam

24 × 14 oz. tins Ryvita
2 × 5 lb. tins Assorted Cheese
  Biscuits
10½ lb. Digestive Biscuits
6½ lb. Marie Biscuits
4¼ lb. Lincoln Biscuits

2 lb. Tea
24 × 8 oz. tins Nescafé
12 × 1 lb. tins Bournville
  Cocoa
6 tins Drinking Chocolate
6 × 1 lb. jars Horlicks

288 Oxo Cubes
6 × 1 lb. jars Bovril
6 × 1 lb. jars Barmene

1 × 5 lb. tin Maggi Mushroom
  Soup
1 × 5 lb. tin Maggi Oxtail Soup
1 × 5 lb. tin Maggi Romany
  Soup
1 × 5 lb. tin Maggi Tomato
  Soup
2 doz. pkts. Spring Pea Soup
  Powder

6 × 10 oz. jars Pickled Onions
2 lb. Ground White Pepper
6 × 1½ lb. tins Cerebos Salt
2 × No. 3 bott. Parsley
14 lb. Curry Powder, Bolst's
  Hot
7 lb. Ground Chillies
12 × 7 oz. bott. Chef Tomato
  Sauce
3 × 7 oz. jars Heinz Salad
  Cream
14 lb. Roasted and Salted
  Cashew Nuts
14 lb. Roasted and Salted
  Peanuts

12 × 1 lb. jars Lifeboat Barley
  Sugar

4 × 1 lb. jars Bicarbonate of
  Soda
1,000 Ascorbic Acid Vitamin C
  tablets
900 Yeast tablets
500 Calcium tablets
1,000 Glucose tablets

1 case Martell Brandy
1 case Grant's Scotch
120 cans Tennant's Lager
1,000 Benson & Hedges
  cigarettes
1,000 State Express cigarettes,
  tipped
1,000 Senior Service cigarettes,
  tipped

12 large tubes Gibbs S.R.
  Toothpaste
12 large tubes Maclean's
  Toothpaste
12 Toothbrushes
1 Razor blade (5 dozen
  intended)
12 bott. Salt Water Soap
18 rolls Toilet Paper

B. MEDICAL STORES

The Ship Captain's Medical Guide
St. John Ambulance Brigade First
  Aid Manual

1 pkt. Solprin tablets
1 pint Kaolin Stomach Mixture
6 ampoule syringes Omnopon
100 tablets Al. Hydrox*
1 bot. Oil of Cloves
1 bot. antiseptic eyedrops*
50 Codeine tabs.*
1 pkt. Cirotyl
5 mls. Otosporin drops
2 tubes Cetrimide cream
1 tube Tinefax
10 suture strips

2 sutures with needles
3 crepe bandages*
4 oz. cotton wool*
1 lge. pkt. small wound dressings
1 oz. white petroleum jelly*†
1 triangular bandage
2 thermometers*
5 safety pins*
1 pr. tweezers
2 tins Elastoplast dressings*
2 rolls Elastoplast
1 tin Stabodor*
4 pints ether*‡
1 hypodermic syringe*§
12 needles for above*§

* Items made use of during
   voyage
† Used on aerial connections
‡ Used for starting engine
§ Used for removing bubbles from
   compass, oiling, etc.

C. CHANDLERY

20 sailmaker's needles ⎫
2 sailmaker's hooks   ⎪
4 sewing palms   ⎬ Sail-
6 skeins sailtwine   ⎪ maker's
2 skeins roping twine ⎪ bag
2 lb. beeswax   ⎪
36 spare sail slides   ⎭

36 spare shackles   ⎫
12 snap shackles   ⎪
3 swivel snap shackles ⎪
3 wire splicing spikes ⎪
1 rope fid   ⎪
12 1 in. thimbles   ⎬ Bosun's
12 2 in. thimbles   ⎪ Bag
6 balls tarred marline ⎪
2 marline spikes   ⎪
1 rope gauge   ⎪
2 serving mallets (1 in. ⎪
   and 2 in.)   ⎭

7 lb. Stockholm Tar
1 gal. boiled linseed oil
12 yd. canvas
1 ball caulking cotton
7 lb. white lead
10 lb. tallow
4 tins grease
2 Senhouse slips
8 bottle screws
1 set caulking chisels
7 lb. marine glue
18 tins flexible seam stopper
1 30 lb. CQR anchor
1 sea anchor
120 fathoms 2 in. polypropylene
   rope
220 fathoms 1 in. nylon rope
40 fathoms 2 in. terylene rope
100 fathoms 1 in. flexible steel
   wire rope
1 leadline
1 boat lamp
2 N.U.C. lamps
1 gal. glass fibre resin
12 yd. glass fibre tape
1 spare bilge pump (Whale 25)
1 deck scrubber
1 set signal flags
2 Red Ensigns
1 Red Ensign (storm)
Assorted burgees
1 foghorn
1 10 ft. rubber pipe, fibre-
   reinforced (bilge pump) $1\frac{1}{4}$ in.
   internal diameter
6 lb. steel wool
8 tins Brasso
3 gal. paint (assorted colours)
2 sets spare parts for Primus
24 mantles for pressure lamp/heater
8 gal. Teepol
3 buckets
2 × 1 gal. tins household
   disinfectant
7 dishcloths
4 dishmops

24 teatowels
6 boxes lifeboat matches
48 boxes safety matches
4 large polythene bags
24 candles

1 self-inflatable 1-man emergency
  lifeboat (complete)
1 inflatable rubber dinghy
  (complete)
12 distress rockets
12 white handflares
6 red handflares

D. TOOLS

1 set spanners for engine
1 spare set of Whitworth spanners
2 Stillson pipe wrenches
1 adjustable spanner
3 ring spanners
1 brace and full set wood bits
1 hand drill and 2 set drills $\frac{1}{32}$ $\frac{1}{4}$ in.
1 wood plane
4 wood chisels, $\frac{3}{8}$ in, $\frac{1}{2}$ in., $\frac{3}{4}$ in.
  and 1 in.
1 wood mallet
3 hammers
2 hacksaws with spare blades
1 wood saw
6 screwdrivers, various sizes
  (including electric)
3 pairs pliers
1 portable vice
3 metal files
1 wood file

1 wire brush
2 cold chisels
2 oil cans
1 box assorted nuts, bolts, washers,
  brass screws, etc.
1 hydrometer

E. FUEL, ETC.

100 gal. Diesel fuel (70, tanks;
  30, containers)
35 gal. petrol
5 gal. SAE 30 lubricating oil
35 gal. paraffin
4 gal. methylated spirits
2 gal. distilled water
6 × 6-volt Silver Exide batteries

F. RIFLE, UNDERWATER GEAR, ETC.

1 ·303 rifle
160 rounds ·303 ammunition
1 Nemrod Crucero Speargun
1 pair diving goggles
1 diver's knife
Miscellaneous trolling lines,
  hooks, etc.

G. CAMERAS, ETC.

1 Nikonis camera
1 Rolleiflex camera with Rollei-
  Marine Underwater Housing
Film for above
1 Sanyo cassette tape recorder
  (with various tapes)   ●

Appendix II

Navigational Stores and Equipment

A. MANUALS, ETC.

Admiralty Pilots

27 Channel Pilot vol. I
28 Channel Pilot vol. II
1 Africa Pilot vol. I
2 Africa Pilot vol. II
39 South Indian Ocean Pilot
13 Australian Pilot
51 New Zealand Pilot
9 Antarctic Pilot
6 South American Pilot vol. II

Admiralty Lists of Lights

A. British Isles
D. Eastern Shores of the North and South Atlantic Oceans
G. Western Side of South Atlantic Ocean and East Pacific Ocean, East Coast of South America ... West Coast of South and North America
K. Indian and South Pacific, South and East Africa ... Australia, New Zealand and South Pacific Islands
Admiralty Manual of Navigation vol. 2
Admiralty Manual of Seamanship vol. 3
Admiralty List of Radio Signals: vol. II Radio Beacons vol. V Time Signals

Ocean Passages of the World
Meteorology for Mariners
International Code of Signals
List of Ships' Stations 1963
Norie's Nautical Tables
1968 and 1969 Admiralty Nautical Almanacs
The Ship's Compass (Routledge and Kegan Paul)

B. CHARTS

3934 The World
2 The British Isles
32 Falmouth Harbour
1598 English Channel and Western Approaches
1 Portsmouth to the Azores and Canary Isles
4011 North Atlantic Ocean – Eastern Portion
2202A South Atlantic Ocean – Eastern Portion
2202B South Atlantic Ocean – Western Portion
748A Indian Ocean – Southern Portion
2759B Australia – Southern Portion
1695B Bass Strait – Western Sheet
1695A Bass Strait – Eastern Sheet

3634 New Zealand – South Island

788 South Pacific Ocean – Western Sheet

789 South Pacific Ocean – Eastern Sheet

1373 South Eastern Part of Tierra del Fuego

539 Puerto Santa Cruz to Cabo Pilar, including Falkland Islands

1185 River Thames – Sea Reach

1607 Thames Estuary – Southern Part

1828 The Downs

1895 Dover Strait

1610 North Foreland to Orford Ness

536 Beachy Head to Dungeness

2450 Anvil Point to Beachy Head

C. EQUIPMENT

1 Plath sextant
1 chronometer
1 barometer
1 handbearing compass
1 set parallel rules
1 pr. dividers
3 ball-point pens and 48 refills
12 B pencils
12 HB pencils
6 Chinagraph pencils
3 India rubbers
6 notepads
1 ream foolscap

Appendix III

Book list

Holy Bible
W. B. Alexander: *Birds of the Ocean*
James Boswell: *London Journal, 1762–3*
Emily Brontë: *Wuthering Heights*
Charles H. Brown: *Nicholls' Seamanship and Nautical Knowledg*
Samuel Butler: *Erewhon* and *Erewhon Revisited*
Boys' Brigade Ambulance Handbook
Thomas Carlyle: *The French Revolution*
Rachel Carson: *The Sea Around Us*
 The Sea
Apsley Cherry-Garrard: *The Worst Journey in the World*

Charles Darwin: *The Voyage of the Beagle*
Fyodor Dostoevsky: *Crime and Punishment*
R. J. Eaton: *The Elements of Transport*
George Eliot: *The Mill on the Floss*
John Evelyn: *The Diary of John Evelyn* (vol. 1). Ed. W. Bray
Henry Fielding: *Tom Jones*
G. W. Gaunt: *Elementary Calculus*
J. Green: *A Biology of Crustacea*
Golden Treasury of English Verse
J. L. Hanson: *A Textbook of Economics*
Eric C. Hiscock: *Around the World in Wanderer III*
Captain F. N. Hopkin: *Business and Law for the Shipmaster*
David Lewis: *Daughters of the Wind*
H. R. Light: *The Legal Aspects of Business*
N. B. Marshall: *Aspects of Deep Sea Biology*
Herman Melville: *Billy Budd, Sailor, and Other Stories*
J. R. Norman: *A History of Fishes*
J. R. Norman and F. C. Fraser: *Giant Fishes, Whales and Dolphins*
Oxford Illustrated Dictionary
Rabelais: *Collected Works*
Ray and Ciampi: *Underwater Guide to Marine Life*
Fred Reinfield: *Chess in a Nutshell*
Samuel Richardson: *Clarissa*
Jean-Jacques Rousseau: *Confessions*
Bertrand Russell: *History of Western Philosophy*
Christopher I. Savage: *An Economic History of Transport*
William Shakespeare: *Complete Works*
H. A. Silverman: *The Substance of Economics*
Joshua Slocum: *Sailing Alone Round the World*
J. L. B. Smith: *Fishes of South African Waters*
Laurence Sterne: *Tristram Shandy*
      Sentimental Journey
W. M. Thackeray: *Vanity Fair*
      The History of Henry Esmond Esq.
Mike Tinbergen: *The Herring Gull's World*
Leo Tolstoy: *War and Peace*
Anthony Trollope: *Orley Farm*
Mark Twain: *Tom Sawyer*
     Huckleberry Finn
Brian Vesey-Fitzgerald: *The World of Fishes*
H. G. Wells: *Outline of History*
Gilbert White: *The Natural History of Selborne*

Index

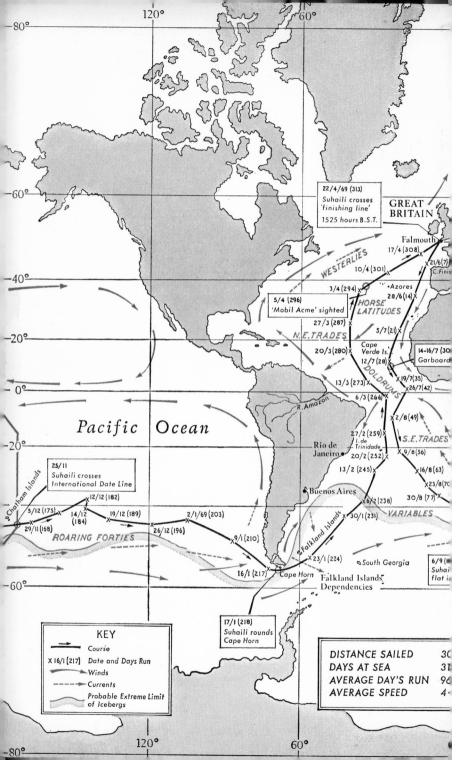

80°

120°   60°

GREAT
BRITAIN

22/4/69 (313)
Suhaili crosses
'finishing line'
1525 hours B.S.T.

Falmouth

17/4 (308)

21/6/(7)
C. Finis

WESTERLIES

10/4 (301)

28/6/(14)

3/4 (294)   • Azores

5/4 (296)
'Mobil Acme' sighted

HORSE
LATITUDES

5/7 (21)

27/3 (287)

N.E. TRADES

Cape
Verde Is.

14-16/7 (30
Garboard

20/3 (280)

12/7 (28)

19/7/35

DOLDRUMS

26/7/(42)

13/3 (273)

6/3 (266)

2/8 (49)

R. Amazon

S.E. TRADES

27/2 (259)
I. de Trinidad

9/8 (56)

Rio de
Janeiro

20/2 (252)

Pacific Ocean

16/8 (63)

13/2 (245)

23/8/(7

25/11
Suhaili crosses
International Date Line

Buenos Aires

30/8 (77)

VARIABLES

12/12 (182)

Chatham Islands

5/12 (175)

14/12
(184)

19/12 (189)

2/1/69 (203)

Falkland Islands

6/2 (238)

30/1 (231)

6/9 (8
Suhai
flat i

29/11 (168)

26/12 (196)

ROARING FORTIES

9/1 (210)

23/1 (224)

South Georgia

16/1 (217)   Cape Horn

Falkland Islands
Dependencies

KEY

——→   Course
X 16/1 (217) Date and Days Run
⇝   Winds
- - -→   Currents
      Probable Extreme Limit
      of Icebergs

17/1 (218)
Suhaili rounds
Cape Horn

DISTANCE SAILED   30
DAYS AT SEA   31
AVERAGE DAY'S RUN   96
AVERAGE SPEED   4

80°   120°   60°